A PICTORIAL
HISTORY
OF
IMMIGRATION

A PICTORIAL HISTORY OF IMMIGRATION

OSCAR HANDLIN

CROWN PUBLISHERS, INC./NEW YORK

ACKNOWLEDGMENTS

The publisher is grateful to the following individuals and organizations for their generous assistance in the accumulation of pictures for this book: Association of American Railroads; Columbia Records; Richard W. Cull, Jr.; Cunard Line Ltd.; Harvard University, Social Ethics Collection; Henry Street Settlement-Urban Life Center; Illinois State Historical Library; Kansas State Historical Society; Library of Congress, Prints and Photographs Division; Metropolitan Museum of Art; Montana Historical Society; Museum of the City of New York; The National Archives; National Park Service; Nebraska State Historical Society; The New-York Historical Society; New York Public Library, Picture Collection; Richard Santerre; Sikorsky Aircraft Corporation; Smithsonian Institution; United States Department of Agriculture.

Picture Researcher: Lenore Weber.

Manufactured in the United States of America
Published simultaneously in Canada by General Publishing Company Limited

Contents

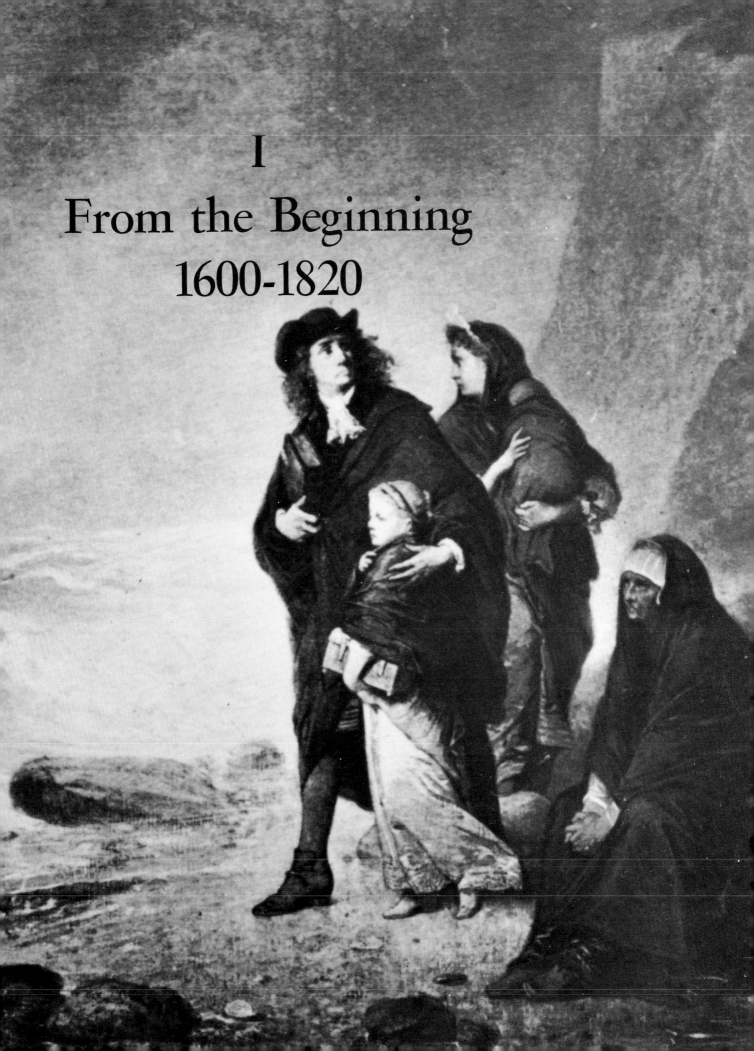

I
From the Beginning
1600-1820

A romantic evocation of nomadic Indian life on the Minnesota River. (Drawing by S. Eastman, Photoworld)

1

Even the Indians Were Newcomers

The course of the first migration to the American hemisphere is lost in the mists of prehistory. The peoples who occupied the two continents before the arrival of the Europeans at the end of the fifteenth century developed complex cultures but had an imperfect sense of history and left no written records of their past. Information about the origins and·wanderings of the pre-Columbian Americans must be gleaned from archaeological survivals and from the informed guesses of anthropologists.

At some point—probably not before 30,000 B.C., nor later than 13,000 B.C.—little bands of men and women made the hazardous crossing over the Bering Strait from Asia to Alaska. They appear to have been a homogeneous group with Mongoloid antecedents, nomads who eked out an existence by hunting and fishing. Slowly they spread down along the Pacific Coast, drawn, as the centuries passed, to the ever warmer climate of the south. The move extended over thousands of years, for the numbers involved were small and it took a long time to adjust to changing conditions. It seems likely that settlement had spread into Venezuela by about 11,000 B.C. It was several millennia more (6000 B.C.) before it reached to the Strait of Magellan.

There may have been subsequent additions to these numbers from across the Pacific. One such party, for instance, seems to have arrived in South America at about 2500 B.C. These contacts were, however, not significant

and the offspring of the original stock increased only slowly.

The vast spaces of the Western Hemisphere sheltered only a small population by the time the Europeans began to arrive. In the fifteenth century, there were no more than twenty million human beings in the whole area between the Aleutians and Cape Horn. These people, whom the Europeans would call Indians, were relatively few and were dispersed over great distances. Since there were substantial climatic and physiographic differences among the various parts of the hemisphere, the residents of each region developed distinctive cultures to cope with the environment. Furthermore, travel was slow and difficult so that the Indians had little contact with one another. Each small, isolated group acquired its own linguistic, social, and cultural characteristics. At Columbus's arrival there were perhaps nine hundred different languages spoken by the Indians. Each tongue served only a few thousand people, for the important activities of life were conducted within small, intimate tribal organizations.

Anthropologists have classified the numerous American tribes into various linguistic groups, three of which were important in the territory that would later form part of the United States. In the northeast and in a band of settlement across Canada to the Pacific were the Algonkian tribes, who lived in the forests and subsisted from agriculture. In the Great Plains and down through

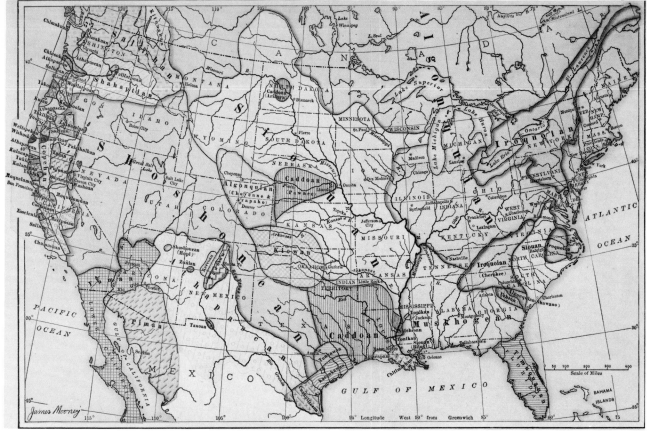

Distribution of Indian linguistic stocks in the United States. (E. M. Avery, *A History of the United States*, Cleveland, 1904)

Hokan Siouan buffalo-skin tents. (*Harper's Monthly*, July, 1853, New York Public Library)

Long birchbark lodge of the Northwest Indian. (New York Public Library)

the Mississippi Valley were the Hokan Siouan groups, who depended for food and clothing largely on hunting and who therefore were less sedentary than the Algonkians. And in the Southwest was an extension of the Azteca-Tanoan grouping, the main elements of which were farther south in Mexico and Central America. This group had developed a highly advanced civilization, were proficient in science, and capable of making striking artistic achievements. It was among them that the pre-Columbian Mayan and Aztec empires developed. But only the remote outposts of those empires extended into the territories that later became the United States.

The predominant Indian population Europeans encountered along the Atlantic Coast of North America had a rudimentary culture, economy, and political order. Nevertheless, it made important contributions to the life of the colonists and later of the nation.

When the first Europeans had reached across the Atlantic, at the end of the fifteenth century, there were fewer than nine hundred thousand Indians in the territory that ultimately became the United States. Their number was stable, increase being limited by the undeveloped economy that kept their food supply and shelter restricted, and by recurrent plagues and intertribal wars. This great area was less densely settled than almost any comparable part of the earth.

Tents of skin of the Plains Indians. (New York Public Library)

An Aztec city—an imaginative portrayal of the highly advanced civilization of Mexico. (Nostalgia Press, Inc.)

A Navaho hogan, or hut, made of sticks and earth. (New York Public Library)

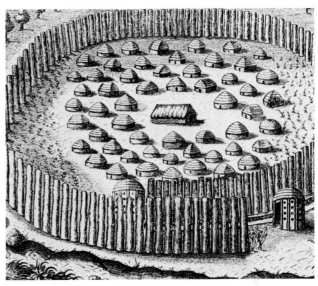

A fortified Indian village in Florida. (After a sixteenth-century etching, New York Public Library)

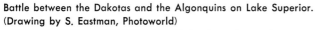

Battle between the Dakotas and the Algonquins on Lake Superior. (Drawing by S. Eastman, Photoworld)

A Virginia Indian village, showing a cornfield. (From an engraving by DeBry of the original drawing by John White in 1590)

An eighteenth-century Mohawk village in New York State showing the making of a birchbark canoe. (New York Public Library)

Southwest Indian pueblos. (E. M. Avery, A History of the United States, Cleveland, 1904)

Pueblo terraces at Zuni, New Mexico. (E. M. Avery, A History of the United States, Cleveland, 1904)

Pueblo at Walpi, Arizona. (E. M. Avery, A History of the United States, Cleveland, 1904)

Also, the heaviest concentrations of Indians were out of reach of most Europeans; the most thickly occupied region was the Pacific Coast. The Southwest had considerably fewer inhabitants, and east of the Mississippi there were only scattered handfuls of red men.

In all areas, the Indians had long since ceased to be nomads. At their first arrival, they had lived by hunting and by gathering nuts and edible berries. Their only domesticated animal was the dog. But sometime at about the beginning of the Christian Era, they had taken to agriculture. In the fifteen hundred years that followed they had developed a remarkable technique for domesticating plants; they had contrived digging tools and grinding stones, and, in some places, had even worked out elaborate irrigation projects. As a result, they raised abundant crops of corn, potatoes, and tobacco, which they were to introduce for the first time to the Europeans. Close at hand were the means for supplementing this diet—from continued hunting for small game in the east and for buffalo in the Great Plains. The Indians had also learned to take fish from the rivers and seas, which further enriched their food supply.

They generally moved little, for there was plenty of space even within a circumscribed area to sustain this way of life. But there was some mobility over limited distances. The red men had learned how to make the birchbark canoes that allowed them to traverse the rivers, and in the sixteenth century those in the western plains adopted the horse from the Spaniards.

The Indians were less proficient in other forms of technology. In the Southwest, traditional skill went into the making of the pueblos—intricate dwellings that housed whole groups. The arts of making baskets and pottery and of working on metal were quite advanced. Although very little is known about them, it is probable that the mysterious mound builders of the Ohio and Mississippi valleys exercised highly developed techniques. By contrast, the eastern Indians lived in rude bark-covered common houses or huts and for clothing depended only on the skins of animals.

Indian basketwork and weapons. (Drawing by D. Lancelot, Brown Brothers)

In the light of the crisis that befell them after 1492, the greatest deficiency of the Indians inhabiting the area that became the United States was their inability to develop any comprehensive social order. The basic communal group was the tribe or the clan, which rarely numbered above a few thousand, and which depended largely on informal personal relationships. Its authority was thus limited. The family was strong, its solidarity confirmed by the economic system that emphasized the small group. But the force of tribalism stifled the development of any loyalty to a larger unit. As a result, the Indians north of the Rio Grande were even less prepared for the invasion of the Europeans than those of Mexico and the south.

Occasional efforts at federation, such as that of the Siouan Iroquois under the leadership of Hiawatha, showed that Indians could mobilize power. The Iroquois were able to assert their dominance over a large area, pushing out the Algonkians who were their enemies. But such episodes were limited and exceptional. To the Indians, war was a game closely related to religion and occupied a good deal of attention and energy. As yet, it generally lacked political purpose.

Political weakness was by no means a racial characteristic; the experience of the Cherokee and other tribes later showed the capacity for communal organization. But before most Indians realized that war was more than a game, they had to deal with much larger and more powerful groups of immigrants from across the Atlantic.

Northeastern Indians beside their mat-covered wigwam. (Smithsonian Institution Diorama)

Lodge of a Mandan chief. (Drawing made in the 1830s, New York Public Library)

An Iroquois longhouse. (E. M. Avery, *A History of the United States*, Cleveland, 1904)

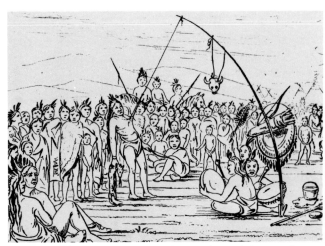

An Indian religious ceremony, perhaps a form of the sun dance. (Drawing about 1830 by George Catlin, New York Public Library)

An Indian battle scene. (Drawing about 1830 by George Catlin, New York Public Library)

The Grave Creek Mound built by Indians from whom the Cherokees may have descended. (E. M. Avery, *A History of the United States*, Cleveland, 1904)

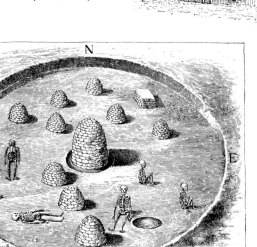

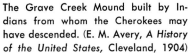

The Nelson Mound in North Carolina. (E. M. Avery, *A History of the United States*, Cleveland, 1904)

Reconstruction of a mound. (Drawn by DeBry, E. M. Avery, *A History of the United States*, Cleveland, 1904)

2

The Old World Spreads Out

Occasional Europeans had penetrated the great ocean to the west before the end of the first millennium of the Christian Era. It is possible that the ancient legend of the voyage of St. Brendan, the Irish monk, had a foundation in fact. The Norse sagas, which refer to a settlement in Vinland, very likely also described a historical occurrence. Indeed, there may well have been other ventures, allusions to which were preserved only in half-forgotten myths.

But these tentative explorations lacked significance and established no permanent connection between Europe and the unknown world beyond the Atlantic. These were daring feats—to leave behind the sight of land and plunge through unknown waters in defiance of the winds and of the mysterious creatures of the deep. But these were personal acts without consequence, which simply merged into the legends that sustained the dread Europeans felt about the boundless ocean to the west. Such casual probes left the Indians in unchallenged possession of the Western Hemisphere.

A dramatic discovery was not in itself enough to set the tides of mass migration in motion. The explorer mapped the way; others followed because great social and intellectual changes had prepared thousands of men and women to depart from ancestral homes and challenge the hazardous wilderness. Both conditions were necessary—the vision that inspired an individual to sail where no one had gone before, and the readiness of many ordinary people to move in his wake.

Columbus's voyage had momentous results while those of St. Brendan and Leif Ericsson did not, because the Europe of 1492 was prepared, as it had not been earlier, to exploit the discovery. The eyes of its people were already turned outward when Columbus demonstrated that the direction in which to look was westward. The pathbreaker and the followers were alike the products of change that had long been transforming the Old World.

The Genoese mariner was an experienced seaman who inspired the confidence of his Spanish backers. He had passed his fortieth birthday when he finally persuaded the Queen of Castile to fit out three little ships for him, and he knew as much about the geography of the world as any contemporary. Nevertheless, it was not practical information that told him where his destination lay, but rather an essentially mystical vision. This hard-headed sailor expected to arrive at a terrestrial paradise that he thought existed somewhere south of the known areas of Asia. It was his destiny, he believed, to redeem that heaven on earth for Christianity. Not until after he had returned from his first successful voyage was he aware that he had discovered an altogether new continent.

Europe was ready for the revelation. Vast social

9

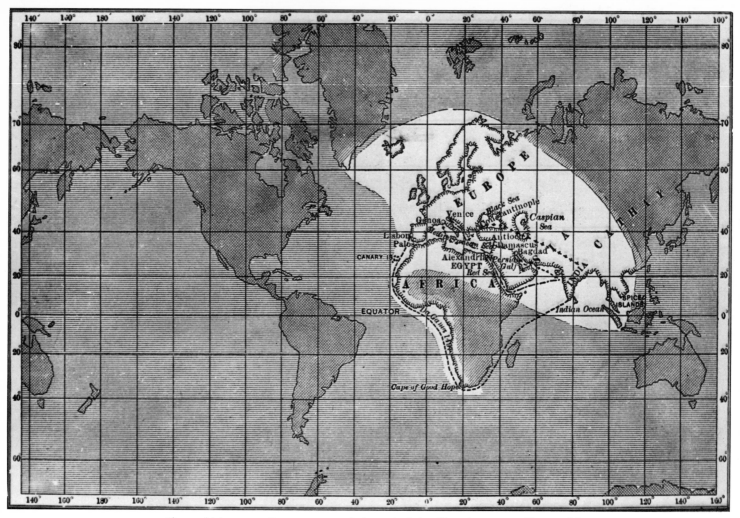

The world known to Europeans toward the end of the fifteenth century. (Photoworld)

Leif Ericsson landing in America. (Painting by DeLand, Library of Congress)

A Viking ship. (Harper's Encyclopedia of United States History, New York, 1906)

A Norse ship. (Justin Winsor, The Memorial History of Boston, Boston, 1881)

Christopher Columbus—the imaginative Montanus engraving. (New York Public Library)

Columbus setting sail. (A nineteenth-century drawing, New York Public Library)

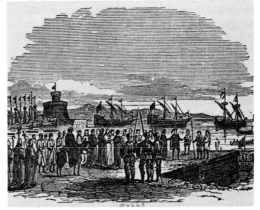

The fleet of Columbus approaching America—an imaginary view. (*Harper's Encyclopedia of United States History*, New York, 1906)

The *Pinta*, the *Santa Maria*, and the *Nina*. (New York Public Library)

Columbus landing in America. (A painting by G. Adolf Closs, 1892, New York Public Library)

Columbus taking possession of the New World. (New York Public Library)

Columbus explaining his discovery to Ferdinand and Isabella. (Idealized drawing by John Gilbert, *Harper's Weekly*, May 30, 1868, New York Public Library)

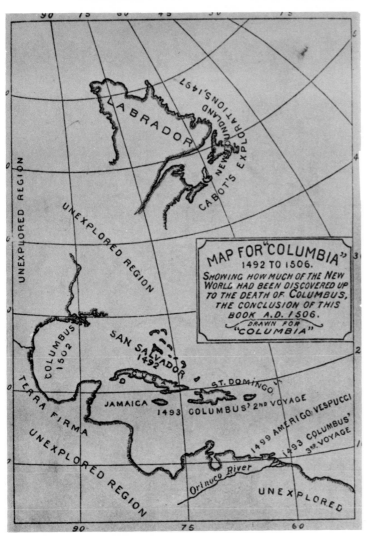

The known outlines of America at the death of Columbus, 1506. (New York Public Library)

Traditional European agriculture. (Smithsonian Institution)

changes had shaken up customary ways of thinking and acting. Men of dynamic personality, discontent with things as they were, eagerly sought opportunities for achievement. America supplied some of them with outlets for their energy.

For centuries, the people of Europe had lived by agriculture in small communities cut off from one another and from the outside world. Their self-sufficient little villages had long resisted change. Each family passed along its landholding and status from generation to generation so that there seemed an inevitability to every man's place and station. In the good years, abundant harvests yielded food for all and the population increased; in the bad years, famine and plague decimated the households. Prudent men knew there was little they could do to control their fate; the husbandman planted with no certainty that he would ever reap, and the merchant dispatched his ship without assurance that it would return. Since man's control over his fate was limited, it was best to cling to habit and seek relief, or at least consolation, in prayer. It was wisest also not to tempt Providence by wandering, but to stay in one's place, to shun strangers, and to act according to the dictates of tradition. Power too was local. The priest in his church and the noble in his hall ruled the spiritual life of the parish and the material life of the district.

The ways of acting and thinking in urban places differed somewhat from those in the countryside. The prelates and functionaries and the merchants and craftsmen who attended the cathedrals, the universities, the fairs, and the great courts knew the arts of calculation and were familiar with distant places. But the towns were small and their influence was limited as long as rural society remained isolated.

The Crusades had begun the slow process of dissolving the isolation of the Europeans. The mission of redeeming the holy places from the infidels justified the journeys of large numbers of men whose startled eyes fell upon the wonders of the more advanced Islamic and Byzantine civilizations. The succession of expeditions, from the eleventh to the thirteenth centuries, brought back exciting information about glamorous and remote countries, familiarized people with the possibility of movement over long distances, and created demands for the exotic goods of the Orient. The volume of trade between east and west rose steadily. Long afterward, when the crusaders' tales had passed into legend, there persisted a restless longing for the opportunity to win glory and to gain relief from boredom through similar exploits.

In the fourteenth and fifteenth centuries, the Europeans pushed out ever farther into the world around them. They left home out of discontent with the humdrum sameness of everyday life; or out of the Christian obligation to convert the heathen throughout the world; or simply out of avarice; or, most often, out of some combination of these motives.

The main channel of long-distance travel was the Mediterranean, which led to Constantinople and to both the Near and the Far East. The powerful mercantile

The magistrates and citizens of Frankfurt am Main, Germany, assemble in the public square, 1745. (Engraving by W. C. Mayr, from a drawing by J. G. Fünck, Library of Congress)

Eighteenth-century state banquet in Frankfurt, 1742. (Engraving by Michael Rössler, from a drawing by J. G. Fünck, Library of Congress)

The First Crusade. (By Emile Bayard, New York Public Library)

The harbor of Genoa. (Edwin Markham, *The Real America*, New York, 1914)

Venice in the fourteenth century. (From a manuscript in the Bodleian Library, New York Public Library)

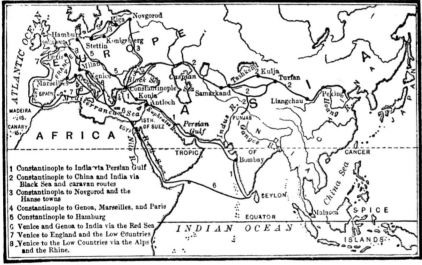

1 Constantinople to India via Persian Gulf
2 Constantinople to China and India via Black Sea and caravan routes
3 Constantinople to Novgorod and the Hanse towns
4 Constantinople to Genoa, Marseilles, and Paris
5 Constantinople to Hamburg
6 Venice and Genoa to India via the Red Sea
7 Venice to England and the Low Countries
8 Venice to the Low Countries via the Alps and the Rhine.

Medieval trade routes. (A. B. Hart, *Essentials in American History*, New York, 1905)

states of the Italian peninsula—above all Genoa and Venice—controlled the trade and profited from it. Western Europe was on the frontier of this world. The merchants and princes of Spain, Portugal, France, and England were envious but lacked the means of breaking into the eastern trade.

In the fifteenth century, the center of political and economic power began to shift toward the Atlantic as the western countries gained strength from the transformation of their societies. Centralized political states and national institutions appeared while Italy still remained divided. The monarchs of the West joined forces with the urban middle classes to reduce the influence of the feudal nobility and to create effective governments. In

Spain and Portugal the struggle against the Moors was the rallying ground. In France and England, aggressive new dynasties—the Bourbons and the Tudors—provided the impetus. In each case the result was the creation of a powerful political force capable of furthering its interest in expansion through the support of overseas trade.

In the fifteenth and sixteenth centuries a new intellectual and cultural spirit also stimulated expansionist influences. The Renaissance persuaded many Europeans that innovation and reason were superior to habit and tradition as guides to action. Once men gained confidence in their ability to solve problems by knowledge and understanding, newness was no longer frightening.

Daring people ceased to depend on custom and began to make decisions based on science, that is, on rationally organized bodies of information. Examining anew their habitual activities, they devised improvements in techniques that transformed many aspects of life. Movable type thus permitted the printed book to replace the manuscript; new maps, charts, and navigational devices enabled seamen to move more freely than before, and the telescope shortened distances. As the new instruments added to the available data, men revised theretofore accepted ideas about the world around them. Observing the movement of the heavenly bodies, for instance, forced them to abandon the old view of the earth as the center of the universe and to adopt the Copernican concept of a solar system within which the earth was but one of several planets.

Before long, the new ideas led to a questioning of conventional religious wisdom. If the sun did not revolve around the earth, then other doctrines affirmed by the priests and the Bible might also prove incorrect. The authority of the church could not make Galileo wrong, and its attempt to do so only undermined a willingness to accept its verdicts without question. People did not lose religious faith. But they were unwilling any longer to regard the church simply as an institution to be accepted as inherited, without question. They wished to

The expulsion of the Moors from Spain. The conflict between Christians and Moslems had lasted for centuries, but finally ended in the very year of the discovery of America. (New York Public Library)

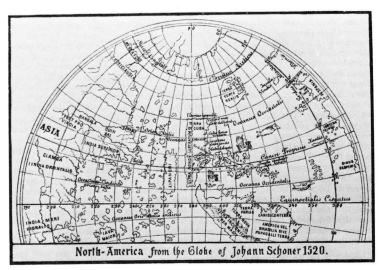

North-America from the Globe of Johann Schoner 1520.

The globe of Johann Schoner showing North America, 1520. (*Harper's Monthly*, September, 1882, New York Public Library)

Genvesa world map, 1457. (Library of Congress)

find a larger meaning in it and to make it a dynamic power in the world. This desire was expressed both in the Protestant Reformation and in the Catholic Counter Reformation; one of the results among all Christians was a determination to spread the true faith to every part of the world.

These tendencies were already at work when Columbus set sail. They continued to operate in the sixteenth century. The power of the state, the desire for trade, the Renaissance spirit, and the missionary impulse carried Europeans outside their own continent to the unexplored places of Africa, Asia, and America. The transfer of population that settled the United States was part of the process of European expansion.

Looking outward from their homes in Spain or France or England after 1500, the adventurous could perceive a host of attractive opportunities. The most enticing areas were those in which possibilities for trade already existed. The Baltic states and Russia, for instance, produced valuable timber and furs. The Near East was a source of textiles, metalwork, and gems. East Asia produced spices, tea, and silk, and Africa, gold and ivory.

America was viewed in the same light—as a land with resources to enrich the conquering Europeans. The

Sixteenth-century seamen studying navigation. (New York Public Library)

Seventeenth-century armillary sphere. (From M. Blundeville's treatise on cosmography, 1636, New York Public Library)

Drawing for a seventeenth-century telescope. (By A. Stech, Library of Congress)

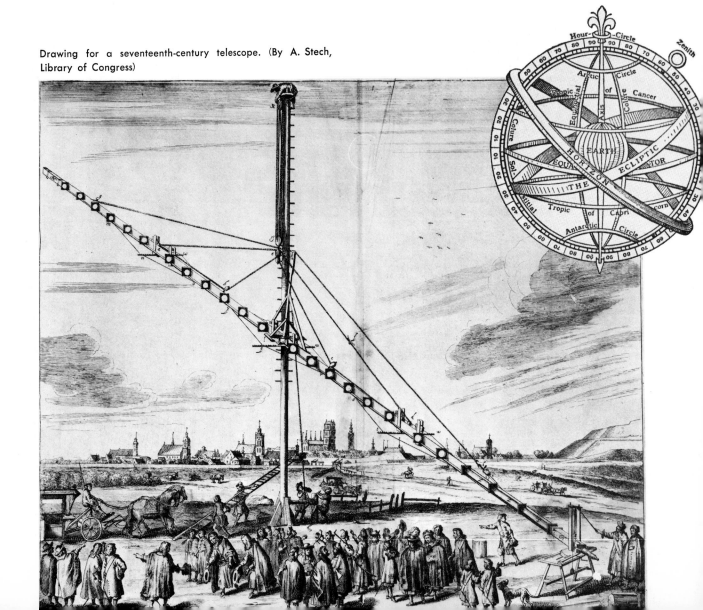

Galileo Galilei. (Engraving,
Library of Congress)

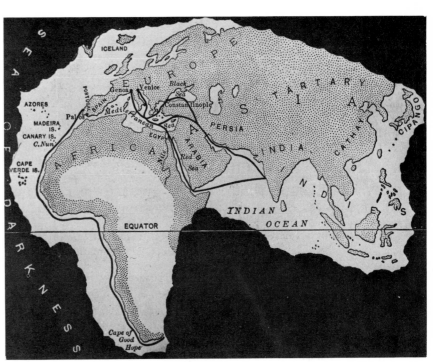

Trade routes to the East, 1490. (Photoworld)

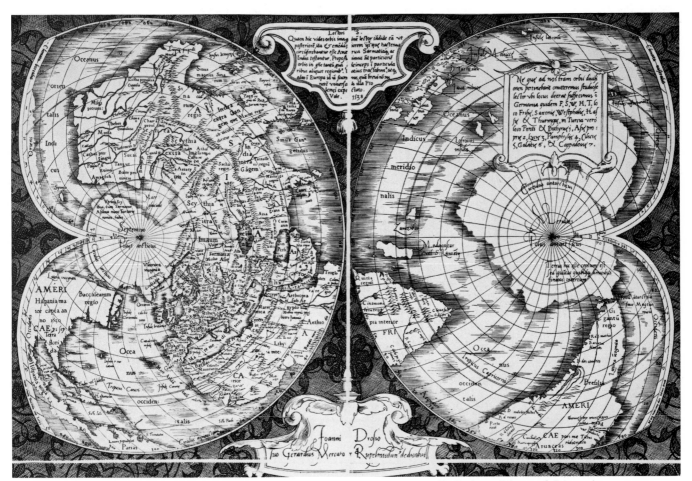

Mercator map of 1538, which applied the name America to the Western Hemisphere. (Library of Congress)

Spaniards, Dutch, and Portuguese led the way in exploitation. In the sixteenth century they carved out the most desirable parts of the Western Hemisphere for themselves. The great Spanish empire stretched from the West Indies across the Caribbean through Mexico down to the very tip of South America. The conquistadores sent home not only the gold and silver seized from the Aztecs and Incas of Mexico and Peru but also precious cargoes of sugar raised in the West Indies. The Portuguese found in Brazil a counterpart of their extensive East Indian and African possessions. At the end of the sixteenth century these provinces, which were more valuable than the territory later to become the United States, were already preempted. France and England, weaker powers, for the time being had made little headway in America.

Nevertheless, by 1600, they too were making ready to move forward; and they would profit from the advances in navigation and shipping that the Spanish and Portuguese experience encouraged. For two centuries more the crossing would remain long, hazardous, and painful; in time of war, pirates and enemy cruisers were a danger, and treacherous weather was an ever-present menace. But by the opening of the seventeenth century, when the English embarked upon large-scale colonization, some of the terror of the transatlantic journey had subsided. Dependable charts and chronometers, the magnetic compass, and the astrolabe guided the mariners. Also, the three-masted square-rigged sailing ships developed during the sixteenth century were more appropriate to the winds and waters of the Atlantic than the little barks that had once beat their way around the Mediterranean shore. Above all, word was spreading—through the printed page and the spoken tale—of a destination so attractive that thousands would consider the risks of the voyage worth taking.

An Italian astrolabe, 1558. (Photoworld)

Pirates. (Drawing by Howard Pyle, *Harper's Monthly*, February, 1895, New York Public Library)

A square-rigged sailing ship. (New York Public Library)

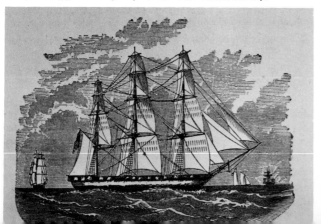

A medieval bark. (New York Public Library)

John Smith and a map of the coast he explored, 1614. (New York Public Library)

3

The English Heritage

Immigrants from many lands participated in building the American nation. But the arrivals from England played a critical role in the process. Since they established the colonies out of which the United States developed and since they and their offspring formed the largest component in the population of the Republic, the foundations they laid influenced all subsequent comers.

Furthermore, peculiar circumstances at the opening of the seventeenth century forced into the ranks of those who migrated from England not only adventurers in search of fortune, but also families in quest of homes. In America, as in colonies elsewhere in the world, administrators tarried for a while in the remote place from which they expected to return enriched to their true homes. But some of the people transplanted from England to the New World came with the intention of staying permanently, and they established an enduring society in the wilderness. They successfully adapted their institutions to the strange environment so that their settlements thrived, and expansion in time opened the way for the reception of other Europeans as well.

The presence of men like John Smith (1580–1631) among the English settlers was not surprising; his counterparts existed also in Spain and France. A restless adventurer, eager to earn a gentleman's status by his sword, he fought against the Turks in Hungary and wandered belligerently about Europe before joining the first expedition to Virginia. But immigrants of the caliber of John Winthrop (1588–1649) and John Bishop were less usual. Winthrop was the son of a gentleman, had studied at the university in Cambridge, and had gone on to a successful career in the law before he decided to come to America. Not personal ambition, but religious conviction dictated his move. And John Bishop, the date of whose birth was not known because he was only a poor servant in England, was transported to Virginia as a bondsman by Thomas Gray. Yet he became a landowner of means, and in time sat in the colony's House of Burgesses. All three types contributed to the planting of civilization on the inhospitable coast north of Florida.

In the fifteenth and sixteenth centuries, England had been the frontier of Europe. Separated from the Continent by the Channel, its population was relatively small and its social and economic development lagged behind that of the Mediterranean countries. But there were also advantages to its remote island situation. Secure from foreign invasion, its people developed maritime skills that would stand them in good stead when political, economic, and religious conditions turned their attention to overseas expansion.

The rise of a unified and central government eradicated some of the old local feudal restraints. The Tudors were strong monarchs; Henry VIII and Elizabeth I created an effective state that assured internal order and

22

John Winthrop. (New York Public Library)

Henry VIII. (Painting probably by Luke Hornebolt in National Portrait Gallery, London, Library of Congress)

Elizabeth I. (Engraving by John Sartain after Zucchero, Library of Congress)

John Cabot in America. (Imaginative wood engraving from *Ballou's Pictorial*, 1855, Library of Congress)

The Spanish Armada, 1588—the culminating effort of Philip II of Spain to subdue England. The fleet of 160 vessels went down to defeat. (Nostalgia Press, Inc.)

kept the nobility within check. Yet English constitutional development had also produced parliamentary institutions and a system of law that set some checks upon the arbitrary use of power. The state thus exercised a stabilizing force, favorable to economic development.

The crown acquired an interest in overseas expansion as it gained power, partly to keep pace with the acquisitions of other monarchs, partly out of the belief that this was a means of increasing the wealth of the whole nation. That conviction induced Henry VII in 1497 to send John Cabot on a voyage that established a claim to the North American coast. Nothing much came of the venture, for the time being, beyond a legal claim. England's economy was agricultural and underdeveloped; it supplied raw materials to the more advanced producers of the Low Countries and Italy, but lacked the capital for extensive undertakings to rival the Portuguese and Spaniards. But it was clear that a strong state would be ready to lend political support when conditions were ripe for colonization.

Changes during the sixteenth century produced the necessary capital and men. The Reformation and confiscation of the wealth of the Church, warfare with Spain and piracy, the conversion of marginal arable lands into pastures profitable for grazing, and the increase of trade left substantial surpluses in the hands of the gentry and merchants; increasingly these enterprising investors longed to use their funds overseas.

Paradoxically, a surplus of people also developed. The signs were clearest after 1600 when a great depression swept through much of the kingdom and particu-

A peasant dispossessed for nonpayment of rent. (A nineteenth-century painting by David Wilkie, Library of Congress)

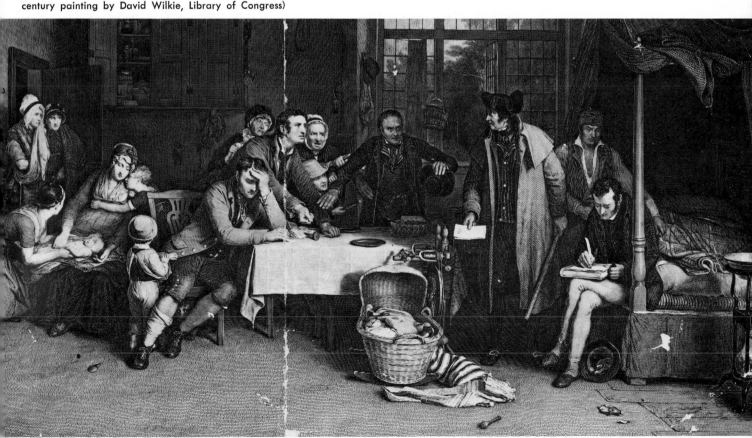

Religious persecution in the sixteenth century. In this drawing, Catholics boil, singe, hang, and quarter Protestants.

larly through the district known as East Anglia. But the basic forces were already at work earlier. The landlord who wished to graze sheep on his estate was impatient with the little plots cultivated inefficiently by scores of peasant families. If he had influence enough, he persuaded Parliament to pass an enclosure act that enabled him to combine the little holdings, even though that meant the displacement of large numbers who could no longer draw a livelihood from the soil.

Increasingly, sturdy vagabonds without employment wandered through the countryside. To control them the law provided that every man had to take service with some master, if in no other way than through public auction of his labor. The only place of refuge was London where people without places could lose themselves in the anonymity of the city. As a result the metropolis gained steadily in population, despite the efforts of the government to limit its size. These depressing conditions created a multitude ready to migrate. Yeomen in danger of losing their positions were willing to take the risk; and servants who had nothing to lose were prepared to follow any glimmer of hope, if only the way was laid open for them.

Religious disorder added an important ingredient to the migration from England. The Reformation had been relatively slow in coming to that country and took a distinctive form there. Under the leadership of the crown, the Church of England dissolved its ties to Rome, but the separation did not completely satisfy the demand for reform. The Puritan movement aimed to carry forward the task of perfecting the faith.

Puritans destroying the cross in London's Cheapside, a symbol of episcopacy. (New York Public Library)

Puritanism was a complex doctrine that included many shades of opinion. It stemmed from the teachings of John Calvin who argued that men were predestined either to salvation or to damnation. The true church, therefore, was not a comprehensive institution that included the whole community; only those men and women destined to be saved, the saints—as the Puritans called themselves—could be members. It followed that the church ought not to be hierarchical, governed by bishops appointed by the king. Rather its essential form had to be congregational, drawing its authority from the members. Some Puritans wished to work for moderate, gradual reform within the existing church. Others wished to separate themselves completely, protesting against any participation in a corrupt institution. Still others followed their consciences to depart from accepted views on the nature of baptism and other theological doctrines.

Ultimately, in the 1640s, the Puritans under Oliver Cromwell gained control of the English state. But in the 1620s the power of the king and bishops still seemed so great that an early improvement in religious conditions appeared unlikely. As a result, many Puritans sought an escape, and migration to a new country offered them a

A narrow London lane in the nineteenth century. (Drawing by J. T. Smith, 1804, New York Public Library)

Oliver Cromwell. (Engraving by E. Scriven, Library of Congress)

John Calvin. (New York Public Library)

Symbolic portrayal of English Puritans escaping to America. (New York Public Library)

The arrival in the New World. (Nineteenth-century drawing by O. C. Darley, New York Public Library)

The Pilgrims' first Sunday in America (New York Public Library)

means by which they could worship in their own way and yet avoid the risks of disloyalty.

Distinctive social conditions in England thus paved the way for a substantial shift of population to America. Gentlemen like John Smith came in pursuit of fortune; thoughtful Puritans of good family like John Winthrop followed the dictates of conscience. And poor people like John Bishop moved because a spark of hope flickered across the ocean while there was none at home.

The chartered company or corporation provided the form which made settlement by these people possible. The company was a political and military, as well as a commercial, organization. The king assigned it a territory within which it could make and enforce laws; it assembled capital from investors; and it recruited men to set up a plantation or trading colony overseas. The gains were then divided according to the contributions of the participants. Through this device, adventurers—merchants or gentlemen with funds to gamble—put up the capital necessary to gain the colonies a foothold. Planters—soldiers and clerks—risked their lives. Servants who worked for the company provided the labor force. Such enterprises were chartered to do business in Asia and Africa, and also in America.

In 1607, the Virginia Company established the first permanent English settlement across the Atlantic at Jamestown. The enterprise never earned its promoters a profit, but it did provide the basis for a thriving community. The natural wealth and the rich trade with the natives never materialized, but slowly a permanent settlement took root.

There was a striking indication of the change in emphasis when the Company sent over a shipload of maidens in 1619 in order to tie the settlers' minds to Virginia by the bonds of wives and children. The colonists no longer were regarded as transient exploiters of the country, but as residents who would make homes there.

The English arriving in Virginia. (New York Public Library)

The English off Roanoke Island. (From DeBry's engraving of John White's painting, New York Public Library)

The settlement of Jamestown, 1607. (New York Public Library)

Arrival of a shipload of maidens in Virginia, 1617. (New York Public Library)

First labors at Jamestown. (New York Public Library)

For more than a decade the men in the lonely outposts had continued to hope that they might fetch away a treasure equivalent to that of Mexico or Peru. But they had learned that they would have to raise food to survive and to cultivate the tobacco they found if they wished to export to Europe. They had learned, too, that the Indians would not do their work for them as they had at first confidently expected, but that they would have to attract labor from home. Published tracts praised the country and persuaded some yeomen to come; to draw still more, the company offered without charge fifty acres for each soul brought over. The people for whom there was no room in England could become independent landowners in America if only they could pay their way across.

There was a chance even for those without funds. A man who signed an indenture or contract to work for a specified number of years would have his passage paid; his master would receive the fifty-acre headright in addition to the labor, and the servant would be a free man when the term expired. Under this system, a steady flow of men and women settled the colony.

The company was dissolved in 1625, but Virginia was then firmly established and growing. By 1642, it had a population of about ten thousand, by 1664, of about thirty-eight thousand. Settlement had spread out as numbers increased. The yeomen moved up the rivers in search of fresh land, and each family learned to live on its own farm, remote though that might be from neighbors. Nearby Maryland, although founded not by a company but by a single proprietor, Lord Baltimore, followed essentially the same pattern.

The experience of New England was somewhat different. Little groups of fishermen and traders had appeared along these northern coasts in the first two decades of the seventeenth century. But there was no

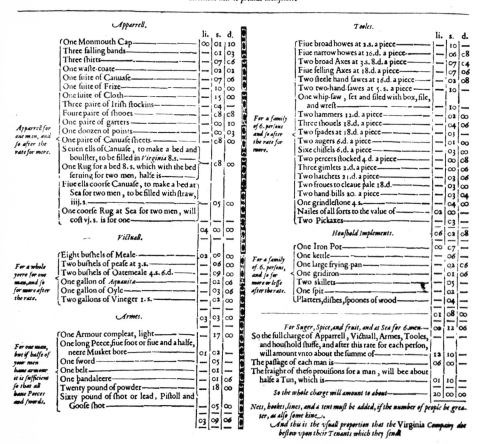

A tract in praise of New York, 1670. This pamphlet was representative of the promotional literature that appeared in all the colonies. (New-York Historical Society)

Instructions for migrants to Virginia, 1622. (Smithsonian Institution)

Jamestown in 1622, just before dissolution of the company. (*Harper's Encyclopedia of United States History*, New York, 1906)

Arrival of the Catholics in Maryland, 1634. (New York Public Library)

George Calvert, Lord Baltimore (c. 1580–1632). (New York Public Library)

Laying out the town of Baltimore, 1730. (New York Public Library)

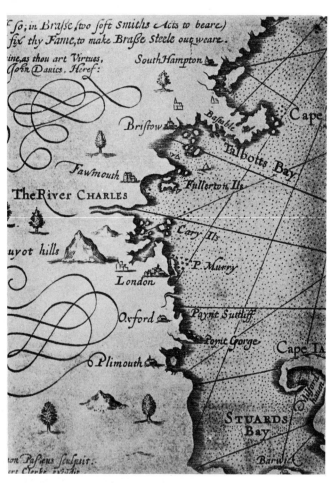

John Smith's map of Massachusetts Bay, 1614. (Justin Winsor, *The Memorial History of Boston*, Boston, 1881)

The *Mayflower*. (A. B. Hart, *Essentials in American History*, New York, 1905)

permanent community in the region until the arrival of the Pilgrims in Plymouth in 1620. These extreme Puritans, unwilling to compromise at all with the Church of England, had fled first to Leiden in Holland and then across the ocean. On the *Mayflower,* which brought them to the New World, they had joined in a compact to form a civil body politic; and they remained a small tightly knit society for the next seventy years.

Ten years later, in 1630, a settlement undertaken by the Massachusetts Bay Company overshadowed the Plymouth plantation. The Massachusetts leaders, like John Winthrop, were Puritans, and their carefully planned colony recruited many Englishmen who despaired of the state of religion at home. In addition, a depression in the cloth trade and poor harvests in East Anglia induced others, less moved by theological scruples, to join the migration. In 1630 alone, two thousand people came to Massachusetts; in the next decade, hundreds of ships brought almost twenty thousand more.

Puritanism was the dominant force in Massachusetts and Plymouth, as it was in Connecticut, Rhode Island, and New Hampshire. John Winthrop had enjoined his fellow passengers on the way over that they were to be knit together as members of the same body, for the eyes of all people were upon them. They were establishing a model commonwealth, governed by God's will, that would be a city upon a hill for the rest of mankind. Therefore, men were not to run off, each in search of his own interest, but were to live together in towns, where the community could supervise their labor, family life, and worship.

The commitment to that discipline was an important source of strength in the wilderness. The New Englanders lived by trade as well as by fishing and farming. But they did not scatter or cast off the bonds of discipline. As a result, one of the immigrants proudly pointed out, in a little more than a decade a few fugitives were able to create an orderly commonwealth. They lacked the gold, silver, and royal support of the foreign plantations. But in a place that had never afforded the natives better than the flesh of a few wild creatures and parched Indian corn eked out with chestnuts and acorns, they had become the rivals of the mother country in fertility.

After 1640, New England grew without the massive addition of new immigrants. The outbreak of the Puritan revolution in England dried up one source of potential settlers, and religious zealots who controlled these colonies were suspicious of the orthodoxy of any outsiders. Individuals and small groups continued to arrive, but in far fewer numbers than formerly.

The restoration of the Stuarts in 1660 led to the

Idealized painting of the Pilgrims embarking on the *Mayflower*. (Painting by Wapper, 1888, New York Public Library)

The Mayflower Compact. (Painting by T. H. Matteson, 1903, Library of Congress)

The Pilgrim landing. (A nineteenth-century painting by Rothermel, New York Public Library)

The Puritan migration to Connecticut. (New York Public Library)

Roger Williams in Rhode Island. (A nineteenth-century painting by O. C. Darley, New York Public Library)

First settlement of Boston. (New York Public Library)

A New England farm, 1770. (New York Public Library)

Puritans going to church. (Painting by George H. Boughton, 1880, New York Public Library)

creation of two new colonies which, however, were not equally attractive to immigrants. The courtiers who had returned to England with Charles II were eager to make the most of the power they had regained. Among their schemes was a project for a great feudal colony in Carolina. Although in time part of their grant prospered, it received its population not from Europe but from the West Indies and Africa.

By contrast, another proprietary colony became the most attractive area of America for people who could choose their destination. Its founder and proprietor was William Penn, son of an admiral and a student at Oxford when the writings of George Fox won him over to Quaker doctrines. The Friends believed that every man could commune directly with the divine spirit, that all could be saved, and that any form of compulsion was wrong. Subjected to persecution in England and in the existing colonies, they made several efforts to establish a settlement of their own. Penn's influence in court gained him a charter in 1681.

Pennsylvania thrived. Its situation was strategic, its soil was fertile, and it enjoyed good relations with the Indians. In addition, its proprietor made a determined effort to attract immigrants through the assurance of religious freedom for all and through liberal land grants. Prosperous farms in the interior and profitable trade in Philadelphia reflected the success of this policy. Through the eighteenth century, a stream of newcomers continued to raise the population of the colony.

Charles II. (Library of Congress)

Colonization of the Carolinas, 1675. (Etching by Oliver Dapper, New York Public Library)

William Penn receiving the charter of Pennsylvania from Charles II. (Library of Congress)

George Fox. (Lithograph by A. Newsam, Library of Congress)

The *Welcome*, which brought Penn on his first voyage to America. (*Philadelphia: Its Founding and Development, 1908*)

Penn's colonists arriving on the Delaware River. (New York Public Library)

The *Welcome* departing from England. (Painting by Howard Pyle, New York Public Library)

Penn landing in Pennsylvania. (*Harper's Encyclopedia of United States History*, New York, 1906)

Penn welcomed in Philadelphia. (New York Public Library)

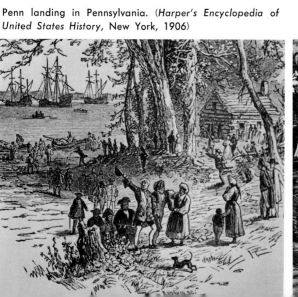

Eighteenth-century Philadelphia. (Engraved by B. F. Lazelt, Library of Congress)

Colonial Quakers on the way to church. (*Harper's Encyclopedia of United States History,* New York, 1906)

In the eighteenth century the flow of immigration from England was less dramatic than formerly. Even Georgia, founded in 1732 as a philanthropic refuge for poor debtors, did not attract many newcomers. It drew most of its people not from across the ocean, but from internal migration within the continent.

Englishmen now found fewer reasons to migrate. The Glorious Revolution of 1688 had stabilized politics and created a tolerant attitude toward dissent, at least among Protestants. The development of industry provided an outlet at home for the labor of peasants pushed off the soil.

The parliamentary supremacy established in 1688 also put in charge of the government the gentry and merchants who strengthened the empire, within which they allowed the American colonies to thrive in salutary neglect. Gradually, the settlements acquired a character of their own as they adapted inherited ideas and practices to wilderness conditions.

Society, politics, and religion were less subject to control and therefore freer than in Europe. Poor strangers could earn a livelihood and rise in rank; representative institutions gave the populace a share in governmental decisions; and different sects learned to coexist without persecuting one another. These qualities attracted immigrants from many parts of Europe and also strengthened the colonies in conflicts with the nearby Dutch, French, and Spanish possessions.

Philadelphia harbor in 1760. (A rare print in the possession of Parker Galleries, London, United Press International)

Arrival of the colonists in Georgia. (New York Public Library)

A quarrel between the English and the Dutch on the New York-Connecticut frontier. (New York Public Library)

James II, removed from the throne of England by the Glorious Revolution of 1688. (Edwin Markham, *Dueling for Empire*, New York, 1912–1914)

The English tear down the Dutch arms and take possession of Saybrook, Connecticut. (New York Public Library)

The British colonies on the eve of the Revolution. (Library of Congress)

4

The Varied Breeds of New Men

By the middle of the eighteenth century, the British government controlled the North American continent east of the Alleghenies and between Florida and Canada. The institutions developed under its suzerainty thereafter remained basic to American society. Yet the growing population of the area had ceased to be purely English. Increasingly the colonists were conscious that they were somehow set apart from the people of the mother country. By the time the conflict with Britain erupted in 1774, the Americans knew they were a distinct nation—even the loyalists who wished to preserve a connection with the crown.

The transformation of English colonists into Americans was due in part to the fact that other breeds of men had been drawn into the society. In 1775, when J. Hector St. John de Crèvecoeur asked, "What then is this new man, the American?" he answered his own question: "They are a mixture of English, Scotch, Irish, French, Dutch, Germans, and Swedes. From this promiscuous breed, that race, now called Americans, have arisen."

The process that permitted the peaceful mingling of people who in Europe had fought each other for generations was not the result of plan or conscious policy. The English were quite ethnocentric and convinced of their own superiority. Their willingness to share the land with others was forced upon them by the circumstances of settlement.

To make themselves masters of the country, the British had to conquer the colonies established by the Dutch and the Swedes. The task proved not difficult. Yet the original settlers remained where they were so that the absorption of the seized territory injected alien elements into the English population of America.

On the Hudson River, the Dutch in 1620 had established New Netherland as an adjunct to their operations in the West Indies. The little town of New Amsterdam on Manhattan Island was the headquarters from which they expected to trade legally with their South American and Caribbean colonies and illegally with those of Spain. Farmers on Long Island and up the Hudson supplied agricultural goods for consumption in the city and for export; and there were a few outposts for trade with the Indians in the vicinity of Albany. The Dutch West India Company welcomed anyone, and New Amsterdam developed into a thriving commercial city, composed of a mixture of many peoples. In the 1650s, it was said, eighteen languages were spoken there. Trade was the main concern of these colonists and they often felt neglected by the company in Amsterdam. In 1650, for instance, they complained that the government was inefficient and that settlement proceeded more slowly than in Virginia or Massachusetts. As a result, the capitulation to the attacking English forces in 1664 troubled only the testy governor, Peter Stuyvesant. Most of the seven thousand people in the colony were as content to live under British as under Dutch rule.

The influence of the Netherlands nevertheless en-

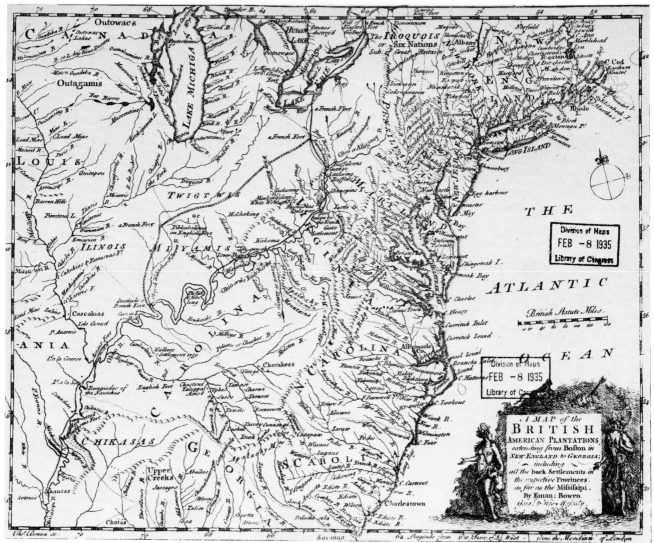

A contemporary map of the country from Boston to Georgia, together with the back settlements, 1754. (By E. Bowen, Library of Congress)

Dutch settlers in Manhattan. (New York Public Library)

The earliest view of New Amsterdam. (Joost Hartger, Amsterdam, 1651, in Albert Ulmann, *A Landmark History of New York*, New York, 1901)

View of New Amsterdam in the seventeenth century. (Brown Brothers)

Ships in the harbor of New Amsterdam, 1656. (*Harper's Encyclopedia of United States History*, New York, 1906)

Peter Stuyvesant and his council in 1652. (From a picture by T. D. Bray in 1663, Library of Congress)

John De Pyster. Dan Van Buskirk. Philip Van Renssellear. Peter Stuyvesant. William Sturtevant. Michael Dykeman.

Surrender by the Dutch to the English. (New York Public Library)

William of Orange. (John L. Motley, *Dutch Nation*, New York, 1908)

Landing of the Swedes at Paradise Point on the Delaware River, 1638. (A nineteenth-century representation, New York Public Library)

The Old Swedish Church at Wilmington, Delaware, built in 1698. (Photograph from Edwin Markham, *On Savage Shores*, New York, 1914)

dured. The existing population long retained its character, and the Dutch language and churches persisted into the nineteenth century. Accommodation was easy because Holland in any case became an ally after 1688, when William of Orange mounted the throne of England, and because of the similarity of religious and cultural institutions in the two countries.

Farther south on the Delaware River a Swedish commercial company had established Fort Christina in 1638. The colony grew slowly; its population never went above five hundred, most of them Finns, for its promoters thought of it only as a trading post. It therefore lacked the strength to fight off its ambitious neighbors. In 1655, the Dutch under Peter Stuyvesant, who had always resented the presence of the Swedish settlement, moved down and swallowed up the colony. As a result,

this area, too, became British nine years later when New Netherland's turn came to yield to a conqueror.

Voluntary immigration was, however, a more important source of aliens than conquest. The English colonists proved willing to accept substantial numbers of people different from themselves. The Puritans were at first suspicious of any strangers who might undermine the effort to build a Bible commonwealth in the wilderness. But time somewhat weakened even their distrust of outsiders. Other colonists felt no such scruples. The Virginia Company early made strenuous attempts to attract skilled artisans from Europe and brought over occasional Dutchmen, Frenchmen, Germans, Italians, Poles, and even a Persian. Anyone who could help develop the country was welcome.

This receptive attitude was the product both of the

Evacuation of Fort Christina by the Swedes, 1655. (New York Public Library)

A gallery of early colonial leaders, most of them gentlemen by origin. Stuyvesant is in the middle of the right-hand column. (New York Public Library)

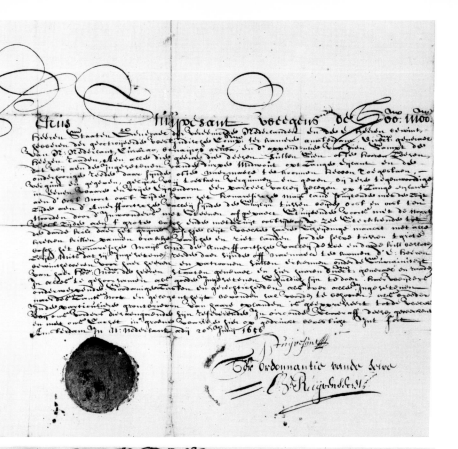

Grants of land, as in this deed, June 20, 1656, to the settlers of Midwout (later in Kings County, New York), were important in attracting settlers. (Smithsonian Institution)

New York State continued the pre-revolutionary land grant policy as in this deed for territory in Montgomery County, New York, 1790. (New-York Historical Society)

Broadside encouraging settlers by grants of land in New York, 1738. (New-York Historical Society)

Encouragement given for People to remove an settle in the Province of New-York i America.

The Honourable *George Clarke*, Esq; Lieu Governour and Commander in chief o the Province of *New-York*, Hath upon the Pe tition of Mr. *Lauchline Campbell* from *Ifla, North Britain*, promised to grant him Thirty thoufan Acres of Land at the *Wood-Creek*, free of a Charges excepting the Survey and the King Quit-Rent, which is about one Shilling an Nine Pence Farthing *Sterling* for each hundre Acres. And also, To grant to thirty Familie already landed here Lands in proportion t each Family, from five hundred Acres unt one Hundred and Fifty only paying th Survey and the King's Quit-Rent. And al *Proteftants* that incline to come and fettle in thi Colony may have Lands granted them fron the Crown for three Pounds *Sterling* per hun dred Acres and paying the yearly Quit-Rent.

Dated in New-York this 4th Day of December, 1738.   GEORGE CLARKE

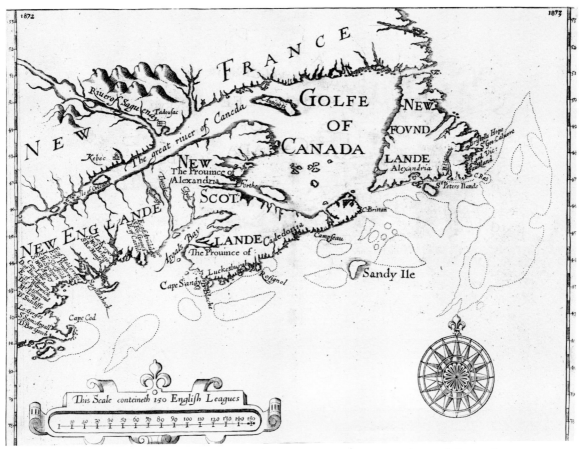

Map of New England and New Scotland (Nova Scotia), 1625. (Library of Congress)

need for labor and of the loose social institutions of the colonies. Land was plentiful, hands were not. In 1680, after seventy-five years of effort, there were fewer than two hundred thousand souls in all the provinces. Migration from England alone would not fill up the country. Immense resources awaited exploitation, and as long as the shortage of labor persisted, place of birth mattered little.

Furthermore, there was space within which different peoples could live side by side without disturbing one another. Certainly in the west, in the interior of Pennsylvania or Virginia, there was room enough so that each family could work and worship and raise its children in its own way. In the closer quarters of the cities, more regard was necessary for the sensibilities of neighbors. But even there, no group had power enough to sustain a single standard of propriety. Tolerance was not so much a principle as a practical necessity. The established churches did not prosecute dissenters; there were no guilds of consequence, and cultural, philanthropic, and social organizations were voluntary. In all these matters, people could follow their own preferences, a condition consistently attractive to immigrants.

Subjects of the British monarch, though not English, had a right to move into the colonies that owed him allegiance. In the seventeenth and eighteenth centuries, the

efforts of the crown to consolidate its hold over Scotland, Ireland, and Wales created serious economic and political dislocations and displaced many people. Significant numbers from all these areas had arrived in the American colonies by the time of the Revolution.

The union of Scotland with England in 1707 had immediate and perilous social consequences. Trade barriers thereafter no longer protected the Scottish farmers and artisans in the Lowlands who found it difficult to compete with the more advanced English economy. On the other hand, there were opportunities for migration to the south; Scots soon became familiar figures in the trades and professions of London and the smaller cities. Some of these restless men also made the more hazardous move to America.

At first the union did not affect the remote Highlanders. Economically self-sufficient and organized in closely knit clans, these people were accustomed to go their own way, without regard for the outer world. But they were fiercely loyal to the House of Stuart and refused to accept the Hanoverian George I, who ascended the English throne in 1714, as their proper king. Their uprising a year later failed. Severe repressive measures then broke up their clans and forced many families to leave, some of them for the hilly interior of Carolina. Movement from both sources continued through the

Highland Scots in the eighteenth century. (New York Public Library)

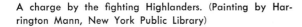

A charge by the fighting Highlanders. (Painting by Harrington Mann, New York Public Library)

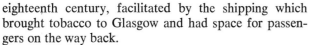

eighteenth century, facilitated by the shipping which brought tobacco to Glasgow and had space for passengers on the way back.

More important than the direct migration from Scotland was the flow of people of Scottish origin who had already moved once before and were willing to make a second change. In the seventeenth century, the English government, determined to keep the Catholic Irish under control, had transplanted thousands of doughty Scottish Presbyterians from the Lowlands to Ulster, in northern Ireland. Belfast was the chief city through which the new arrivals fanned out into the countryside, once that was pacified. The Scots soon multiplied beyond the capacity of their little farms to support them, even though some eked out a livelihood by linen weaving. Furthermore, few owned the plots on which they labored, for they had been accustomed to renting on terms that were at first easy in order to attract them. When their leases "fell in" and the absentee landlords refused to renew, they had no alternative but to seek new homes.

Their situation became calamitous after a series of crop failures in 1716 and in the years that followed. The poorest faced the prospect of certain starvation unless they got away. Wandering down to the docks of Belfast and Londonderry, where the ships from Philadelphia unloaded cargoes of flaxseed, they sold themselves to any captain for the cost of their passage. He in turn would auction off their services once he reached the New World; and they would labor a term of years to redeem themselves from their purchasers. The redemptioners were very much like the indentured servants of the preceding century, except that the promise of free land was no longer involved, the headright system having fallen into disuse.

Small groups found homes in Massachusetts and New Hampshire. But most of the Scotch-Irish went to Pennsylvania and, once free of their service, headed for the frontier; life in Ulster had prepared them for the wilderness. They settled in the interior and moved down the great valley into Virginia and the Carolinas. By the middle of the eighteenth century the movement snowballed as ship captains sent agents into the rural Irish countryside to spread information about the virtues of America. By the time of the Revolution, about three hundred thousand Scotch-Irish had made the crossing. Some who came as servants were able to rise in the world. Charles Thomson, for instance, became secretary of the Continental Congress. Most remained frontier farmers, tough, resolute, and independent.

The Presbyterian faith to which the Scotch-Irish had clung in all their moves imbued them with a consciousness of their own sinfulness and a fear of God's wrath. Individualistic and aggressive, they looked to religion

Charles Thomson, 1729–1824, American patriot. (New York Public Library)

A Quaker family. (Drawn by Benjamin West, Brown Brothers)

for stern discipline and found an emotional outlet in periodic revivals. Their needs shaped the career of William Tennent, a graduate of the University of Edinburgh and an ordained priest in the established Protestant Church of Ireland, who came to Philadelphia in 1716 at the age of forty-three. Two years later he became a Presbyterian minister and labored at the task until his death in 1745. A fiery evangelical, he founded the "log college" in 1736 at Neshaming, Pennsylvania, where he trained his sons and others to keep the gospel alive.

Immigrants from other parts of Ireland were more difficult to identify. A number of Quakers from that country followed Penn to Pennsylvania. No doubt, some Catholic Irish also came as servants to New York, Pennsylvania, and Maryland. But they were difficult to trace, either because they were not distinguished from the Scotch-Irish, or because they were reticent about their identity in communities that still regarded Catholicism with distrust. There were also some natives of Wales

A cottage in County Cork, a Catholic area of Ireland that remained unchanged through the centuries. (Photoworld)

Arrival in America of the Huguenots under Jean Ribault in the sixteenth century. (New York Public Library)

Protestant conception of the tortures facing the Huguenots in the seventeenth century. (New York Public Library)

among the Pennsylvania Friends. They were joined in the eighteenth century by small groups of other Welshmen who established firm little centers of settlement in that colony.

There was room also for foreigners who were not even subjects of the king. Protestant sympathies thus created a favorable environment for the French Huguenots. These Protestants had been tolerated in Catholic France by virtue of the Edict of Nantes (1598), the revocation of which in 1685 threw them into peril. Great numbers left their homelands, some to come to America. By the end of the century, they were found in every colony from Massachusetts to South Carolina.

Religious forces also influenced the migration of Germans. In the eighteenth century the parts of Europe inhabited by German-speaking people were politically disorganized, economically unstable, and intellectually volatile. Divided among a dozen large states and hundreds of autonomous principalities and free cities, the vast

area between Alsace in the west and Poland in the east was subject to fitful changes in government and to unpredictable fluctuations in trade and agriculture. All too often the region provided the battlefields for the wars that intermittently desolated the Continent. And since some places were Catholic and others Protestant, transfers of territory often created conflicts of loyalty.

This was fertile soil for religious dissent. Men and women, distressed by the recurrent disasters of the material world, sought spiritual consolation, which the formal established churches—Catholic or Lutheran— seemed incapable of providing. Such people longed for an immediate experience and tried to attain direct communion with the divine spirit through acts of piety, fervent emotional worship, and deeds of benevolence. That was why the Quakers were able early to find support in Germany, and why other pietistic sects animated by similar aspirations gained members from every level of society there.

Huguenot refugees after the revocation of the Edict of Nantes, 1685. (Painting by E. J. C. Hamman, New York Public Library)

Faneuil Hall, Boston. Used for public meetings during the events that led to the Revolution, this famous building was erected with a gift from a Huguenot family that settled in Boston. (Engraving by John McRae, Library of Congress)

The city of Magdeburg besieged by the army of the Flemish Field Marshal von Tilly, 1631. The experience of war was common to many German towns of the seventeenth century. (New York Public Library)

An embarkation scene in the early eighteenth century. (New York Public Library)

Plan for the layout of Philadelphia and the settlement of Pennsylvania under William Penn. Note the township set aside for the Germans. (Library of Congress)

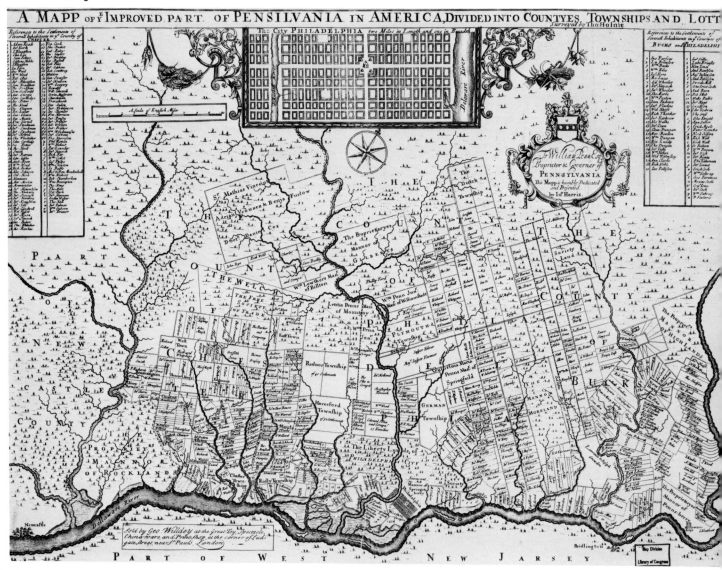

Religious persecution in the sixteenth century.

Migration to the New World offered many advantages to the members of such sects. They could escape the hazards of religious persecution, leave behind the corruption of the Old World, and find space in the New for life in accordance with their ideals. The prospect of an escape from privation was an additional inducement.

Francis Daniel Pastorius, a university graduate in law, who was converted to the doctrines of the Society of Friends, led a group of Mennonites (an older sect with similar views) to Pennsylvania where they laid out a successful settlement in Germantown. They spread through the colony and later into the interior of the country; the Amish were one of their offshoots. The Moravians and the Schwenkenfelders were other groups that joined the migration.

Other refugees fled out of desperation even though no religious vision of a regenerate life drew them on. When the conquering armies of Louis XIV swept through the Rhineland during the War of the Spanish Succession, thousands of Protestant Palatines fled to London. In 1708 and 1709, many of them were transported to New York in the hope that they would raise naval stores along the Hudson for the British. The scheme never worked and scores of the hapless Palatines perished of illness and hunger. The rest made their way to the frontier, forming tiny settlements along the Mohawk and Susquehanna valleys where they at last found a tolerable livelihood. So, too, in the 1730s about a thousand Lutheran Salzburgers, driven away by a Catholic bishop, found refuge in Georgia, in the vicinity of Ebenezer.

The majority of the Germans, like other eighteenth-century immigrants, however, were simple peasants and artisans forced to migrate by economic hardship. Like the Scotch-Irish, many of them came as redemptioners.

A regular system developed after the Treaty of Utrecht in 1713 brought a period of peace to the Continent. Dutch merchants in Amsterdam and Rotterdam sent scores of agents down the Rhine to enlist hundreds of men and women by unstinting praise of the new land. Many a poor soul cursed the Newlanders, as the agents were called, while he suffered the hardships of the sea voyage and while he toiled for strangers in a far distant world. But the promises became real often enough to keep hope alive and to sustain the traffic. Despite the interruptions caused by war in 1742 and 1753 the number transported increased steadily and reached a peak in the decade after 1763.

Germans who were not members of a pietistic sect also felt the need of religious organization, a need Henry M. Mühlenberg helped to satisfy. One of nine children left impoverished by the death of their father, Mühlenberg nevertheless fought his way to an education and became a Lutheran pastor, intending to do missionary work. After considering the East Indies as a field, he accepted a call to Pennsylvania in 1741, at the age of thirty. He put the affairs of the colony's three little existing churches in order, brought in helpers, and developed the denomination. Mühlenberg married the daughter of Conrad Weiser, the frontiersman, and their eleven children became influential in their group and in the nation.

Even Jews, who suffered from political and social disabilities in every other part of the world, found refuge in the colonies. The twenty-three who arrived at New Amsterdam from Brazil in 1654 were Portuguese. In the next century coreligionists from Holland, Germany, England, and Poland joined the first arrivals. This was not a mass migration, but one composed mostly of merchants. At the Revolution, there were only about

Interior of a Dutch Mennonite home. (*Harper's Monthly*, May, 1880, New York Public Library)

The Moravians left their mark on Bethlehem, Pennsylvania, on into the nineteenth century. Scenes of Moravian home and religious life. (*Harper's Weekly*, April 18, 1874, New York Public Library)

The Amish retain a strong sense of community. A barn-raising in Lancaster County, Pennsylvania, in 1968 shows the strength of cooperative habits. The traditional hats of the men are in marked contrast to the modern tractor. (United Press International)

Louis XIV, King of France, 1643–1715. (Nostalgia Press, Inc.)

The Salzburgers, 1732. The lower picture is a view of the town they left behind. The upper picture shows two emigrants. The legend warns them not to flee in the winter or on the Sabbath; the motto affirms that only the gospel drives them into exile, and although they leave the fatherland, they remain in God's hands. (*Ausführliche historie derer emigranten oder vertriebenen lutheraner aus dem ertz-bissthum Saltzburg*, Leipzig: J. M. Teuber. Library of Congress)

The Salzburgers pass through Frankfurt, 1733. (New York Public Library)

Sixteenth-century peasant rebels in Germany.

The departure of emigrants on the way to America from Basel, 1805. (Woodcut by Johan Heinrich Heitz, in *Briefe aus Amerika von einem Basler Landmann*, Basel, 1806, Library of Congress)

Henry M. Mühlenberg. (Reproduction of a painting by Charles W. Peale in Independence Hall, Philadelphia, Library of Congress)

The old Jewish cemetery of New York, first used in 1656 and still a setting for prayers in 1926. (United Press International)

two thousand Jews in all the colonies. Yet they had organized congregations in New York, Newport, Savannah, Philadelphia, Charleston, and Richmond; and they had acquired the civic rights of residing where they wished, of engaging in any trade, of voting and of holding public office.

The favorable treatment accorded the Jews showed the extent to which the colonies had departed from European precedent even before the Revolution. The willingness to accept settlers of all origins had a profound influence upon American society. It stimulated growth and was an important factor in the fourfold increase of population in the half century after 1713. Moreover, it gave colonial life a pluralistic flavor. The degree of homogeneity varied from place to place, with Connecticut the most purely English and Pennsylvania the least. But everywhere the character of the population necessitated some modifications in the institutions brought over from Britain. Sometimes the result was bitter sectional and ethnic conflict. But, more often, shared experiences forced dissimilar peoples into neighborly tolerance. Even the residual hostility to Catholics, while fed by old Puritan tradition, was less religious than national in character. Prejudice against the Papists remained alive not out of dislike of the small groups of Catholics in the colonies but out of real fear of the French and Spaniards on the frontiers.

The first Jewish cemetery in New York City, established under the Dutch. (Photograph of 1900, Albert Ulmann, *Landmark History of New York*, New York, 1901)

Juan Ponce de León (1460?–1521), discoverer of Florida. (*Harper's Encyclopedia of United States History*, New York, 1906)

5
The Spaniards and French on the Frontiers

Spain and France were the strongest European powers in the seventeenth and eighteenth centuries. Their population was larger, their wealth greater than England's, and both ruled extensive empires around the world. Furthermore, a family alliance united the two countries after 1700 when Philip V, grandson of Louis XIV, mounted the throne of Spain. Thereafter the French and Spanish branches of the Bourbon family generally cooperated against their common English enemy in battles fought on European as well as on Asian and American soil. Yet the Bourbons proved incapable of ousting the British from North America and, in time, lost their own foothold there.

The Spaniards had gained most by the initial acts of discovery and settlement; in the sixteenth century, there was no question of their dominance in America. However, the wealth of the Indies, which enriched Spanish society, also sapped its vigor and deprived it of incentive toward enterprise or adventure. Increasingly, Spaniards chose to enjoy past gains rather than to take the risks of seeking new ones; and they allowed cautious or corrupt bureaucrats to administer the empire. In any case, America for the residents of Madrid or Seville brought to mind the fortunes in gold, silver, and sugar of Cuba, Mexico, and Peru. Whatever energies they devoted to the New World, Spaniards expended it south of the Rio Grande.

Their migrations therefore left only feeble marks on the area that became the United States. Florida, which had been discovered by Juan Ponce de León in 1513, was first settled in 1565, and then only in order to keep out intruding Huguenots. The colony remained a backward military outpost, with Saint Augustine its only important town. Spain held possession until 1819, except for twenty years of English control after 1763. But the settlements were always small, incapable of growth, and dependent on subsidies from Madrid. Louisiana also passed briefly into the hands of the Spaniards at the end of the eighteenth century. But the territory soon reverted to the French who in turn relinquished it to the United States in 1803. There were few traces there of the Spanish occupation.

The greatest Spanish impact on future United States territory was along the southwestern frontier. The legendary Seven Cities of Cibolá (its streets were reported to be paved with gold and silver) drew the conquistadores northward, from Mexico City, to establish the settlement at Santa Fe in 1610. But only a few hundred Spaniards moved into New Mexico; the population remained largely Indian.

More than a century later, the Spaniards pushed out of Mexico toward California. By 1770 Don Gaspar de Portolá and Fra Junípero Serra had reached San Diego and Monterey, and Juan Bautista de Anza had arrived in San Francisco in 1776. Most of the people in these places were, however, Indians. The Spaniards who provided the military force of the presidio and the religious authority of the mission were a small minority. Yet since

Map showing French and Spanish territories after the Revolution, 1783. (Library of Congress)

Fernando de Soto, leading a Spanish expedition, arrives at the Mississippi in 1541. (A nineteenth-century painting by W. H. Powell, New York Public Library)

De Soto's party descends the Mississippi after his death in 1542. (New York Public Library)

The first settlement of St. Augustine by the Spaniards, 1565. (New York Public Library)

A view of St. Augustine. (*Harper's Encyclopedia of United States History*, New York, 1906)

Spanish troops assault the British fort at Pensacola, 1781. The explosion shown in the picture killed more than 100 defenders and resulted in the surrender of the fort. (Engraving by N. Ponce, Library of Congress)

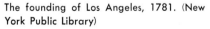

THE LOUISIANA PURCHASE.
MESSRS. MONROE AND LIVINGSTONE COMPLETING NEGOTIATIONS WITH TALLYRAND, APRIL 30, 1803

James Monroe, Robert R. Livingston, and Charles Maurice Talleyrand complete the negotiations for the purchase of Louisiana, 1803. In the painting by H. C. Whorf, Jefferson and Napoleon look benevolently on. (Library of Congress)

The founding of Los Angeles, 1781. (New York Public Library)

Monument to Fra Junipero Serra in Monterey, California. (Library of Congress, Wittemann Collection)

first Spain and then Mexico controlled the area until 1848, when war transferred it to the United States, Hispanic culture left a permanent impression there.

The cultural influence of France also survived in some parts of North America long after it lost its most important continental possessions. Its claims went back to the voyage of Jacques Cartier in 1535; and its rulers aggressively tried to maintain and expand the colony in Canada, the chief cities of which were Montreal and Quebec. The French had the advantage of an effective, centralized colonial administration. The crown provided substantial military and financial support. Resourceful and devoted Jesuit and Sulpician missionaries carried the faith to the Indians and won their loyalty. And courageous explorers penetrated deep into the continent.

René Robert Cavelier, Sieur de la Salle, evoked the vision of a great French empire in America. He had been a Jesuit, but had left the Society to earn glory in the world. Having spent ten years in Canada, he became familiar with the interior and conceived the idea of link-

ing the settlements on the St. Lawrence with those of New Orleans, on the Gulf of Mexico, by way of the Great Lakes and the Mississippi. In 1679, at the age of thirty-six, he started on a long arduous journey to mark the route. Although he was later killed by his mutinous men, he had succeeded in demonstrating the feasibility of his dream.

In the next half century, the French continued their effort to develop a line of fortified posts between Montreal and New Orleans that would give them control of the continent. They expected thus to exploit the fur trade and keep the English penned up east of the Allegheny Mountains.

The scheme failed. Back in 1609 the French had earned the bitter enmity of the Iroquois when Samuel de Champlain joined their Algonquin enemies in battle against them. The redoubtable warriors of the Iroquois confederation thereafter fought French control of the interior and the fur trade. These Indians would prove useful allies of the English.

Spanish mission of the Alamo. (Wood engraving from Augustus L. Mason, *Romance and Tragedy of Pioneer Life,* Cincinnati, 1883, Library of Congress)

Jacques Cartier taking possession of New France, 1534. (New York Public Library)

La Salle landing in Texas, 1682. (New York Public Library)

La Salle leaving Fort St. Louis in Texas, 1687. (New York Public Library)

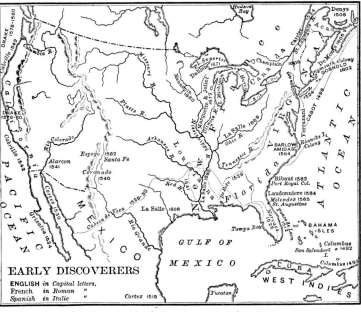

French explorations in North America. (Nostalgia Press, Inc.)

Champlain helps the Algonquins defeat the Iroquois, 1609. (From Champlain's own drawing, New York Public Library)

Samuel de Champlain. (Harper's Encyclopedia of United States History, New York, 1906)

Defeat of Braddock's expedition by the Indians, 1755. In the first stages of the French and Indian War, the British troops, unfamiliar with wilderness warfare, were victims of a disastrous ambush by the Indian allies of France. The incident showed the advantage familiarity with the forests gave natives, red or white, over European troops. (Wood engraving by John Andrew in Ballou's Pictorial, July 7, 1855, Library of Congress)

Moreover, Canada never developed the population capable of supporting Bourbon ambitions. On the eve of the French and Indian War (1754–1763), which was the decisive contest for the mainland, there were just about fifty-five thousand French colonists to oppose well over a million English. Canada had not received the stream of immigration that strengthened its neighbors to the south. Until 1789, the law limited the rights of peasants in France to leave their land and barred foreigners and Protestants from the colonies. Furthermore, within the province of Quebec, the seigneurial system created a kind of feudal tenure unattractive to men who sought freedom and status as well as economic betterment. The immigration that strengthened the English colonies passed the French by.

At the end of the century, Napoleon briefly revived

The embarkation of the Acadians, 1755. The French residents of Nova Scotia were expelled when the English captured the territory, many of them moving to Louisiana. H. W. Longfellow's poem made the incident famous. (Nostalgia Press, Inc.)

the dream of an American empire, but also proved incapable of carrying it forward. The legacy of France in New Orleans and Quebec was therefore cultural rather than political. Long after the Bourbons and the Bonapartes had vanished from the scene, traces of the French presence lingered in Louisiana—in the language, the cuisine, the parish boundaries, the law, and the leisurely patterns of Creole life.

Neither France nor Spain profited from the migrations that enabled Britain to settle and keep the mainland. The Bourbons could win occasional battles; they could not win the war. Their colonists were mostly administrators, soldiers, and priests who did not strike roots. The French and Spanish, who were fighting for empire, were at a disadvantage in the contest with people who were fighting for homes.

French quarter of New Orleans, showing the characteristic balconies and ironwork. (*Harper's Monthly*, December, 1858, New York Public Library)

French church in Louisiana, built 1688. (New York Public Library)

The festivities of the early French of the Mississippi Valley. These settlers left an impression of gaiety that contrasted with the seriousness of their British rivals. (New York Public Library)

60

A nineteenth-century slave market on the Gambia River, Africa. (Engraving by Andrew and Filmer in Richard Drake, *Revelations of a Slave Smuggler*, New York [1860], Library of Congress)

6
Immigrants in Bondage

One current in the general flow of peoples to the New World early acquired a distinctive character. Migration from Africa followed a course different from that out of Europe. Although the divergence was scarcely apparent at the start, it grew steadily in importance as colonial society developed.

The colonists of the early seventeenth century recognized various degrees of freedom and servitude. All men were bound by some obligations and enjoyed some privileges, but it was assumed that those duties and rights, far from equal, would vary from person to person according to rank and position. This was the point of view of a society that took differences of status for granted. It was God's will, John Winthrop once explained, that "in all times some must be rich, some poor, some high and eminent in power and dignity, others mean and in subjection."

Winthrop's contemporaries thought that their community was organized in a set of graduated steps with the greatest freedom above and the greatest servitude below. Nobles, gentlemen, and great merchants occupied places near the top. Below them were yeomen, traders, and artisans. Still less free were various dependent persons—children, apprentices, servants—all subject to the discipline of the master in whose household they lived.

There was thus nothing unusual about the status of the servants who came to America. Nor was it surprising that they occupied the lowest position in society. The only uncommon aspect of their situation, for which experience in Europe offered little precedent, was the probability that some of them would rise after they finished their terms of service.

Any individual's chances of getting ahead depended upon the conditions of his bondage. Englishmen or other Europeans who signed contracts voluntarily in order to come to the New World exercised some control over the terms of their service. The landowners who needed labor, the ship captains who needed passengers, and the agents who recruited the migrants all had an interest in making favorable arrangements so as to stimulate the movement of people. The length of servitude rarely exceeded seven years and often was as low as four; and there was sometimes provision for a stake at the attainment of freedom. Such servants were therefore ready to strike out on their own and to advance in status once their terms were over.

By contrast, men whose migration was not voluntary but a product of force had no choice and therefore no control over their future. Lacking any contract, they were unable to influence the conditions of their labor or the length of their terms. These helpless victims went where they were led, worked as long as their masters insisted, and had only faint prospects of improving their lots.

Many different types of people found themselves

New England yeomen. (Brown Brothers)

First landing of slaves in Jamestown. (From the drawing by Freeland A. Carter, in Edwin Markham, *The Real America*, New York, 1912)

The poor of London—seeking refuge. (New York Public Library)

among the involuntary immigrants. In England itself hundreds of men, women, and children were at the mercy of local authorities. Paupers and orphans, servants who could find no masters, and vagrants without places crowded the workhouses and jails, along with respectable folk confined because they were unable to pay their debts. It seemed plausible to ship such dependents off to America rather than to support them indefinitely out of taxes. Sometimes, for the same reason, convicted criminals were sent to the colonies where they would work for their keep instead of subsisting in idleness. An act of Parliament in 1717 provided for the punishment of felons by transportation instead of by hanging and in-

creased the numbers bound to service in the New World whether they willed it or not.

Prisoners taken in war sometimes met the same fate. It was a deed of generosity to capture rather than to kill an enemy and it seemed fitting that the lucky survivor pay in labor for his life thus spared. The practice was not questioned in the seventeenth century. The colonists, where they could, applied it to the indigenous Indians. The red men, however, were few in number and so familiar with the country that they generally escaped back into the wilderness. By contrast, Irishmen and Scots captured in the intermittent wars of the seventeenth century and sold in America, though considered as uncivilized as the Indians, had no alternative but to work for their masters.

Occasionally, also, European shipmasters trading off the coast of Africa purchased from local chieftains the prisoners seized in tribal battles. In the first half of the seventeenth century, these captives were usually sold in Caribbean and South American markets. But, now and again, after 1619, a cargo of Africans appeared for sale in Virginia or its neighboring colonies. Until 1660, however, the numbers were small and the status of black servants was not markedly distinct from that of whites.

After that date, the fate of the Negroes began to diverge radically from that of other servants. The process was gradual, but the trend was unmistakable. The result was the emergence of the institution of black slavery.

Insofar as there was any choice, every settler preferred servants of an origin similar to his own. The conditions of life in the wilderness were difficult, housing was crowded, and there was no police force to maintain orderly rules of conduct. Survival seemed to depend upon common habits, language, and culture that enabled people to live together. The colonist therefore wished to

An Indian captive being sent into slavery. (New York Public Library)

A nineteenth-century slave market in Zanzibar. (Sketch by Lieutenant Henn, *Illustrated London News,* June 8, 1872, New York Public Library)

Slaves being prepared for the voyage. (W. O. Blake, *The History of Slavery,* Columbus, Ohio, 1857–1860)

Gang of African captives on the way to the coast. (New York Public Library)

Slaves being paddled and whipped. (Schomburg Collection, New York Public Library)

Slaves being branded. (W. O. Blake, *The History of Slavery,* Columbus, Ohio, 1857–1860)

Slave-driving in central Africa. The practice still continued in the nineteenth century, conducted largely by Arab dealers. (Nostalgia Press, Inc.)

take into his household servants from his own district or at least from his own country; and if these were not available, he sought a stranger as much like himself as possible. In the eyes of an Englishman, his own countrymen were most desirable, then Scots, Welsh, Scotch-Irish, Protestant Europeans, other Christians, and Jews. Least desirable, because most alien, were Africans.

Reflecting these preferences, the law attempted to encourage white and to discourage black immigration. The colonial governments were solicitous of the rights of European servants lest an evil reputation halt their movement. On the other hand, there was no limit to the power masters exercised over Africans, who sent no letters home and whose migration was not in any case a matter of free choice. As a result, the conditions of the favored group improved steadily, that of the disfavored deteriorated. By the end of the seventeenth century, there was a clear distinction between the white servant who worked for a term and then became free and equal and the black slave who was a chattel, bound for the whole of his life, and whose servitude passed to his children.

By then, the trade in Negroes had boomed. Slavery was not new to Africa. But until the seventeenth century captives either had been held locally by the tribe that captured them or they were sent overland to Arab markets. In either case, the numbers involved had been small. But the appearance of the Europeans and the development of traffic with America expanded the demand, and greedy chiefs hastened to provide adequate supplies, even at times selling off their own people. Most of the human cargoes were destined for the West Indies, where the demand and the ability to pay were greatest. But there was also a rising flow to the mainland colonies, either directly from the Guinea coast or from the Caribbean islands.

The appearance of the plantation system in South Carolina, Virginia, and Maryland toward the end of the seventeenth century, and later in Georgia, created an insatiable demand for servile labor and dissolved the earlier hostility to the importation of Negroes. On the great estates given over to the cultivation of tobacco, rice, indigo or cotton, gangs of slaves toiled under rigid discipline, which relieved their masters of anxiety about conduct or profit. Meanwhile, white indentured servants who had a choice about their destination began to avoid the plantation colonies, preferring to go to Pennsylvania

A nineteenth-century sugar plantation. (New York Public Library)

Scenes from a cotton plantation. (New York Public Library)

Scene in the hold of a slave ship. (Engraving in Richard Drake, *Revelations of a Slave Smuggler*, New York [1860], Library of Congress)

Field work on a nineteenth-century cotton plantation. (New York Public Library)

or New York where they could look forward to becoming free landowners. As a result, the planters became still more dependent on Negro labor.

The slave trade increased rapidly in the eighteenth century. The Middle Passage now acquired its dread reputation; every crossing of the Atlantic was uncomfortable and dangerous but the perils and sufferings were immeasurably multiplied in the voyage from Africa. The slaves were wedged into the holds so tightly that they could scarcely move at all. Vessels of one hundred to two hundred tons commonly carried four hundred to five hundred Negroes, in addition to the crew and provisions. Cooped up for week after week of the long journey, deprived of air and sustained on mea-

Slaves in chains. (*Harper's Monthly*, 1864, New York Public Library)

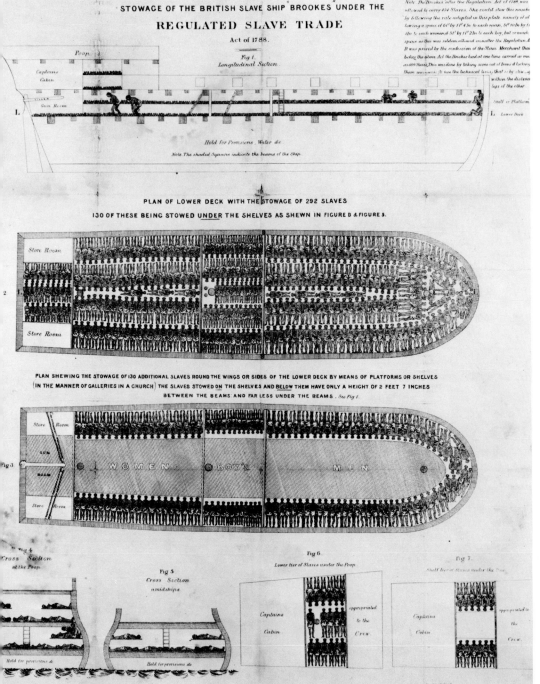

Method of stowing slaves aboard a British ship in the eighteenth century. Hundreds of slaves could be transported by utilizing every inch of space. (Library of Congress)

ger rations, the unhappy captives sickened and died at a fearsome rate. The ships that carried them were always at the mercy of the weather, of hostile cruisers during war, and of pirates during peace. And some masters were not above simply tossing their cargoes overboard when it suited their convenience.

The slave trade thrived through the eighteenth century. There was no precise count of the number transported to the mainland colonies; the best estimate is that about two hundred thousand people from Africa came ashore in the area between Maine and Georgia. A few thousand Negroes landed in the cities and in the northern colonies. But the overwhelming majority found homes in the South where their presence effected a social and economic transformation. With the aid of the new labor force, the great plantation soon overshadowed the yeoman farm as the determining element in the life of the region.

Africa thus made a substantial contribution to the American population. By the time of the American Revolution there were about five hundred thousand Negroes in the colonies, the natural increase having more than offset deaths. The great majority were slaves. The unique qualities of this migration had by then planted the seeds of a difficulty that would permanently mark the nation.

Even before the Revolution, some Americans expressed discomfort with the slave system. A few conscientious Quakers like John Woolman and the Puritan Samuel Sewall advocated the abolition of this form of bondage. In actuality the roots of slavery were growing deeper, yet it seemed not compatible with the ideas of freedom that were widely spread in the colonies. And as the revolutionary crisis approached in the 1760s and 1770s, the discrepancy between slavery and the ideals of the Republic became ever more glaring.

Slave labor on a cotton plantation. (W. O. Blake, *The History of Slavery*, Columbus, Ohio, 1857–1860)

Samuel Sewall, early critic of slavery. (Justin Winsor, *The Memorial History of Boston*, Boston, 1881)

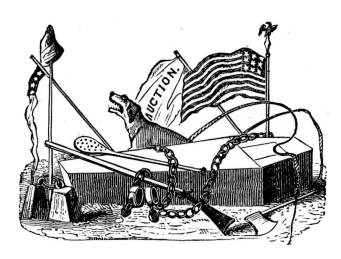

Antislavery cartoon. (Engraving in *The Oasis*, 1834, Library of Congress)

A cartoon mocking George III, who holds in his hand a copy of Thomas Paine's book, *The Rights of Man*, published in England in 1791. (Etching, Library of Congress)

7
The Revolution and American Nationality

The War for Independence gained the colonies sovereignty by casting off their ties to Britain. But the nation already existed in 1774. The Revolution, a contemporary wrote, had been effected in the hearts and minds of Americans before the first shot was fired. The desire for independence did not arise simply from grievances against George III. It sprang also from a devotion to the basic principles enunciated in the Declaration of Independence and a national sentiment that made the English connection irksome.

The United States emerged from the war with an expanded capacity for future growth. Between 1770 and 1820 the Americans created enduring federal and state governments, and developed a thriving economy. The population rose from about 2 million to more than 9 million, and the line of settlement pushed westward to beyond the Allegheny Mountains. Immigrants participated in these efforts; their presence had a symbolic value for the whole country. The cooperation of people from many parts of Europe was proof of the distinctive nationality of the United States and a token of the unlimited promise of its future.

During the war, there was some division of opinion among immigrants about the wisdom of independence. But the colonists of German or Scotch-Irish birth or antecedents had no sense of loyalty to the crown or affec-

tion for Britain. They were less likely, therefore, than people of English origin to become Tories.

The ideology of the Revolution attracted men of every origin. The appeal of the Declaration of Independence to the opinion of mankind struck a responsive chord throughout Europe, and devoted sympathizers hastened across the ocean to fight for the new republic. They agreed with Thomas Jefferson that the cause of America was the cause of all mankind.

Thomas Paine, for instance, reached Philadelphia from England in November, 1774, thirty-seven years old and a consistent failure. He had been a corset maker, a privateer, a teacher, a civil servant, and a grocer; he had married twice without luck; and he had drifted into bankruptcy. He brought with him letters of introduction from Benjamin Franklin, whom he had met in London, an understanding of the revolutionary crisis, and a gift for sharp utterance. *Common Sense,* published in January, 1776, sold 120,000 copies in a few months because it explained to Americans that they were fighting not for easier taxes but to lead the world into a new era.

The Marquis de Lafayette was at the opposite social pole from Paine. Scion of a wealthy noble family, married at the age of seventeen, he had everything his heart desired, except glory for which he lusted all his life. Revolution was the way to fame for a young man reared

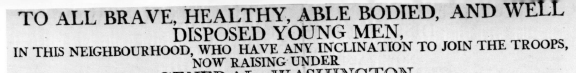

TO ALL BRAVE, HEALTHY, ABLE BODIED, AND WELL DISPOSED YOUNG MEN,

IN THIS NEIGHBOURHOOD, WHO HAVE ANY INCLINATION TO JOIN THE TROOPS,
NOW RAISING UNDER

GENERAL WASHINGTON,

FOR THE DEFENCE OF THE

LIBERTIES AND INDEPENDENCE
OF THE UNITED STATES,

Against the hostile designs of foreign enemies,

TAKE NOTICE,

THAT .... Tuesday, Wednesday, Thursday, Friday and Saturday at Spotswood in .... county, attendance will be given by Lieutenant Reading .... with his music and recruiting party of .... company in Major Shute's Battalion of the 11th regiment of infantry, commanded by Lieutenant Colonel Aaron Ogden, for the purpose of receiving the enrollment of such youth of SPIRIT, as may be willing to enter into this HONOURABLE service.

The ENCOURAGEMENT at this time, to enlist, is truly liberal and generous, namely, a bounty of TWELVE dollars, an annual and fully sufficient supply of good and handsome cloathing, a daily allowance of a large and ample ration of provisions, together with SIXTY dollars a year in GOLD and SILVER money on account of pay, the whole of which the soldier may lay up for himself and friends, as all articles proper for his subsistance and comfort are provided by law, without any expence to him.

Those who may favour this recruiting party with their attendance as above, will have an opportunity of hearing and seeing in a more particular manner, the great advantages which these brave men will have, who shall embrace this opportunity of spending a few happy years in viewing the different parts of this beautiful continent, in the honourable and truly respectable character of a soldier, after which, he may, if he pleases return home to his friends, with his pockets FULL of money and his head COVERED with laurels.

GOD SAVE THE UNITED STATES.

A broadside announcing the visit of a recruiting officer for the revolutionary army. The appeal stresses the leadership of General Washington, the objects of the war—liberty and independence—and the bounties as inducements to enlist. (Engraving by B. Jones, Library of Congress)

Scene in a Hessian home, where a father is being conscripted for service in America. Some of the Germans who arrived under these circumstances remained to become citizens of the United States. (Brown Brothers)

Thomas Paine. (Lithograph by L. Rosenthal from a drawing by P. Kramer, 1851, Library of Congress)

Benjamin Franklin occupies the central point in this stylized painting in the United States Capitol of the scene of the adoption of the Constitution. His prominence in the picture reflected the reputation he had acquired for wisdom and sagacity. (Library of Congress)

on the philosophers of the Enlightenment. Lafayette was not yet twenty years old when he appeared in Philadelphia to accept a commission as major general in the Continental Army; his service to the American cause cost him $200,000 of his own funds. Later he participated in the French revolutions of 1789 and 1830, seeking to apply to the land of his birth the ideals he had seen realized in his adopted country.

The Baron Friedrich Wilhelm von Steuben, by contrast, was almost fifty when he received his commission as major general. He was born to a military career, for his father had been a professional soldier. Trained in the Prussian army, Von Steuben wandered about Europe after he left the service in 1763. The position he took with the Americans in 1777 he probably regarded as just another job, although he must have had some faith in the cause for he did not bother to negotiate his salary but staked his reward on the outcome of the war. He spent the hard winter at Valley Forge drilling the miserable patriots, and turned the raw troops into an orderly army. After the peace, he decided to remain in the United States, spending his winters in New York City and his summers on an estate near Utica.

Baron von Steuben. (*Institute of the Society of the Cincinnati*, New York, 1886)

Lafayette. (A nineteenth-century engraving by De Mare of a drawing by Chappel, Library of Congress)

The winter in Valley Forge became the symbol of revolutionary devotion and patriotism. Here Washington encourages his suffering troops. (Lithograph by P. Haas from the drawing by A. Gibert, 1843, Library of Congress)

Thaddeus Kosciusko. (Lithograph from the drawing by A. Girard, 1839, Library of Congress)

Haym Salomon. (Smithsonian Collection of Business Americana)

Thaddeus Kosciusko, the Polish patriot, was less fortunate than Von Steuben. A gentleman educated as an engineer, he was sensitive to the call of the Revolution in 1776, particularly because he was suffering from an unhappy love affair. Borrowing the cost of his passage, Kosciusko came to America and provided valuable aid on the techniques of fortification. But his efforts to gain freedom also for his native Poland failed, and he wandered back and forth across the Atlantic for the rest of his life, feeling at home nowhere.

Another Polish advocate of liberty suffered under czarist control, both as a Pole and a Jew. Haym Salomon, despairing of improvement in Europe, came to New York in 1772 and, after the British seized the city, fled to Philadelphia. He was an agent for the French and

Dutch in getting supplies to the Americans. Impoverished by his willingness to advance gold in order to sustain the Continental paper currency, he died two years after the victory to which he had contributed.

Men of foreign birth were only a small minority among those who struggled for American independence. Yet their presence was a heartening assurance that the former colonists did not stand alone against a great empire. Thousands of people elsewhere wished them success in the conflict.

For the citizens of the new republic, the link to the outer world through immigration was also an important symbol of their unique nationality. They were not simply rebellious Britons but a new people; "Europe, and not England, is the parent country of America," wrote Thomas Paine.

That belief compelled Americans to think about nationality not as a characteristic inherited by birth or by attachment to a specific territory. People of heterogeneous antecedents who were all relative newcomers to the continent were Americans by virtue not of common descent or common heritage, but rather of common destiny. The nation was the product not of its roots in the past but of its prospects for the future.

It followed from that basic assumption that the United States should be open to the immigration of anyone who wished to share that future. No doubt there were both advantages and disadvantages to this receptive attitude. The newcomers would help settle the empty lands and contribute scarce capital and labor to the economy. On the other hand, their foreign ways and irritating clannishness sometimes led to local quarrels. Yet in any calculation of potential gains and losses, the weightiest factor was the ideological commitment to free immigration. After all, the Declaration of Independence had condemned the king for endeavoring to prevent the increase of population by obstructing laws for the en-

The modern ark. This drawing in which Uncle Sam welcomes aboard a multitude of strange peoples illustrates the ideological commitment to free immigration, born in the revolutionary era and sustained through the nineteenth century. (Drawn by Sol Eytinge from a sketch by E. S. Bisbee, *Harper's Weekly*, May 6, 1871, New York Public Library)

The opening of the first Continental Congress, 1774. (New York Public Library)

An impressment scene. American seamen are seized on the docks and forced into the British naval service. This was a denial of American nationality. (United Press International)

couragement of immigration and for easy naturalization. The Republic would certainly not repeat the errors of the monarchy.

Congress immediately wrote the principle of the open gates into legislation, which remained unchallenged for more than a century. Furthermore, it made naturalization easier than in any other country in the world. The only requirement for citizenship was a brief period of residence as a test of sincerity.

The American naturalization and expatriation policies rested on the belief that every man had the right of his own free will to bestow his allegiance on the country of his choice. The concept ran counter to the prevailing European practice in which allegiance was an unshakable bond. The result sometimes was an open conflict.

The British, for instance, insisted that "once an Englishman, always an Englishman," and therefore impressed for service in the Royal Navy naturalized citizens taken from American ships. Impressment was one of the factors that led to the War of 1812.

Attachment to the principles of free immigration and easy naturalization also had an effect on domestic politics. The Federalists, who sponsored the one challenge to those principles in the Alien and Sedition Acts (1798), met defeat in the election of 1800 as a result, and never recovered as a national party thereafter.

Americans who believed in human freedom could not close their eyes to the discrepancies between ideals and reality in their own society. The continued existence

THE IMPRESSMENT OF AN
American Sailor Boy,
SUNG ON BOARD THE BRITISH PRISON SHIP CROWN PRINCE, THE FOURTH OF JULY, 1814
BY A NUMBER OF THE AMERICAN PRISONERS.

THE youthful sailor mounts the bark,
  And bids each weeping friend adieu :
Fair blows the gale, the canvass swells :
  Slow sinks the uplands from his view.

Three mornings, from his ocean bed,
  Resplendent beams the God of day :
The fourth, high looming in the mist,
  A war-ship's floating banners play.

Her yawl is launch'd ; light o'er the deep,
  Too kind, she wafts a ruffian band :
Her blue track lengthens to the bark,
  And soon on deck the miscreants stand.

Around they throw the baleful glance :
  Suspense holds mute the anxious crew—
Who is their prey ? poor sailor boy !
  The baleful glance is fix'd on you.

Nay, why that useless scrip unfold ?
  They damn'd the "lying yankee scrawl,"
Torn from thine hand, it strews the wave—
  They force thee trembling to the yawl.

Sick was thine heart as from the deck,
  The hand of friendship wav'd farewell ;
Mad was thy brain, as far behind,
  In the grey mist thy vessel fell.

One hope, yet, to thy bosom clung,
  The captain mercy might impart ;

Vain was that hope, which bade thee look,
  For mercy in a Pirate's heart.

What woes can man on man inflict,
  When malice joins with unheck'd power ;
Such woes, unpitied and unknown,
  For many a month the sailor bore !

Oft gem'd his eye the bursting tear,
  As mem'ry linger'd on past joy ;
As oft they flung the cruel jeer,
  And damn'd the "chicken liver'd boy."

When sick at heart, with "hope defer'd."
  Kind sleep his wasting form embrac'd,
Some ready minion ply'd the lash,
  And the lov'd dream of freedom chas'd.

Fast to an end his miseries drew :
  The deadly hectic flush'd his cheek :
On his pale brow the cold dew hung,
  He sigh'd, and sunk upon the deck !

The sailor's woes drew forth no sigh ;
  No hand would close the sailor's eye :
Remorseless, his pale corse they gave,
  Unshrouded to the friendly wave.

And as he sunk beneath the tide,
  A hellish shout arose ;
Exultingly the demons cried,
  "So fare all Albion's Rebel Foes !"

Battle between the *Bonhomme Richard* and *Serapis*, 1779, in which the American vessel commanded by John Paul Jones won a notable victory. (Painting by J. O. Davidson, 1876, New York Public Library)

A slave coffle passing the United States Capitol in Washington. The internal slave trade continued down to the Civil War although the importation of Africans was forbidden. The sight of the slaves in the nation's capital was particularly offensive to abolitionists. (New York Public Library)

This painting of George Washington and Casimir Pulaski after the Battle of the Brandywine showed the continuing popularity of the concept that the American and European revolutionary causes were linked. (Painting by A. Szyk)

of slavery ran counter to the proposition that all men were created equal and endowed with the rights to life, liberty and the pursuit of happiness. Few before 1820 could yet see how to secure the abolition of slavery without impoverishing the freed men or plunging the whole society into turmoil. Emancipation would have to wait for the future. But the slave trade was susceptible to immediate control. The constitution permitted its abolition after twenty years, which result was achieved in 1808. Occasional illegal cargoes thereafter slipped into southern ports, but the organized trade came to an end. This tragic episode in the history of immigration was effectively over.

The volume of immigration remained low in the whole period between 1774 and 1815, averaging fewer than ten thousand entries a year. The decline was not due to any lack of attractiveness of the country, but rather to the difficult conditions of travel. Naval warfare during the Revolution interrupted traffic across the Atlantic, as did the long series of Franco-British conflicts after 1792. Furthermore, in the quarter century after 1790 Europe suffered from repeated laceration by armies in battle. The desolation of the countryside and the break of communications shattered the organized pattern of the old redemptioner trade and put obstacles in the way of other types of migration.

The revolutionary disturbances in Europe did bring to America a group of colorful and influential refugees. The belief that the United States was to be an asylum for anyone in flight from Europe's despotic shores was scarcely challenged in these years. George Washington in 1783 had given it his authoritative support: "The bosom of America is open to receive not only the Opulent and respectable Stranger, but the oppressed and persecuted of all Nations and Religions; whom we shall welcome to a participation of all our rights and privileges if, by decency and propriety of conduct, they appear to merit the enjoyment."

Each uprising in Europe brought a wave of fugitives to America. Successive changes in the French government forced first the royalists, then the moderate revolutionaries, then the enemies of Napoleon and, finally, the Bonapartists to emigrate; between ten and twenty-five thousand of these people found refuge in the United States. Other Frenchmen fled to the same destination from the Black Revolution in Hispaniola after 1791.

Repercussions of the revolution spread to England after 1792. The British government persecuted French sympathizers and other dissidents, who sought safety in escape across the Atlantic. Joseph Priestley, the chemist, and Thomas Cooper, a fiery politician and scientist, were the best known. The journalist Joseph Gales, the Welsh minister Morgan John Rhys, and many others who feared the extinction of liberty in their native land also escaped to America.

Joseph Priestley (1733–1804) devoted himself to science. He wrote on electricity, was one of the discoverers of oxygen, and was elected to numerous learned societies. In 1794 he came to western Pennsylvania. (New York Public Library) ▶

A Napoleonic battle, 1809. The extensive use of artillery caused heavy damage in the countryside. (*Figaro Illustré*, April, 1908, New York Public Library)

Archibald Hamilton Rowan (1751–1834), who fled from Ireland to Philadelphia. (Drawing by Comerford, engraved by Cooper, 1825, New York Public Library)

John Jacob Astor. (Engraving by George E. Perine, New York Public Library)

In 1798 the Society of United Irishmen launched a revolt against Britain. The failure of that insurrection forced into exile a band of defiant rebels. They joined Wolfe Tone, Napper Tandy, and Hamilton Rowan who had earlier fled to the United States.

The political radicals were not the only Europeans to respond to the attractions of the New World's liberty and opportunity. A poor boy of seventeen, for instance, left his home in Baden in 1780 and worked his way to London where he dreamed of America and saved every penny he earned in order to pay for passage. Three years of determined effort gave him the passage money; a four-month crossing carried him to the United States. It took him two years more and a lucky marriage to get established in the fur trade. By 1800, John Jacob Astor had his fortune, $250,000. But he discovered he could not be content and restlessly reached for more, trading with the Far West and the Orient, investing in urban real estate. When he died in 1848, he was the richest man in the country, very much an American although he had never shed his German accent.

Liberty thus had a varied meaning to the immigrants of the late eighteenth century. The number of such people was, however, in any case small. The long-term effects of the political and economic changes in European society would not be felt until after 1815. The flow of immigrants would then assume altogether new proportions. By then, the American republic had developed the capacity to receive and absorb the newcomers.

II
Peasants in a New World
1820-1880

The launching of *The Great Republic*, the largest merchant ship in the world in 1853. Popular interest reflected the rising commerce of the United States in the early nineteenth century. (New York Public Library)

1
Land of Liberty

The battle of Waterloo and the final downfall of Napoleon brought peace to Europe. After 1815 trade within the Continent and across the Atlantic resumed its earlier course and increased in volume. Expansion in America and industrialization in Europe swelled the streams of commerce; a growing fleet of vessels carried cargoes of cotton, wheat, and timber from the New World to exchange for the manufactured goods of the Old.

Shipping was therefore available to carry a renewed movement of Europeans to the United States. The number of arrivals was at first relatively small. There were a few thousand in each of the years just after the Napoleonic Wars, about eight thousand in 1820. Then the totals mounted steadily—23,000 in 1830, 85,000 in 1840, 369,000 in 1850, and a peak of 427,000 in 1854.

After this tremendous outpouring, there was a decline, which deepened during the Civil War; in 1862 only ninety-one thousand newcomers sought admission. Fear of the fighting and of the disturbed conditions in America persuaded some prospective immigrants to stay home. More important, the initial burst had carried across those most eager to come, and it took time for a second wave to prepare itself.

After the restoration of peace in 1865, the tide of migration resumed its flow. The number of entries had climbed to 387,000 in 1870 and reached a new peak of 459,000 in 1873. Then again, the movement subsided, although it persisted at a declining rate through the rest of the decade. In the sixty years between 1820 and 1880, more than 10 million immigrants entered the United States. Their arrival contributed substantially to raising the population of the whole country from fewer than 10 million at the start of the period to more than 50 million at its end.

The immigrants of these decades were an extraordinarily varied lot. Some were gentlemen or people learned in the professions; others were skilled artisans or husbandmen with money gained from the sale of their land; many were desperately poor fugitives from hunger. Motives for making the journey were therefore quite diverse. The desire for bread or fortune, the lust for adventure or the fear of punishment for a crime, religious persecution or political dissent were among the reasons men left their homes for America.

One constant element drawing all these people westward was the reputation of the United States as the land of liberty. Throughout the nineteenth century romantic Europeans echoed the words of Goethe:

> *Amerika, du hast es besser—*
> *als unser Kontinent, das alte.**

This was also the sentiment of Isaac M. Wise, a young rabbi in Bohemia, who founded Hebrew Union College

---

* America, you have it better than our continent, the old one.

Statistics kept with some accuracy from 1820 showed the rising volume of immigration into the United States in the nineteenth century. (E. A. Ross, *The Old World in the New*, New York, 1914)

Year ending Sept. 30

1820	8,385
1821	9,127
1822	6,911
1823	6,354
1824	7,912
1825	10,199
1826	10,837

Year ending Sept. 30

1827	18,875
1828	27,382
1829	22,520
1830	23,322
1831	22,633

15 months ending Dec. 31

1832	60,482

Year ending Dec. 31

1833	58,640
1834	65,365
1835	45,374
1836	76,242
1837	79,340
1838	38,914
1839	68,069
1840	84,066
1841	80,289
1842	104,565

9 months ending Sept. 30

1843	52,496

Year ending Sept. 30

1844	78,615
1845	114,371
1846	154,416
1847	234,968
1848	226,527
1849	297,024
1850	310,004

3 months ending Dec. 31

1850	59,976

Year ending Dec. 31

1851	379,466
1852	371,603
1853	368,645
1854	427,833
1855	200,877
1856	200,436
1857	251,306
1858	123,126
1859	121,282
1860	153,640
1861	91,918
1862	91,985
1863	176,282
1864	193,418
1865	248,120
1866	318,568
1867	315,722

6 months ending June 30

1868	138,840

The Good Time Coming, wood engraving from *Harper's Weekly*, October 31, 1868, reflects the optimistic mood of post-Civil War reformers. People of all nations enter the scene to move through the bustling factories and on to the schoolhouse, while the spirit of peace, union, and fraternity drives away the clouds of anarchy and disloyalty. (By Thomas Hogan, Library of Congress)

The wide variety of immigrant types appears in this photograph of immigrants landing in Battery Park, New York, in 1894. (United Press International)

In a strange land—asking the way, newly arrived German immigrants in transit between the ship and the railroad. (Drawing by Thomas Worth, *Harper's Weekly*, 1879, New York Public Library)

Rabbi Isaac M. Wise (1819–1900), who arrived in the United States in 1846. (New York Public Library)

Louis Philippe (1773–1850) in 1830, the year in which he mounted the throne of France. (Engraving by Pauquet, Library of Congress)

Napoleon III (1808–1873). (Photograph by Neurdeix, Library of Congress)

in 1875. The spiritual attractions of the New World fascinated him, so that in 1846 emigration seemed to him a divine commandment he was obliged to obey at any cost.

Many shared his faith and experience. Again and again liberal revolutionaries looked to the United States for refuge when their efforts to reshape the Old World failed. The generation that matured after Waterloo refused to accept the conservative settlement and still hoped to transform Europe. Liberals aimed to liquidate the remnants of the old regime. Nationalists sought to liberate dependent territories and to unify them into sovereign states. Agitation directed toward those goals reached the height of intensity in the decade of the 1840s, when Young Italy and Young Ireland and their counterparts in Germany and Hungary launched movements that were at the same time liberal, national, and revolutionary.

For a moment in 1848, a successful revolution throughout Europe seemed within reach. An outbreak in Paris toppled Louis Philippe from his throne and similar eruptions took place in Ireland, Italy, Germany, and Hungary. Frustration followed. Everywhere the rebels met defeat, and even in France the only outcome of an initial success was the creation of the gaudy empire of Napoleon III. These disappointments infected thousands with America fever; escape across the ocean seemed the only way to the liberty unattainable at home.

The Irish refugees found in America not only an asylum, but also a sympathetic environment. Anti-English feeling was strong in the United States. Memories of 1776 and 1812 kept alive the dislike of British tyranny, of which the Irish patriots and the Founding Fathers alike seemed victims. Furthermore, the émigrés found support among substantial numbers of their countrymen who had migrated to the United States for other reasons.

The careers of John Mitchel and Thomas F. Meagher showed, however, that it was no simple matter to adapt the outlook of a European revolutionary to life in America. Both were flaming Young Irelanders, determined to effect the repeal of the Act of Union with Britain, by violence if necessary. Both were convicted in 1848 and sentenced to transportation to Australia. Each escaped and made his way to the United States. Yet Mitchel never found a place for himself while Meagher, though less gifted, won immediate success.

Mitchel had been the more famous in Ireland, a lawyer and journalist whose name was well known in America even before his romantic escape. In New York, he edited *The Citizen,* a paper that achieved a wide circulation, but he was pugnacious and restless and threw it all up to move to Tennessee. Paradoxically, he became a pro-slavery man and, during the Civil War, a strong partisan of the Confederacy. For a time he edited *The Richmond Enquirer,* then, finally, returned to Ireland. He was never at home in the United States, for the central element in his life was hatred of England.

Massacre of Irish Catholics in 1641. Drawings such as these kept alive the memory of persecution by the Protestants.

John Mitchel (1815–1875). (New York Public Library)

Thomas F. Meagher (1823–1867). (*Harper's Encyclopedia of United States History,* New York, 1906)

Carl Schurz as a major general in the Union Army. (Photograph by Julius Brill, Library of Congress)

Garibaldi at Rome, 1849. (Painting by G. H. Thomas from a sketch made during the siege of the city, *Illustrated London News*, July 1, 1854, New York Public Library)

Meagher, by contrast, got ahead fast. He was not yet thirty years old when he arrived in New York in 1852, and he used his revolutionary experience as a means of pushing himself ahead in his adopted country. An orator rather than a writer, outgoing rather than introspective, he was more inclined to calculating future prospects than to brooding over past wrongs. He practiced law in New York, acquired a popular following and, when the Civil War came, gathered an Irish regiment. By the time of the peace, he had advanced to the rank of brigadier general.

The German exile, beguiled by old visions, also had difficulty in the New World. But he would find support among numerous countrymen in America if he shifted his sights to their problems. Carl Schurz, for instance, had come to America in the aftermath of a romantic escapade. A nineteen-year-old student at the University of Bonn, he had rushed to arms during the futile revolution of 1848. Dismayed by failure, he nevertheless resolved to rescue his beloved teacher, Professor Gottfried Kinkel, who was imprisoned in the Prussian fortress at Spandau. Nine months of scheming and a feat of daring brought the old man out; and Schurz escaped to Paris and London, a hero. But when Napoleon III seized power, the revolutionary dream faded and in August, 1852, Schurz left Europe.

At that point he cut his ties to the Old World. Others continued to scan the skies for signs of a revolutionary revival in the Fatherland or conceived airy plans for a new Germany-in-exile. But he knew that his future was American. From Philadelphia he moved to Wisconsin, which then was receiving hundreds of German farmers. Schurz entered politics, helped swing the German vote to Lincoln, and then went on to become minister to Spain, a major general during the Civil War, a senator,

and secretary of the interior. He also found time for a distinguished career as a journalist before he died in 1906. Many of the two thousand Forty-eighters, whose migration, like his, grew out of revolutionary failure, also exercised influence far beyond their numbers.

There were also stray individuals from other nations among the rebels. Giuseppe Garibaldi, for instance, lived in Staten Island, New York, while plotting his return to Italy after the fall of his Roman republic in 1849. Small groups of refugees from France, Poland, and Hungary likewise made their way to the American republic.

For some revolutionaries America was not a last but a first hope. Europe was too crowded with old institutions for those who hoped totally to reconstruct the social system. The United States, by contrast, offered empty space in abundance for experiment both by natives and immigrants.

The decades after 1820 bubbled with schemes to rebuild society; and the land of liberty seemed an appropriate place to put utopian projects into practice. New England transcendentalists formed such colonies—in Massachusetts at Brook Farm, Hopedale, and Fruitlands.

But there was room enough also for European visionaries. The tempestuous Scotswoman, Frances Wright, for instance, founded Nashoba in Tennessee in 1826 to train slaves for freedom. She was twenty-three when she first came to the United States in 1818, and the new country never lost its fascination for her. Nashoba was unsuccessful, but her books and lectures continued to argue that here man would first awake to the full knowledge and the full exercise of his powers. And woman, too!

Garibaldi enters Naples as a hero. (Sketch by T. Nast, *Illustrated London News*, September 22, 1860, New York Public Library)

Portraits of Hungarian officers who still lived in exile in New York in 1870. (New York Public Library)

Frances Wright (1795–1852). (Engraving by J. C. Buttre, after J. Gorbitz, Library of Congress)

Robert Owen (1801–1877). (Engraving by H. Scher, New York Public Library)

Étienne Cabet (1788–1856), the founder of Icaria. (Harper's Monthly, December, 1904, New York Public Library)

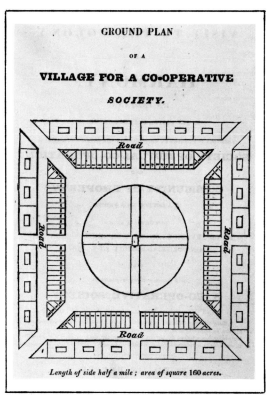

Plan for a utopian community. (Library of Congress)

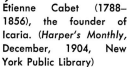

Fanny Wright had found a model for her community when her lecture tour took her through the prospering Rappite settlements. George Rapp had been almost fifty years old when in 1804 he led three shiploads of German sectarians to Butler County, Pennsylvania. He was the absolute dictator of a theocracy pledged to celibacy and a total community of goods, but not to asceticism; members regularly put away five full meals a day. Father Rapp lived to be ninety, and the Rappites became wealthy from the sale of their wine, whiskey, and woolens.

On the other hand, the Indiana land the Rappites sold to Robert Owen, the English philanthropist, was the site of an unfortunate experiment. Owen was a utopian socialist, convinced that he had a formula for an improved social order. His New Harmony colony, established at considerable expense in 1825, promptly fell upon hard times. The thousand recruits drawn to the settlement arrived full of enthusiasm but deficient in the capacity for work or the management of their own affairs. They flew apart in factional quarrels and, within three years, the experiment was over. Owen's community lacked the religious discipline that held Rapp's together.

Owen's dreams nevertheless inspired Étienne Cabet, a French lawyer and perennial rebel who had fled to London in 1834. Cabet had given form to his speculations in a widely popular novel, *Voyage en Icarie,* and after years of preparation, in 1847 he was ready to put his ideas into practice. Hundreds followed him. A site in Texas proved unsuitable; the colony ultimately acquired Nauvoo, Illinois, just abandoned by the Mormons. Cabet unhappily gained neither peace nor prosperity for his effort. When he died in 1856, the community was torn by dissension.

Other groups like the Rappites, which commanded religious sanctions, were more durable. As long as William Keil lived, his authority held together the immigrants—mostly German—whom he settled in communities in Bethel, Missouri, and in Aurora, Oregon. So, too, the Swedish pietists who followed Eric Janson to Bishop Hill, Illinois, in 1846, were untroubled by internal disputes. Nor were the members of the Community of True

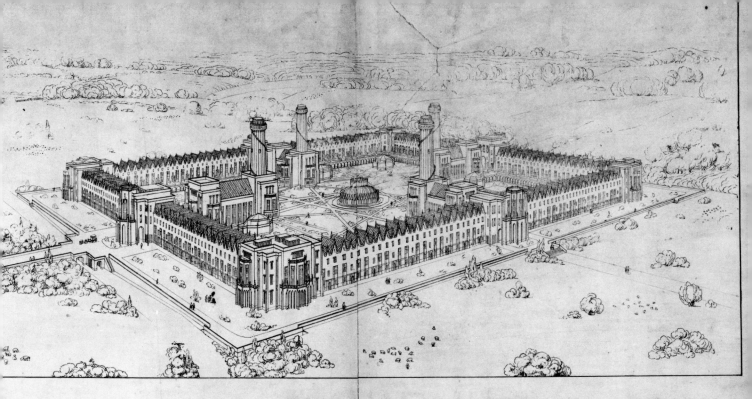

A BIRD'S EYE VIEW OF ONE OF THE NEW COMMUNITIES AT HARMONY.
IN THE STATE OF INDIANA NORTH AMERICA.
AN ASSOCIATION OF TWO THOUSAND PERSONS FORMED UPON THE PRINCIPLES ADVOCATED BY

ROBERT OWEN
STEDMAN WHITWELL, ARCHITECT.

SCITE IS NEARLY IN THE CENTRE OF AN AREA OF 2000 ACRES POSSESSED BY THE COMMUNITY, SITUATED UPON HIGH LAND, ABOUT THREE MILES FROM THE EASTERN SHORE OF THE GREAT WABASH RIVER
TWELVE MILES FROM THE TOWN OF MOUNT VERNON, ON THE RIVER OHIO. BOTH THESE RIVERS ARE NAVIGATED BY STEAM BOATS OF CONSIDERABLE BURTHEN, WHICH MAINTAIN A COMMUNICATION BETWEEN
ORLEANS IN THE GULPH OF MEXICO ON THE SOUTH AND PITTSBURGH IN THE EASTERN STATES ON THE ATLANTIC.
THE GENERAL ARRANGEMENT OF THE BUILDINGS IS A SQUARE, EACH SIDE OF WHICH IS 1000 FEET. THE CENTRES & THE EXTREMITIES ARE OCCUPIED BY THE PUBLIC BUILDINGS. THE PARTS BETWEEN THEM ARE
DWELLINGS OF THE MEMBERS. IN THE INTERIOR OF THE SQUARE ARE THE BOTANICAL & OTHER GARDENS. THE EXERCISE GROUNDS &c. THE WHOLE IS RAISED ABOVE THE LEVEL OF THE NATURAL SURFACE, AND
ROUNDED BY AN ESPLANADE. THE DESCENT TO THE OFFICES IS UPON THE OUTSIDE OF THE WHOLE ── ONE OF THE DIAGONALS OF THE SQUARE COINCIDES WITH A MERIDIAN, AND THE DISPOSITION OF EVERY
ER PART IS SO REGULATED BY A CAREFUL ATTENTION TO THE MOST IMPORTANT DISCOVERIES & FACTS IN SCIENCE, AS TO FORM A NEW COMBINATION OF CIRCUMSTANCES, CAPABLE OF PRODUCING PERMANENTLY,
ATER PHYSICAL, MORAL, AND INTELLECTUAL ADVANTAGES TO EVERY INDIVIDUAL, THAN HAVE EVER YET BEEN REALIZED IN ANY AGE OR COUNTRY.

INGREY & MADELEY, LITHO. 310. STRAND.

An advertisement showing the attractions of the community planned at Harmony upon the principles advocated by Robert Owen. (Library of Congress)

A building erected by Owen at New Harmony and still standing in 1926. (United Press International)

Planting corn at Bishop Hill. (Painting by Olaf Krans, Illinois State Historical Library)

Bishop Hill as it was in 1853—view from north of the Edwards River. (Painting by Olaf Krans, 1911, Illinois State Historical Library)

The Emigrant's Letter. The peasant working his little plot hears the news from America read by his wife. (Engraved by T. L. Atkinson from a painting by J. C. Hook, 1886, Library of Congress)

Inspiration, which had its roots in eighteenth-century Germany. In 1817 Inspiration members received divine instructions through their leader, Christian Metz, to depart for America. For twenty-five years, these humble people saved to acquire the means to transplant themselves to the New World. In 1842, some eight hundred of them moved to Ebenezer, near Buffalo, New York, where they adopted a communist system. A decade later they began to migrate to Iowa, selling their eastern lands and establishing six villages in Amana. The community remained intact until 1932 when losses during the great depression forced it to change into a business corporation.

The United States was not the only soil on which Europeans attempted to establish their heaven on earth. The experiments in America were significant not for their uniqueness but for the tolerance with which they were regarded. In an expanding economy, fostered by free institutions, people were willing to permit newcomers to settle on their own terms. The same attitude

applied also to the much larger numbers who migrated for other reasons.

The political refugees and the utopians were relatively few in number. But their influence was great. The exiles often provided leadership for their countrymen; and both groups were symbols to the millions of other immigrants of these decades that America was a promised land.

In the years after Waterloo the United States was being described also as a utopia of another sort, one which encouraged not communal solidarity but individual opportunity. The Englishman Morris Birkbeck and the German Gottfried Duden, among others, published influential tracts that explained that the land of liberty was also the land of potential riches. Read aloud in village reading clubs, passed from hand to hand, these books, like letters from friends and relatives, diffused the image of a New World capable of rectifying the wrongs of the Old. Thousands of Europeans would soon respond.

German artisans of the 1850s. The two men at left are making candles, those at the right are making soap. (From Wilhelm Oertel [W. D. von Horn], Library of Congress)

2
The Destruction
of Peasant Life

The great migrations of the nineteenth century originated in profound changes in European society. An old order gradually crumbled as its economic foundations shifted. The process, which had already begun in 1820, continued through the next sixty years. It left millions of men and women without places and turned the thoughts of many of them to the possibility of a fresh start in the New World.

A dramatic rise in population was basic to all the changes that transformed European society. The number of people on the Continent had never been stationary, but until the seventeenth century, fluctuations had occurred within a rather narrow range. The total had declined in some periods and risen in others, but usually reverted to a norm that was much the same in 1650 as it had been in 1050. Then in the middle of the seventeenth century, for reasons that remain unclear, the mortality rate declined and the population of Europe began to climb consistently. In the hundred years after 1650, the number of Europeans increased from 100 to 140 million and then almost doubled between 1750 and 1850. The rise continued thereafter despite recurrent wars, famines, and emigration.

The problem of accommodating all these additional men and women was difficult because the existing social and economic systems of Europe passed through a radical transformation in the nineteenth century. Drastic changes in the conditions of life both in the city and in the country prevented millions of families from going on

as their ancestors had. Respectable artisans and farmers faced a painful loss of status, and many of those not content with the prospects at home often decided to emigrate.

The rise in population after 1820 combined with a series of dramatic technological innovations to undermine the position of traditional workers everywhere. Until the eighteenth century, all the necessities and luxuries of life that were not the direct products of nature were the products of a single individual's labor and ingenuity. A skilled handicraftsman, using his own tools and working in his own shop, had shaped shoes to the purchaser's feet; others tailored coats to his measure, or built chairs and chests to his specifications. The Industrial Revolution, which had begun in eighteenth-century England, made such headway after 1820 as to threaten the livelihood of all artisans.

Increasingly, in the nineteenth century, great factories using machinery, steam or waterpower, and cheap unskilled labor turned out immense quantities of goods at prices with which craftsmen could not compete. The new mode of production had appeared first in England, but its advantages were so compelling that it spread eastward. Everywhere in Europe it threatened the ruin of traditional enterprises.

Some of the artisans could find employment in the new plants. But most people with skills who had once been or aspired to be their own masters were unwilling to sink to the lower social status of the factory worker,

German papermakers of the 1850s. (From Wilhelm Oertel [W. D. von Horn], Library of Congress)

German coachmakers of the 1850s. (From Wilhelm Oertel [W. D. von Horn], Library of Congress)

German shoemakers of the 1850s. (From Wilhelm Oertel [W. D. von Horn], Library of Congress)

English glassmakers of the eighteenth century. (*Universal Magazine*, November, 1747, Library of Congress)

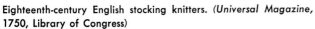

Eighteenth-century English stocking knitters. (*Universal Magazine*, 1750, Library of Congress)

German weaver of the 1850s. (From Wilhelm Oertel [W. D. von Horn], Library of Congress)

or to accept the meager pay of these jobs. Nor were they willing to look to a future in which they would have to rouse their children "at the Sound of a bell from their beds and Drag them through the pelting storm of a Dark winters morning to earn a small pittance at a factory."

Some of the weavers or smiths who faced such uncomfortable choices expressed their fury in riotous, but futile, efforts to destroy the machines. Others who learned that there was still a shortage of labor in the New World were attracted by the opportunities for a fresh start. And even those unwilling themselves to make the break sometimes realized that their sons would do better to leave than to stay at home.

The collapse of the traditional structure of European agriculture also complicated the effects of population growth after 1820. Until then, farming had been a communal undertaking. The peasants lived in villages within which they organized their economic, social, and religious life. Each family was a household, a unit that held together in work, in prayer, in the joys of birth or marriage, and in the sorrows of death. All the families together formed a community of shared activities.

In most areas, the cultivated land was divided into small plots, scattered throughout the village. Elsewhere, as in Ireland or Norway, each peasant worked a single, consolidated tract. But in either case, it was likely that the community also possessed sizable common fields, from which each member could take food, cut hay, or graze cattle. Even the landless cottier, who rented a few acres, if he had place for a cow or a pig and a little kindling for the fire, could make ends meet by hiring out his labor.

The rise in population created serious problems for

A peasant farmyard. (New York Public Library)

Sunday morning in the olden time, a sentimental portrayal of the English scene. (Lithograph by Nathaniel Currier after the painting by William Collins, Library of Congress)

The meeting on the country road, a European village of the seventeenth century. (Painting by Jan Breughel, New York Public Library)

The village fete, sixteenth century. (Etching by Daniel Hopfer, Library of Congress)

European peasant communities. Every additional child was another claimant to a share in his father's patrimony. To take care of the more numerous offspring, plots were repeatedly subdivided, so that farms dwindled in size as they passed from one generation to the next. Some heirs received so little they could not possibly feed themselves from the produce. Yet they made every effort to remain where they were, displaying a "rooted antipathy to locomotion," for by leaving permanently, they would leave not only their claim to a scrap of land but also their place in the community. The peasants were immobilized because they could not conceive of life apart from the village and because survival seemed to demand that they stay where they were.

The cultivation of the potato was evidence of the determination to force the soil to support greater numbers than before. Though less nourishing than grains, it became the staple of the peasant diet in Ireland and Germany in the eighteenth century because it could be raised on any little patch of land.

Yet, in time, to stay where they were proved impossible and wasteful. While the peasants were finding it increasingly difficult to feed their families, the burgeoning cities swelled the demand for foodstuffs. The little plots could scarcely nourish their occupants, much less raise a surplus for sale. The villagers could not increase their output by crop rotation, or by the use of machines, or by new practices of animal husbandry. Their holdings were too small and they lacked capital, even if they could surmount the obstacles of inertia and the reluctance to take risks.

Enterprising owners of large estates did perceive the new possibilities. Already in the eighteenth century in some districts they had converted arable land into pasture for sheep and cattle, and they had begun to use the hired labor of cottiers or servants to cultivate large

Two pitchers of soup and one loaf of bread for a family of ten— the rural poor had difficulties even in the late nineteenth century. (*Illustrated London News*, December 2, 1893, New York Public Library)

tracts scientifically. Farms of this sort played an ever more prominent part in nineteenth-century European agriculture, and diminished the space available to peasants.

Often the great landowners thought impatiently of the tracts on which the poor peasants still scrabbled miserably for a mere subsistence. If only the wretched people would disappear, then estates would grow still larger and still more profitable. In some cases it was possible to se-

Irish peasants in the 1880s. By this time a good part of the population had emigrated and the condition of those who remained had begun to improve. But much poverty still existed and the villagers held together. (Library of Congress)

Irish peasants in the 1880s. Cramped quarters in the thatched stone hut held large extended families. (Library of Congress)

cure legislation to divide the common fields and consolidate and fence individual holdings. Enclosure was most advantageous to the large landowners who thereby acquired the tracts on which to conduct modern agriculture. The change was costly to small landowners, who had to pay a share of the expense. But it was most burdensome to the cottiers, who lost their woods and pastures.

But enclosure in itself was not an adequate solution from the point of view of the great landowner. Often he continued to rent tracts to the cottiers, wasteful as that was, because he was personally involved in the village community. His peasants were his responsibility. He could not simply liquidate them even if they had no legal right to their holdings. Sentimentality apart, unless there were some place for them to go, the evicted would simply become charges on charity. It was better to col-

lect a pittance in rent from a tenant than to oust him and then have to pay higher taxes for his support.

The more precarious their situation, the more desperately the peasants tried to hold on, reluctant as they were to abandon their native villages and the only life they knew. The rise in the price of land and of rent only increased their determination. The least afflicted ones sometimes borrowed to make improvements or to increase their holdings in order to match the efficiency of the great estates. The poor often went away as seasonal laborers—from Ireland to England or from Sweden to Denmark—hoping to bring back wages that would help pay the rent. In the meantime, the women and children did the work at home.

The struggle was in vain, however. Improved transportation and lowered tariff barriers further favored the most efficient producers, whose goods penetrated every

Scenes from a rent war in Ireland. At the left, peasants throw down rocks on a party of eviction officers. At the right, an eviction in County Kerry. (*Illustrated London News*, January 29, 1887, New York Public Library)

The eviction. This lithograph, published in 1871 by J. T. Foley in New York from a painting by Powell, is a sentimental version of the scene with which Irish immigrants had too frequently been familiar. The neatly grouped characters are, for instance, heroic rather than despondent. Note also that the houses in the background have grown in size and dignity in the memory of the artist. (Library of Congress)

The young emigrant leaving home, a scene of the 1850s. (Engraved by F. E. Jones after G. Bartsch, Library of Congress)

A party of refugees wandering through the city. (New York Public Library)

Paupers in the great city—houseless and hungry. (Drawing by S. L. Fildes, *The Graphic*, December 4, 1869, New York Public Library)

local market. At the same time factory products also inundated those markets and deprived the peasants of the income some of them had earned by spinning and weaving at home. To hold on became increasingly difficult and crop failures, as in the 1840s in Ireland and Germany and in the 1860s in Sweden, drove those with debts to the wall.

The possibility of emigrating was at first most attractive to those with hope and resources. Children of more prosperous peasants, who realized that they would not be able to occupy the places in society their parents had, might well be tempted to seek an equivalent life in the

new countries beyond the sea where land was available. Or venturesome peasants might decide to sell their holdings while they could, and use the proceeds for a fresh start abroad. Both types mounted steadily in the 1820s and 1830s. In those decades the emigrant ships carried away primarily those who possessed the funds to bring them to their destinations.

The situation of the landless was more desperate. When the common fields disappeared or the landlords refused to rent to these peasants anymore, they would only become paupers or drift about as vagabonds or wander to the cities. The number of these people who managed to get across the ocean remained small until the 1840s.

In that decade, major disasters made them a growing percentage of the migrants. Famine provided the means for evicting them and, at the same time, shipping made possible their transportation at low cost. Once a foothold was established abroad, letters and remittances to relatives and friends back home attracted followers.

The movement of the peasantry was thus more than an idealistic quest for freedom. It was also a response to a profound transformation in the character of European society.

Irish emigrants leaving for America, a scene showing the mail coach setting forth from a village in County Kerry. (*Frank Leslie's Illustrated Newspaper*, January 20, 1866, Library of Congress)

The destruction of the emigrant ship *Ocean Monarch* bound for America. (Lithograph by Maclure, MacDonald, and MacGregor, New-York Historical Society)

3
Crossing by Sail

In 1820, the first little vessel powered by steam had already crossed the Atlantic. Ten years later the railroad began to revolutionize overland transportation. But for a long time these innovations did not affect immigration. Not until the 1860s and 1870s did more traditional means of getting to a port and crossing from the Old to the New World yield to these more advanced methods. Steam helped only the most fortunate newcomers to their destinations. The great majority traveled by foot and by sail.

The harsh voyage took a heavy toll. Statistical records of the time are fragmentary and unreliable, so that it is difficult to measure the incidence of illness and death in the course of a voyage. Contemporary accounts no doubt emphasized the unusual—dramatic cases of shipwreck or plague—and paid little attention to the uneventful journeys. But even the average passage involved real hardship that affected the immigrants' ability to cope with the subsequent problems of American life. At each stage of the voyage, hidden traps endangered the hapless pilgrims on the way to the New World.

The old redemptioner system had disintegrated between 1776 and 1815, and was not revived. War and in-ternal disorder on both sides of the ocean had broken the connections on which it depended. The new migration consisted primarily of individuals who made their way as best they could to the ports and across the sea.

Many old legal restrictions also disappeared after 1815, so that the people of Europe were freer to depart than before. The German states thus disregarded or repealed the statutes that forbade residents from leaving, and the reshuffling of boundaries during and after the Napoleonic era left fewer borders to cross. Also, economic development produced some improvements in roads, river vessels, and canals, and travelers no longer risked encounters with bandits or faced a toll taker at every provincial frontier.

Down to mid-century most immigrants still went on foot or by cart, so that the first steps to America were slow and arduous. Only later did the railroads reach deep enough into the rural interior to offer some relief. The experience of Hollanders, who were, after all, close to the sea, showed the inescapable difficulty of migration. In 1846, a laborer in Drente, who had never seen a ship, much less been on one, decided to go to America. He traveled first to Buinen, then to Assen, and at last to Meppel—to him strange and remote places. At the pier

The launching of a new, iron immigrant ship in England. (*Illustrated London News*, October, 1852, New York Public Library)

An immigration report, 1849, showing the hazards of the crossing. (Smithsonian Collection of Business Americana)

Of vessels with emigrants that have arrived at the port of New-York, in the year 1849, showing the whole number of passengers, the number of sick on arrival, the number of deaths and births, and the ratio of each.

NATION OF VESSEL.	No. of vessels.	Passengers.	Sick.	Deaths.	Births.	Ratio of sick.	Ratio of deaths.	Ratio of births.
American, ...	894	134,657	921	1,556	113	61.100	1,16.100	9.100
British, ...	371	62,463	475	658	76	76.100	1,5.100	12.100
German, ...	85	10,966	66	87	11	60.100	79.100	10.100
French, ...	12	1,779	1	1	1	6.100	6.100	6.100
Belgian, ...	8	810	....	4	....	....	49.100	....
Swedish, Norwegian, &c., ...	581	13,718	18	41	10	....	....	....
Total, ...	1,651	224,393	1,481	2,357	211			

The *Savannah*, the first steamship to cross the Atlantic. (Wood engraving, *Gleason's Pictorial*, 1854, Library of Congress)

An immigrant at the railroad office. Although the new form of transportation was easier than travel by foot, it was still difficult for strangers to find their way. (*Harper's Monthly*, March, 1871, New York Public Library)

A view of seventeenth-century Amsterdam drawn in 1844. (New York Public Library)

Rotterdam in 1892, showing boats from the interior of Europe crowding toward the harbor. (New York Public Library)

Bremerhaven, the new harbor of Bremen, 1852. (New York Public Library)

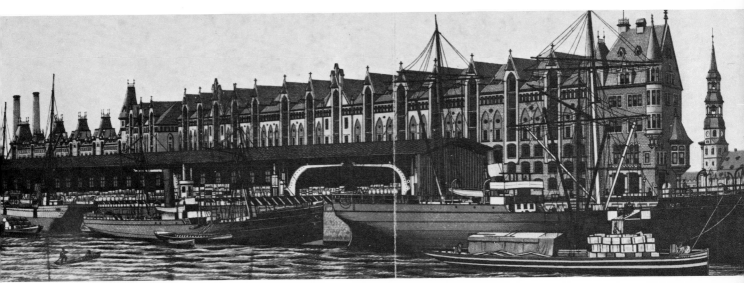

The wharves and docks of Hamburg, 1880. (New York Public Library)

in Meppel, where he took the market boat, mockers covered him with insults for leaving the province. He disembarked in Amsterdam and found his way to a canalboat, which took him overnight to Rotterdam, where he wearily sought out a ship on which to cross the Atlantic, purchased provisions for the journey, and awaited the sailing date. Twenty-two days elapsed from the morning he left home to the moment when his ship finally cleared the English Channel. For people from the interior of England, Ireland, or Germany, travel to the ports was more difficult still.

Few prospective passengers could avoid a lengthy stay in the seaports while they found a vessel, made arrangements, and waited for their departure. For men and women who had never before left their native villages, these strange cities abounded in additional pitfalls.

Rotterdam, Antwerp, Hamburg, and Göteborg were important points of European departure. But the great northern port was Bremen. This Hanseatic free city had suffered from isolation in the first two decades of the nineteenth century, until its merchants set out aggressively to restore its prosperity. In 1827 a treaty of commerce with the United States expanded the possibilities of transatlantic trade; and a new harbor at Bremerhaven, after 1830, permitted the expeditious handling of traffic. The city became the center for the movement of American tobacco—by way of Baltimore to Europe—and empty vessels were available to take immigrants back on the return journey.

Bremen's rival farther to the south was Le Havre, a relatively new city that received strong impetus from industrial development after 1815. It then became the channel for the movement of cotton from New Orleans to the textile factories of France and southwestern Germany. Le Havre's population rose from 28,000 in 1823

to 59,680 in 1851, an index of its expanding business. Here, too, ships having unloaded their cargoes had space for return passengers.

There was some movement to the United States also by way of Cork and Belfast and other English, Irish, and Scottish ports. But the preeminent eastern terminus for transatlantic trade and travel after 1815 was Liverpool. The tonnage that moved through that port to and from America increased steadily, as did its resident population. From just about 100,000 in 1811 it grew to more than 286,000 in 1831 and to 375,000 in 1851. The stranger in search of a vessel found the central quarters of the city crowded with a miserable, sodden mass of humanity housed in cellars, abandoned warehouses, or shabby court tenements. Poverty, drunkenness, crime, and vice were characteristic. An investigation in 1836 counted twelve hundred thieves under the age of fifteen and thirty-six hundred known prostitutes.

But high mortality was the most significant index of social conditions in Liverpool. During the 1840s the death rate per thousand rose from thirty-five to forty-six, while in 1842 the average age of death was seventeen in the city as a whole and less than fourteen in the most crowded ward. These conditions were the worst in England. Yet Liverpool was the most important outlet for passenger traffic from England, Ireland, and Scotland. The city also had important connections with continental Europe, by routes substantial numbers of immigrants took. By mid-century, for instance, it was possible to travel with dependable connections from North Sea or Baltic ports to the English port of Hull, then by canal to Liverpool. After 1845 some fifty thousand passengers passed through the city each month.

Liverpool's great advantage was the frequency with which it offered sailings. It was a tremendous hardship

Immigrants moving through Le Havre on the dock of the Compagnie Générale Transatlantique, 1886. By then, convenient connections made it possible to move directly from railroad car to ship. (E. Clair-Guyot, New York Public Library)

Outward bound, a caricature of an Irish immigrant on the quay of Dublin, 1854. (Lithograph by T. H. Maguire after a painting by T. Nichol, New-York Historical Society)

Immigrants in the port of Le Havre, 1848. (Drawing by Ernest Charton, New York Public Library)

Here and There; Or, Emigration a Remedy. A cartoon of 1848 showing the contrast between poverty and destitution in Europe and prosperity in America. (New York Public Library)

Office of an immigrant agent, 1850. (Brown Brothers)

A winter street scene in London, showing the misery of the poor. (Harper's Weekly, April 2, 1859, New York Public Library)

A banquet given for General Grant in Liverpool in 1878. The luxury of the scene stands in sharp contrast to the misery of the great mass of the population there. (John Russell Young, *Around the World with General Grant*, New York, 1879, vol. I)

The landing stage at Liverpool. (New York Public Library)

A great frost in Liverpool during a hard winter. (*Illustrated London News*, February 5, 1881, New York Public Library)

to spend even a few days in the city's haphazard accommodations. But the stay in other ports might extend for weeks while ill-prepared families waited for a ship to take them away. In the 1840s packet lines, operating on regular schedules, relieved the more fortunate emigrants —those who could afford the passage—of some of the uncertainties of earlier crossings. But the transit through the European seaports always remained a hazardous experience.

For most immigrants, whose imaginations could never fully conceive the trials of the voyage ahead, cheapness was the primary consideration in arranging passage. The cabins of the packet lines were not for them. Knowing that they would need whatever little sums they had for settlement after arrival, they judged the quarters they would occupy only by the standard of low cost. The holds of ships that carried fish or timber or tobacco or cotton, once cleared of the cargoes they carried eastward, could be partitioned into two-tiered bunks, each the home for a family.

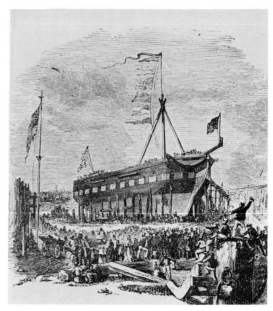

The transatlantic steamship *Liverpool*, 1838. Fully 240 feet long, this ship was a marked improvement over earlier vessels. But it still depended on sails for much of its power. (Lithograph by N. Sarony, Library of Congress)

The launching of a packet ship in 1872. (New York Public Library)

The steamer *Acadia*, 1840. Vessels such as the *Britannia* and *Acadia* were too expensive for most immigrants, but by capturing the business of well-to-do passengers, they left space for the poor on older ships. (Cunard Line)

The grand salon of an American steamer, 1875. (New York Public Library)

The steamer *Britannia*, 1840. (Cunard Line)

The entry of the steamships into transatlantic trade in the 1840s at first affected the immigrants only indirectly. The steamers quickly captured the business of well-to-do passengers and valuable freight. The sailing vessels, therefore, had to seek out immigrants, and often lowered their rates to attract them. In the 1850s it was possible to get passage from England or Ireland to an American port for as little as ten dollars a head, a price that put migration within the reach of even the poorest peasants in those countries.

Under any circumstances, the sea voyage was frightening. But the particular terrors of the immigrant crossing were far from fanciful. The little wooden sailing ships spent months at the mercy of wind and weather. A forty-day passage was not unusual, and some stretched out to sixty or ninety days. Each family fended for itself in the bunk assigned to it, prepared its own food on communal stoves, and tried its own remedies for seasickness or more dangerous illnesses. Often there was no access to the deck, and the hatches, when open at all, provided little ventilation. It was hardly surprising that 10 to 20 percent of those who left Europe failed to survive the voyage.

In the 1860s and 1870s conditions improved. The steamships then began to seek immigrant business. The Cunard Line from Liverpool, the North German Lloyd from Bremen, and the Compagnie Générale Transatlantique from Le Havre were among those active in the trade. When the size of their vessels increased, the companies arranged space in the afterhold, or steerage, where poor families would travel at a very low rate. The dangers of the crossing diminished, but travel in steerage was still painful; in 1874, the young Serbian Michael Pupin, who owned no blanket, had to sleep on deck near the smokestack for warmth. But the sailings were now on dependable schedules and their duration was only a week or ten days. That made all the difference in the world.

Once debarked, the immigrants faced in American cities some of the same problems they had encountered in Europe. The port cities—New York, New Orleans, Boston, Philadelphia, and Baltimore—were crowded and growing, and lacked facilities for receiving the newcomers. Montreal was also a debarkation point. Many immigrants spent costly and uncomfortable days before they emerged from the city in which they landed; some who lost everything in the process were compelled to remain there.

The port cities, fearful of the pestilences steerage passengers might introduce, forced arriving vessels to clear through quarantine. The station on Staten Island, in

Michael I. Pupin after gaining fame. (Photograph by Pach, Library of Congress)

The deck of the Cunarder *Scythia*, 1879. These scenes show the accommodations available to the well-to-do. (New York Public Library)

Steerage emigrants, 1870. (New York Public Library)

The departure, 1840. This drawing shows the dense throng of immigrants on an old sailing vessel and reveals the conditions of the crossing just before the peak of mid-nineteenth-century migration. (Brown Brothers)

An immigrant ship leaving Queenstown, the port of Cork, Ireland. (Nostalgia Press, Inc.)

Immigrants crowded on shipboard, 1871.
(New York Public Library)

The *Bremen*, 1858, the first vessel of the North German
Lloyd Line. (Rudolf Cronau, *Drei Jahrhunderte Deutschen
Lebens in Amerika*, Berlin, 1909)

The *Germanic*, a modern steamship as of
1877. (New York Public Library)

The launching of the C. G. T. *Empress Eugénie*, 1864. (New
York Public Library)

The Cunarder *Aleppo*, 1865. (Cunard Line).

A view of Broadway, New York City, 1880. (Lithograph by J. J. Fogerty, Library of Congress)

A view of Boston, 1848. (Lithograph by N. Currier, Library of Congress)

Philadelphia, viewed from the South Street bridge. (Wood engraving from *Picturesque America,* 1874, Library of Congress)

View of Baltimore and its harbor, from Federal Hill. (Engraved by E. Whitefild, Library of Congress)

Health officers vaccinating Russian and Polish immigrants on the steamer *Victoria* at quarantine in New York City, 1881. (Wood engraving from *Frank Leslie's Illustrated Newspaper*, Library of Congress)

The attack on the quarantine establishment on Staten Island, September 1, 1858. Native residents, fearing contagion, attempted to burn the hospital down. (New York Public Library)

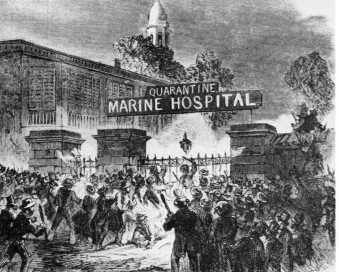

The interior of Castle Garden. The view is of the great hall in which immigrants were processed. (*Harper's Monthly*, April, 1871, New York Public Library)

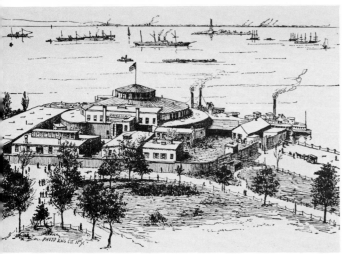

Castle Garden at Battery Park, New York. (New York Public Library)

The labor exchange at Castle Garden. Here potential employers came to interview laborers and servants. (Sketched by Stanley Fox for *Harper's Weekly*, August 15, 1868, New York Public Library)

Customs inspection at Castle Garden. *(Harper's Monthly, June, 1884, New York Public Library)*

Scene at Whitehall at the foot of Manhattan Island where ferries and barges left for other parts of the harbor in the 1860s. (New York Public Library)

New York harbor, where the ill were detained, acquired a fearful reputation; in 1858 it was burned down by rioters who feared a rumored yellow fever epidemic.

But there was long no provision for the reception of immigrants not held in quarantine. The newcomers simply descended to the docks and, unless met by friends, had to find their own way. In 1855 New York turned Castle Garden into a receiving station financed by a tax on each arrival. At the foot of Manhattan, in this large building which had once been a fort and then a theatre, as many as two thousand passengers at a time could prepare for their encounter with America. They could buy fresh bread and milk, wash in free hot water, and, if need be, sleep on the benches or the floor until they were ready to set forth. This was long the best the country offered its prospective citizens.

In the 1840s and 1850s most immigrants remained in the ports of arrival, except for those Irish who landed in Canada and insisted upon getting away from British territory even if they had to walk to do so. Generally, the people who moved beyond the cities were those fortunate enough to have the means to carry them to other destinations. The quality of their further journey depended upon circumstances. Those who imagined at the sight of Staten Island that their troubles were over often discovered that the worst was yet to come. In 1850 it took nine to fourteen days to get from New York to Buffalo by steamer and canalboat, and four days and nights by lake steamer to Chicago or Milwaukee. And then there was still a way to go to a farm site. Railroads, where available, were swifter. But each transfer involved new negotiations and the hazard of being cheated, to say nothing of the ever-present danger of illness or injury.

There were occasional efforts to regulate the traffic. The British took the lead, partly with the intention of diverting the flow from the United States to Canada or Australia. Statutes limited the number of passengers ships could carry and regulated the food and accommodations. Americans were less concerned. Before 1880 the federal government left the matter to the states, which were more anxious to protect the ports of landing than to offer security to the passengers.

More important—and more effective—were the means by which the immigrants gradually learned to protect themselves. By buying tickets that covered passage from point of origin to destination, for instance, they avoided some of the potential dangers that had wrecked many at the points of transfer. Protective societies formed by the immigrants who were already settled offered aid and advice to newcomers. And the slow development of information transmitted through the letters of those with experience taught fellow travelers how best to survive the journey. In their first experience away from home, the immigrants thus learned what it meant to be strangers, to lose the protection of the community, and to have to depend on themselves. Many paid a heavy cost, and all approached the New World, whether in hope or in desperation, already influenced by the profound shock of the crossing.

Immigrants carry their belongings onto the train, about 1850. (New York Public Library)

The Modern Ship of the Plains. This was the caption attached to a drawing of the interior of a railroad car of the 1880s. (Drawn by R. F. Zogbaum for Harper's Weekly, November 13, 1886, Library of Congress)

An immigrant transfer barge docked at Castle Garden, 1874. The sign in German offers to take immigrants from Castle Garden to the Erie Railroad where they can make connections for cities in the interior. (Smithsonian Collection of Business Americana)

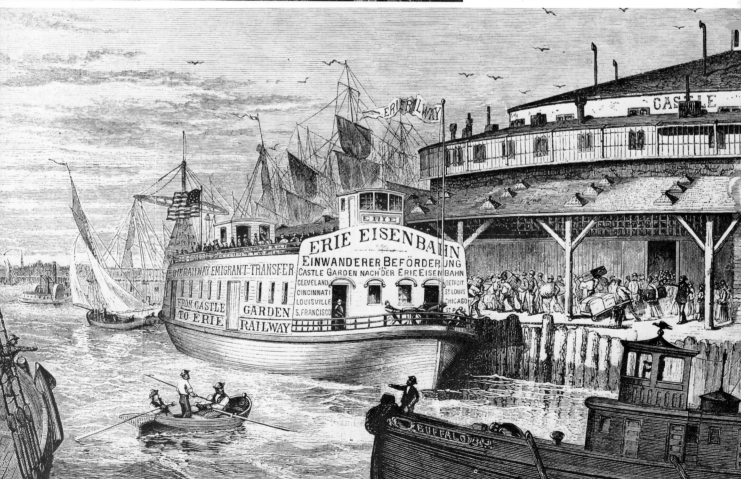

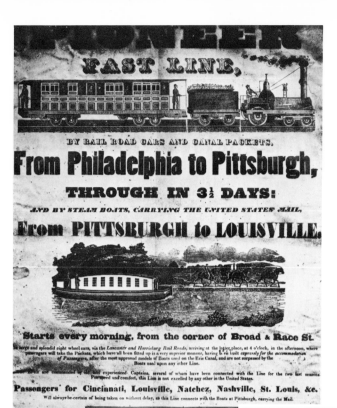

The first locomotive to cross the Allegheny mountains. (Library of Congress)

A railroad advertisement, 1837, offers to carry passengers through from Philadelphia to Pittsburgh and on to the cities of the Middle West. (New York Public Library)

Railroads in operation in the United States in 1840. Most of the lines were then still in the northeast. But some had developed around the Great Lakes and the Ohio River. (Smithsonian Institution)

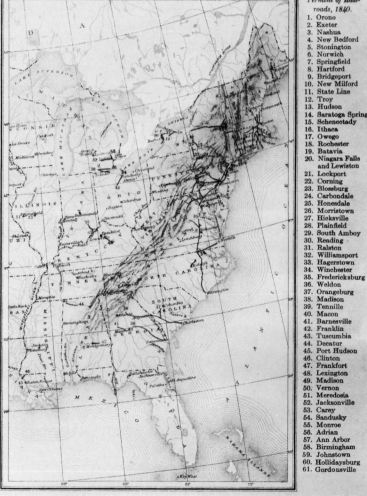

Termini of Railroads, 1840.

1. Orono
2. Exeter
3. Nashua
4. New Bedford
5. Stonington
6. Norwich
7. Springfield
8. Hartford
9. Bridgeport
10. New Milford
11. State Line
12. Troy
13. Hudson
14. Saratoga Springs
15. Schenectady
16. Ithaca
17. Owego
18. Rochester
19. Batavia
20. Niagara Falls and Lewiston
21. Lockport
22. Corning
23. Blossburg
24. Carbondale
25. Honesdale
26. Morristown
27. Hicksville
28. Plainfield
29. South Amboy
30. Reading
31. Ralston
32. Williamsport
33. Hagerstown
34. Winchester
35. Fredericksburg
36. Weldon
37. Orangeburg
38. Madison
39. Tennille
40. Macon
41. Barnesville
42. Franklin
43. Tuscumbia
44. Decatur
45. Port Hudson
46. Clinton
47. Frankfort
48. Lexington
49. Madison
50. Vernon
51. Meredosia
52. Jacksonville
53. Carey
54. Sandusky
55. Monroe
56. Adrian
57. Ann Arbor
58. Birmingham
59. Johnstown
60. Hollidaysburg
61. Gordonsville

Shipping advertisements in the 1880s. (New York Public Library)

An advertisement of an employment office for immigrants, 1832. (Smithsonian Collection of Business Americana)

EMIGRANT OFFICE.

A free Emigrant Office is instituted in Sixth-street, near the Sixth Avenue and Washington Square, for the purpose of giving intelligence, directing to employment, and affording disinterested counsel and advice to all foreigners coming to this country. Persons who want to hire Mechanics, Artisans, Laborers, &c. in any part of the Union, will please to communicate with this Office, free of postage, whose application will be promptly attended to.

Hours of attendance from nine o'clock till two.

New-York, July, 1832.

An immigrant almanac of 1893, issued by an employment office. (Smithsonian Collection of Business Americana)

Immigrants buy boxes of food to take on their journey into the interior. The signs appear in various languages addressed to the numerous nationalities involved by the end of the nineteenth century. (Brown Brothers)

Illustrious sons of Ireland—a patriotic
representation of heroic figures of Irish birth,
including Daniel O'Connell, Edmund Burke,
Marshall Patrick Sarsfield, Henry Grattan,
Oliver Goldsmith, Theobald Wolfe Tone, and
Robert Emmet. (Smithsonian Institution,
Peters Collection)

4

The Exodus from Ireland

Irish society remained sadly divided through much of the nineteenth century and was therefore helpless in the face of its grave problems. The Act of Union of 1803 had incorporated the island into the British polity but did nothing to ease the difficult situation of the people. Instead, by focusing attention on politics, the union had obscured more fundamental issues, which produced the immense migration to America.

At root was the inability of a peasant society to adjust to the nineteenth-century economy. The small group of absentee landlords and gentlemen fixed their eyes on England and regarded their Irish possessions simply as a source of income. The artisans in the towns suffered from competition with the products of factories and lacked either power to protect themselves by tariffs or capital to modernize. Above all, the mass of peasants led lives of hopeless poverty. Most of them were tenants who toiled desperately on patches of ground too small to sustain their families. Their situation sank precipitously through the first half of the century.

The deterioration was due in part to the increase in population which proceeded more graphically and with greater damage in Ireland than anywhere else in Europe. The island held fewer than a million people in 1660; more than 8 million crowded it in 1840. By then about 80 percent of the families were landless cottiers, who rented tiny plots and survived by labor for others. Since their numbers were steadily rising, tenants could be accommodated only by dividing the holdings into ever smaller parcels. Fifteen-acre holdings were most unusual; two- or three-acre parcels were far more common. Such farms were not adequate to feed a family, even one that lived only on potatoes and milk. The peasants survived by whatever they could earn in wages and by seasonal labor in England. Thousands annually crossed the Irish Sea in the hope of bringing back enough cash to pay the rent and eke out the produce they drew from the soil.

Religious prejudice and political subordination made matters worse. The people were Catholics, their rulers Protestants. Persecution no longer took the drastic form it had in Cromwell's time when in ten years a third of the population had perished by the sword and the plague and

110

An Irish peasant family about 1880. (Library of Congress)

Irish peasant types—the impression left on a French traveler by the misery of the cottiers. (New York Public Library)

One hundred drown'd in a River.

Boys forced to kill the Protestants.

Scenes of persecution in Ireland. (New York Public Library)

The clustered huts and narrow fields of a nineteenth-century Irish village. (Harvard University Social Ethics Collection)

The priest's blessing—Irish emigrants leaving home. (*Illustrated London News*, May 10, 1851, New York Public Library)

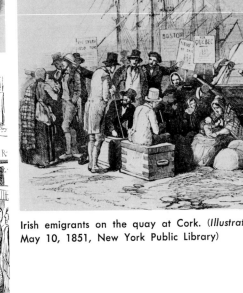

Irish emigrants on the quay at Cork. (*Illustrated London News*, May 10, 1851, New York Public Library)

A court for King Cholera—overcrowding and filth in the Irish slums encourage disease. (New York Public Library)

hunger. But the majority of the population still suffered from disabilities, and a good deal of energy went into the struggle for elementary rights. The achievement of Catholic emancipation in 1828 after a long struggle led by Daniel O'Connell gave the propertied Irish population a voice in Parliament, but the measure had relatively little influence on the peasantry.

Nor did subsequent political agitation improve their lot. The issues about which Parliament argued concerned the small, middle-class groups. These issues rarely dealt with the grievances of the peasants, whose only mode of expression was in occasional, and largely self-defeating, outbursts of violence. The Whiteboys or Black Feet could burn the buildings or ravage the crops of a heartless landlord or take a stick in the dark to a local official. But the people were no better off after the incident than before.

The only way was to get out. The already substantial emigration from Ireland between 1820 and 1845 con-

sisted primarily of artisans and the more prosperous peasants. Such people, discouraged about their own future or the prospects for their children, nevertheless possessed enough funds to permit them to seek relief in the New World.

Then economic disaster struck. There had been hard times earlier, in 1821, for instance, when the potato crop failed. But far-reaching consequences followed the blight of 1845 because by then a movement toward agricultural reform was well under way. Landlords wished to consolidate small holdings, exclude the cottiers, and adopt the efficient methods already proven in England. But the inability to dispose of the excess population had frustrated these intentions. Those forced off the land simply became charges on the local parish funds. As it was, the authorities were already paying the way of surplus people willing to emigrate.

The great potato rot of 1845 touched off a mass migration. That disaster eliminated the sole means of sub-

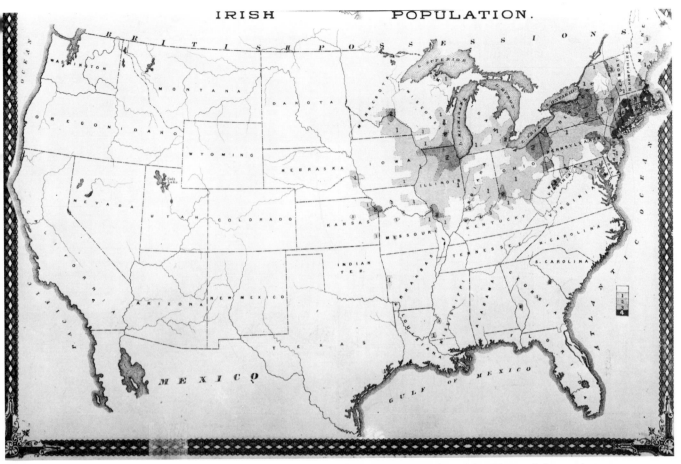

The distribution of Irish population in the United States, 1870. (*Indiana Atlas*, Library of Congress)

sistence of millions of peasants and thrust them over the edge of starvation. For five weary years the crops remained undependable, and famine swept the land. Untold thousands perished, and the survivors, destitute of hope, wished only to get away.

Emigration was the only mode of escape. Starving families could not possibly pay the rent and landlords could evict the useless tenants with the certainty that they would flee. Aid to help them on the way was worthwhile to rid the land of unwelcome occupants.

Immigration to the United States responded to these pressures. The number of Irish arrivals mounted steadily in the 1820s and 1830s. Then, in the 1840s, the movement accelerated; almost 2 million came in that decade. The flow persisted at a high level for five years more, as the first immigrants began to earn the means of sending for relatives and friends. In the decade after 1855 the movement subsided, but smaller numbers continued to arrive after the Civil War. In all, almost 3.5 million Irishmen entered the United States between 1820 and 1880.

The conditions that produced emigration had a pro-

found influence upon the nature of settlement in the New World. The peasants arrived without resources, weakened by the troubles that had driven them away and by the hardships of the journey. Yet they had to begin at once to earn their daily bread. Those who wished to become farmers as they had been in the Old World lacked even the capital to make a start. Instead, they were confined to the cities where they had landed, and few of them ever accumulated the resources to make any meaningful choice about their way of life. Theirs was an adjustment to unending labor and poverty.

Fortunately, the expansion of the American economy created heavy demands for types of work in which muscle alone counted. The great canals, which were the first links in the national transportation system, were still being dug in the 1820s and 1830s, and in the half century between 1830 and 1880 thousands of miles of rail were being laid. There was no earth-moving equipment but the pick and the shovel; everything had to be done by hand. Irish laborers were the mainstay of the construction gangs that did this grueling work. And in the

Immigrants landing in New York City in 1851. (Brown Brothers)

A scene on Pier 6, East River, New York. (*Harper's Monthly*, September, 1877, New York Public Library)

towns along the way, immigrants who decided to stay when the gang moved on formed the nuclei of Irish communities.

There was also a demand for their muscle in all the growing cities. Unskilled labor built new streets and aqueducts; sewerage, lighting, and transit systems; and residential, commercial, and public structures to meet the needs of a soaring population. Masons and carpenters were always in short supply; there was a need too for men who could only carry a hod or wield a shovel. In addition, the great cities had work for porters, draymen, and stevedores, for which skill was less important than a willingness to toil for low wages.

In time entrepreneurs also developed other uses for the labor of the Irish. The immigrants learned to dig coal from the anthracite mines of Pennsylvania, to wield the needle as tailors, and, eventually, to tend the machines in the many factories. In the New England textile mills, they formed a more dependable, more permanent, and less costly labor force than the farm girls whose places they took. And numerous new enterprises that

sprouted with industrialization throughout the country also depended increasingly upon Irish employees.

None of these jobs gave a man an adequate livelihood. Hours were long, conditions harsh, wages low, and periods of unemployment long. As a result, every family required the income of more than one breadwinner to get by. The Irish washerwoman, seamstress, and domestic servant soon became familiar, and occasionally women also found work in the factories. It was a matter of course that children began to earn their keep as quickly as possible.

Nothing in the uses to which America put them helped the Irish reorganize the lives they had upset by migration. Preponderantly city dwellers, they formed between 20 and 30 percent of the population of New York, Boston, Philadelphia, and Baltimore. There poverty forced them into the crowded makeshift tenements of the slums where they were ready victims of illness and high mortality rates. There were few gray-haired Irishmen, an observer noted; so many of them died young. The adults were tempted into excessive drinking

Immigrants landing in New York. (*Harper's Weekly*, June 26, 1858, Library of Congress)

The first street railway in New York. (Painting by Clyde O. De Land, Library of Congress)

Laying the track of the Union Pacific railway. The scene is forty miles west of Kearney, Nebraska, in 1867. (Association of American Railroads)

Driving the last spike on the Southern Pacific Railroad, January 12, 1883. The bridge was two miles west of the Pecos River, near the Mexican border. (Association of American Railroads)

A train and crew of the Punxsutawney, Titusville, and Erie Railroad, 1889. (Smithsonian Institution)

The leveling of Beacon Hill to make room for expansion behind the State House in Boston, 1811. (Drawing by J. R. Smith, Library of Congress)

Moving the Brighton Beach House, New York, 1888. (Library of Congress)

Shipbuilding in East Boston. (Wood engraving from *Ballou's Pictorial,* May 19, 1855, Library of Congress)

The Boston horsecar—a scene in 1872 when an emergency compelled the conductors and passengers to do the pulling. (*Frank Leslie's Illustrated Newspaper,* November 16, 1872, Library of Congress)

Miners and breaker boys in the anthracite fields of Pennsylvania about 1910. (Library of Congress)

The printing room of a large cotton mill in Lawrence, Massachusetts. (Library of Congress)

Women at work—the peeling room of a cannery, 1879. (New York Public Library)

New England bonnet makers. (*Harper's Monthly*, October, 1864, New York Public Library)

A street scene in New York. Note the signs of employment agencies supplying servants. (Brown Brothers)

Youthful factory workers. (A photograph by Lewis W. Hine, Library of Congress)

Working with the flatiron. (Brown Brothers)

and the youths into crime and vice; both responses were a measure of the hopelessness of men unable to conceive of a future free of poverty.

Yet, within a short time of arrival, there were signs of reconstruction. The Irish immigrants possessed cultural resources and developed institutions that helped them face hardship without despair.

To other Americans, who were predominantly Protestant, the distinctive feature of Irish life was its Catholicism. The strange ritual of the "Papist" churches, the hierarchy of priests and bishops, the nuns and convents, and the wild excitement of the St. Patrick's Day parade were regarded as evidence of the separateness of these immigrants.

Long years of English oppression had tested the loyalty of the Irish to Catholicism; in the tolerant environment of the New World, they were not likely to abandon the faith for which they had fought in the Old World. On the contrary, in the face of new tribulations, they sought the same consolation and guidance from religion as they had in their former homes. In some towns they found churches already in existence, and to those they quickly imparted a thoroughly Hibernian character. Elsewhere they laboriously scraped together the money to buy or construct a building. There had been perhaps five hundred thousand Catholics in the United States in 1820; there were more than 6 million in 1880, and much of the increase was the product of Irish immigration.

St. Patrick's Day in America. The picture commemorates the devotion of Irish exiles to their ancient religion and to the redemption of their motherland as a nation. Note the combination of religious and patriotic symbols, Irish and American. (Painting by John Reid, 1872, Library of Congress)

St. Patrick's Cathedral, 1853. (New York Public Library)

Participation in the activities of the church served the social as well as the purely religious needs of its communicants. The priest was a counselor to the parish, and an array of philanthropic and cultural associations connected with it provided activities for the more fortunate, as well as aid for the less well off. Before long, parochial schools supplied a pious education for the children.

The desire to be near the church was a cohesive force. These immigrants had little enough choice about their place of residence. They lived where they could find space at the meager rent they could afford. Irish neighborhoods appeared in the old districts from which former inhabitants had fled, or in shanty towns on the outskirts. But in any case it was best to be with people of one's own kind who could take a glass together in the saloon or who understood the keening at a wake.

In these quarters the young men often formed gangs, and, if they sometimes rioted, at other times lent themselves to more constructive purposes. Occasionally, either away on a construction job or working in the city, they fought in protest against a grasping contractor or struck for better wages. But the desperate need for work deprived these laborers of bargaining power and, as in Ireland, drove them to futile acts of violence. The Molly Maguires, for instance, organized secretly in the Pennsylvania coal mines and used whatever force they could against the owners until an informer and twenty hangings in 1877 put an end to the terror. But up to the time that the teamsters and the workers in the building trades could form effective, legitimate labor unions, the temptation to violence remained.

O'Connell's Call and Pat's Reply, 1843. The cartoon displays the progress made by Irish immigrants in America. (Library of Congress)

A meeting of the Molly Maguire leaders. (Drawn by Frenzeny and Tavernier, *Harper's Weekly*, January 31, 1874, Library of Congress)

At the polls. Rowdyism marked many an election in the immigrant quarters. (*Harper's Weekly*, November 7, 1857, Smithsonian Institution)

Some of the gangs and other local immigrant associations channeled a good deal of energy into politics with a more positive outcome. The arrival of the Irish had coincided with the abolition of property qualifications as a requirement to hold office or vote in the United States. Urban laborers, helpless in any other fashion, could assert through the ballot the power of their numbers. Furthermore, the prospect of a place on the public payroll gave them a direct interest in municipal government; jobs as policemen or street cleaners or, with a nod from an influential patron, with a gas or streetcar company offered security available nowhere else and were therefore well worth fighting for.

High office was as yet out of reach. Not until 1880 did an Irishman, William Russell Grace, venture to run and win the office of mayor of New York; he was far from a typical immigrant, having earned a fortune in

THE NEW YORK HERALD.

NEW YORK, SUNDAY, SEPTEMBER 9, 1894.   PRICE FIVE CENTS.

THE SAME OLD INVITATION.

Peru before coming to the United States. Nor did the Irish invent the political machine. Tammany Hall in New York City had seized power long before Mike Walsh and his Spartan Band gained admission to it. But in every city with a sizable Irish settlement, the immigrants learned to cooperate through ward and county organizations; the process trained leaders who would take power in many places after 1880.

Involvement in American affairs did not weaken ties to the Old Country; the steady flow of remittances to those who stayed behind showed the strength of these attachments. These immigrants also consistently supported movements to loosen the British hold on the island. The Young Irelanders of 1848 had numerous sympathizers in the United States; and in the 1860s the Fenian organization twice launched abortive invasions

Tammany received the blame, some of it deserved, some of it not, for the corruption of municipal politics. (A cartoon in *The New York Herald*, September 9, 1894, Smithsonian Institution)

of Canada to call attention to its demand for a republic.

By then, some immigrants had attained middle-class and professional status and were ready to provide leadership. A few had acquired wealth like W. R. Grace, or Peter Donahue and John Mackay who profited from the gold and silver booms in California and Nevada. Occasional lawyers and contractors achieved local prominence; and, more numerous, skilled craftsmen, grocers, and saloonkeepers became influential among their neighbors. These groups would be the guiding personalities of the future.

The Tammany ball of 1853. (New York Public Library)

A Tammany Democratic procession. (Drawing by A. Boyd Houghton, *The Graphic*, March 26, 1870, New York Public Library)

The grand procession in honor of the Fenian exiles before City Hall, New York City, February 9, 1871. (Library of Congress)

Fenians battle the police near Dublin. (*Illustrated London News,* March, 1867, New York Public Library)

John Boyle O'Reilly. (Bust in the Boston Public Library, New York Public Library)

John W. Mackay. (Sculpture by Gutzon Borglum, 1906, Library of Congress)

Barney Williams in "Dandy Jim." (New York Public Library)

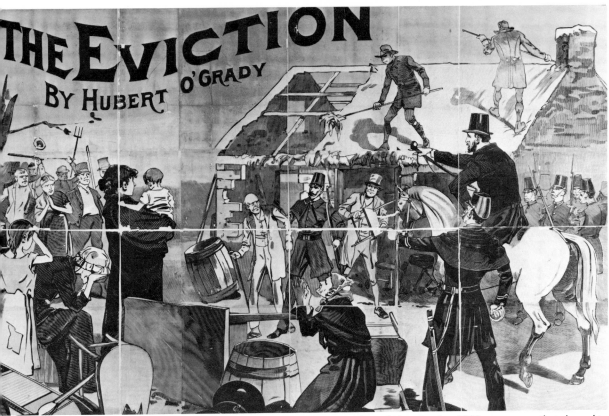

An eviction in the 1880s, a scene that brought poignant memories to many Irish immigrants. (Library of Congress)

Their desire for self-expression showed that the Irish understood their group identity. Poor though they were, they drew strength from a culture that explained their situation in the world and provided spiritual resources to face if not to solve their problems. Apart from the church, the most important media of that culture were the press and the stage. Irish newspapers had either a nationalistic or a religious base. Some were published as church organs, others drew support from patriotic societies. Their newspapers interpreted news, purveyed information, and printed popular poems and stories. John Boyle O'Reilly, for many years editor of *The Boston Pilot,* was representative of the best of the journalists. The stage was even more attractive because it made no demands on literacy and presented to attentive audiences dramas as real as life but not as painful. Barney Williams, the most popular actor, was the comic Irishman, a jaunty victim of the ironies of existence. The more formal dramas of Dion Boucicault treated the same themes realistically; and many Irish actors acquired national reputations.

By 1880 the painful initial Irish transplantation was over. A second and third generation born and educated in America were replacing the immigrants. Their heritage stemmed from the peasants' flight from Ireland and from the hardships of striking new roots in the New World.

The stage Irishman—a character in *Arrah na Pogue,* 1860s. (New York Public Library)

Dion Boucicault as "Conn" in *The Saughraun.* (Photograph by Mora, New York Public Library)

BOSTON PILOT.

Be just, and fear not—let all the ends thou aim'st at, be thy God's, thy Country's, and Truth's.

$2,50 In Advance. BOSTON, MAY 25, 1844. Volume VII-----No. 21.

THE BOSTON PILOT,
IS PRINTED AND PUBLISHED BY THE PROPRIETORS,
DONAHOE & ROHAN,

On every Saturday morning, at No. 1 Spring Lane, near Washington street, Boston, Ms., where all orders and communications (in all cases free of expense) must be addressed.

TERMS.—$2,50 if paid in advance, or $3,00 if not paid within three months from the time of subscribing.

$1.50 for six months. Four months $1.

Any of our present subscribers procuring a new one, and making it known at our office, or to any of our agents, will be entitled to two copies for $4,00, each sent separately.

In order to comply with the above terms, the whole must be paid in advance.

☞ A Postmaster may enclose money in a letter to the Publisher of a Newspaper, to pay the subscription of a third person, and frank the letter, if written by himself.

☞ PARTICULAR NOTICE. In future, no letter (except from Agents) will be taken out of the Post Office, unless the Postage is paid. Our Agents will bear this in mind, and mark the initials to their name on the outside cover of the letter.

Our Jubilee.

Having had some share in freighting the last British steam ship, which left these shores to travel over the unnumbered leagues of the glorious sea, the *corps* editorial of the *Pilot* assembled on the evening of the day, with the contributors, to whom we are so deeply indebted, with many prominent friends of the cause, to celebrate that epoch in American Agitation. The place of meeting was the venerable apartment in which the first club of friends to Repeal ever assembled on this continent, from whose social compact the Boston Repeal Association afterwards emerged into existence. A fine painting of one of our ancestors, mounted on his milk white steed, in the act so minutely described by the legend, of walking the azure waters of Killarney's fairy lake, hung

That emblem once heard through Byzantium, such notes
As those you now utter, from Mosleman throats,
And as it fell prostrate from the domes of the East
A spirit of light bore it off to the West.

Mahomet then trampled it; Heroed before
And the bigot to-day as the Pagan of yore,
But Isreal withered—and the Russian hath trod
The Crescent of Ottoma deep in the sod.

Beware, oh, beware, ye faithless and bold,
Even ye into bondage and chains may be sold.
Place not your proud feet on the trophy of Christ;
But half such a crime for their ruin sufficed.

Are ye mad in your rancor? what harm hath it done—
'Twas that Cross which Columbus to glory led on,
'Twas that Cross which your Lafayette clasped to his breast
When his soul plumed its flight to the homes of the blest.

Blaspheme not your fathers!—foul dastard if they
Could take up once more the cast garment of clay,
It would be to upbraid you, of the wrong and disgrace
You have brought on the fair fame they left to their race.

Shout, louder and louder, and drown if you can
The abhorrence of God and upbraidings of man,
Nor stay your great labor—but finish the work
Which to you was resigned by Jew, Pagan and Turk.

Aye, down with the Cross, let no emblem of love
Be seen the red City of Riot above,
Give to Bigots your cheers, and Religion a grave
"In this land of the free and this home of the brave."

There was silence painful and prolonged, and then the memory of the Revolutionary Fathers was drunk in solemn silence.

"I fear much," said the elder Mr. Redshanks, "that the disgrace of this odious event will be laid upon the whole land, which does not, in truth, de-deserve it. Those who have really had an American ancestry—who have read their country's history—who desire to add each one honorable leaf to its continuation in the 20th century—abhor and abjure such deeds."

"We will want another Bolivar, if these things go on," said M'Manus to the Colonel.

The Riots.

THOUGHTS FOR THE PEOPLE.

All was quiet in our city yesterday. It was a strange thing, however, to see the Military promenading our streets on the Sabbath, but still stranger to feel that their presence was necessary to the maintenance of the public peace! Into all the churches, as the chiming bells pealed out their solemn tones, poured crowd after crowd to give thanks, perhaps, to the Deity for their safety. Into all the churches, we should have said, *excepting*—the Roman Catholic. They stood desolate, silent and untenanted. In obedience to the orders of the Bishop they were not opened for public worship. The solitary tread of the sentinel, or the clank of the musket, was the only sound that disturbed their solitary repose.

And this was a Sabbath picture of the "City of Brotherly Love!" This was a picture of the "Quaker" city! Could William Penn have risen from his grave and looked at such a scene; could he have gazed on the bristling bayonets that offended the quiet eye in almost every direction; could he have been told that this pomp and panoply of war were necessary to secure the liberty of religious opinion; that here, on this very spot where he had planted the Christian banners, which he had made the asylum of the persecuted for opinion's sake, and had peculiarly consecrated to Religious Freedoom; could he have been told that here all this exhibition of military force was required simply to enable men to exercise one of the inalienable privileges of humanity, to worship God according to the dictates of their own consciences, what that great and good man would have said we leave the reader to imagine. He could not have credited the evidence of his senses. He could not have believed his descendants so monstrously degenerated. He

forsooth, where is it? If you are an Atheist, and deny a God, it is well. If you are a Hebrew and deny our Saviour, it is also well. If you are a Musselman and adore Mahomet, it is equally well. The unmolested possession of your opinion is guaranteed to you in Philadelphia. But if you are a brother Christian, differing with us in Biblical interpretations, fly for your life, abandon your home, forsake your altars—we, descendants of Wm. Penn, have but the faggot and the musket for such terrible unbelievers. Our presses shall call you unfitted to share in the blessings of freedom, and our people in the name of the Bible and the American Flag, shall drive you forth by the flame and the sword, lest your presence should contaminate their righteousness!

Alas! this is a contemplation for a Sabbath in Philadelphia. Who feels not ashamed that it is true? Who would not give world's to wipe off this foul blot from the disgraced name of our city, occasioned by a few misled and maniacal leaders? Who knows not that the fiery stain will stick to our people, as did the poisoned shirt to Nessus, hugging to its death their social reputation? And all this, too, at a moment when, after so much trial, Pennsylvania has shaken off the obloquy consequent upon her financial embarrassments. Having taken so much pains to stand erect before the world in her honesty, to be again made the pointed at of nations, the contemned of every liberal and enlightened spirit!—*Philadelphia Spirit of the Times.*

FORBEARANCE. The Philadelphia Catholic Herald says:—

"What we can say fearlessly and sincerely is, that Catholics, as a body, desire to live in friendship with their fellow-citizens, and utterly abhor lawless violence. This feeling is no doubt common to all good

THE BOSTON PILOT.

Methodist Sympathy for Church Burners.

The *Olive Branch*, whilome the defender of Louis Phillippe and Queen Victoria, and no less noted for its learned researches into the origin of the art of printing, has recently eased its troubled bosom much to the disgust of many of its readers, by an elaborate article on the Philadelphia riots. In order to prepare the minds of our readers for the extract we mean to present them, we will relate them a pair of facts relating to this paper, whose name so emblematic of peace and good will amongst men, is every week contradicted by its contents. When it had rushed into a controversy with us on the French question and found itself loosing ground, it then produced a letter from "a Catholic merchant," as it said, of this city—a Mr Leonard. Now this Catholic merchant turns out to be the veritable prophet seer of strange sights, who keeps an apple stall at the old South Church. So much for ingenuity in terms. Now for another *Olive Branch* quibble—More recently we had occasion to reprimand that journal for an uncharitable expression relative to the instructor of Mesmer, the father of Mesmerism, who was a friar named Hell. Fortunately for the *Olive Branch* our compositor misspelled the German name of Gutemberg, one of the discoverers, according to Bayle, *the* discoverer of the Art of Printing. An *n* having been substituted for the letter *m* gave this very fair and candid journal an opportunity to evade the main question and to avoid retribution.

Having explained thus far, our readers will not be astonished at the bitterness and injustice of the following excerpt from the columns of the same organ of a religious sect, which could use such expedients to avoid making the *amende* honorable palpably due on both occasions:—

"We do not intend to palliate the excesses of our native citizens," writes the *Olive Branch*, "nor do we intimate that they were altogether in the wrong. That they had great provocations, is clear from all the statements which we have seen. If it was wrong in them to form a party organization and meet for the advocacy of ultra political principles, it was equally wrong for the leaders of the Catholic party to usurp privileges which are granted to no separate religious sect in this country. That the latter have been striving for a number of years to obtain special advantages, there is no room to doubt. Their fastidious taste would not allow Catholic children to be educated at the public schools of New York, for fear of their imbibing Protestant principles through the ordinary text books introduced into the primary and grammar schools. A portion of the public fund

the past, nor its memorable deeds. Let us not think our cause impregnable, because it was baptised with prayer, because great men like Penn and Washington were its pioneers. It is just as durable as Virtue, as Principle, as reverence for Right is durable in the hearts of the People. It has no roots in the ashes of the dead. It lives in the vital force of the acting generation; it lives with their morality, their truth, their righteousness; it dies when these die out. Let these dwindle and rot, and we are as sure to perish as ever a nation perished in the past. And with all our advantages, and all our anticipations deepening the shame of our fall, others will clap their hands at us and hiss, and wag their heads, saying, "Is this the land of great experiments and lofty principles—of glorious promise and unprecedented opportunities?"

A Word to the Unnaturalized.

FOREIGNERS! Permit us to impress upon your attention the importance of taking an immediate stand in favor of the Constitution of the United States, which invites *all men* to liberty and the pursuit of happiness. Recent events clearly demonstrate that the time has come, when there is developed a wide-spread and connected prejudice against the further growth of an already very numerous foreign population in this country. This feeling is held in common, with the weak-minded, the venal, the bigoted and the interested, who form unhappily, a very large proportion of our American born neighbors. Many of these do not hate you—oh! no, heaven forbid!—but they would fain restrict your political privileges and rights, and *naturalize* you by mingling your bones with the soil of their church-yards; others again there are, who would see you hard-wrought and poor; if you labor, and delve and sweat, and remain poor, not daring to acquire property or raise your heads from the earth your labor, they will be condescending enough to allow you food and lodging in the land; a third and worse division makes up the anti-emigrant party—their principles are written on the height of Mount Benedict, and in the streets of Philadelphia.

Wisdom and self-preservation alike demand, that you shall take such measures as can shield you from this odious combination. The laws, as at present constituted, give you the means of defence; in a year or two you may ask for them, and they may not be in existence; you will then remember with bitterness, the Proberb which wisely says,—"Prevention is better then care." The prevention then, is to be found in one word,

Excerpts from the *Boston Pilot*, May 25, 1844, showing the combination of news and advice to newcomers that made the immigrant newspaper important to those it served.

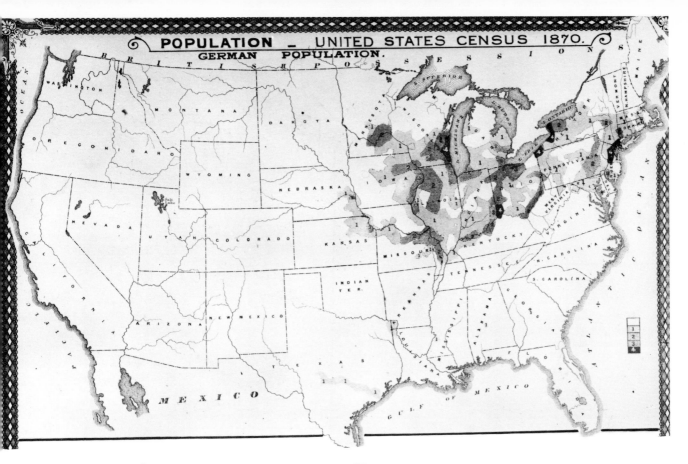

Distribution of the German-born
population of the United States, 1870.
(*Indiana Atlas*, 1876, Library of
Congress)

5

The Germans

Germany, in 1815, was not even a geographical expression. The term, as then used, referred to the lands occupied by German-speaking peoples, which spread from the North Sea to Poland. This area lacked political, cultural, and social unity; a multitude of dialects and religious and regional differences divided the population. Napoleon had finally liquidated the moribund Roman empire but no significant federating arrangement took its place at his downfall. Austria and Prussia were the most powerful states, but many other sovereign jurisdictions shared control in Central Europe until 1870.

Poets, historians, and philosophers nurtured a national sentiment attractive to the middle classes; the desire for unity flickered into life in 1848, but then subsided. Not until the Hohenzollerns and their Iron Chancellor, Bismarck, harnessed nationalism to the ambitions of the Prussian state did it have any practical effect. Then, between 1860 and 1870 patriotic fervor, dynastic ambitions, and economic interest combined in the creation of a unified Germany, which excluded the polyglot Austrian empire.

Until then, forces that produced emigration operated without political control. As elsewhere, the impulse to move was predominantly economic. Population soared in Central Europe, as in the rest of the Continent, and there was no central government that might take steps to ease the impact of change in the system of production. After Waterloo, a flood of cheap English manufactured goods poured into the Continent, ruining local handicrafts and turning the thoughts of artisans to America. At the same time, a growing market for agricultural goods put a premium on more efficient production. Large estates using modern methods squeezed out the peasants, particularly the cottiers. Some drifted to the cities while others migrated eastward; still others made the longer move across the Atlantic. The number of Germans entering the United States rose from about two thousand a year in 1830 to almost thirty thousand in 1840.

As in Ireland, famine, which swept across Central Europe after 1846, accelerated the departures; tens of thousands of victims turned their backs on their homelands. The number of arrivals climbed to a peak of 215,000 in 1854. The movement subsided somewhat after 1855, but resumed at the end of the American Civil War, and remained at a high level until 1880. In all, more than 3 million Germans arrived in the United States within sixty years.

127

German emigrants departing for the United States, late nineteenth century. (Brown Brothers)

Prince Otto von Bismarck, 1815–1898. (New York Public Library)

The emigrants' farewell. (From a painting by Ludwig Bokelmann, Library of Congress)

Americans generally identified the newcomers by language. But the designation "German" obscured real differences among these people and sometimes also encompassed Dutch and Swiss. The immigrants called Germans were therefore far more heterogeneous than the Irish. Among them were Lutherans, Catholics, and Jews; peasants, artisans, and traders; people from the Elbe and the Rhine; townsfolk and countrymen. They spread across the whole United States and became farmers, businessmen, and laborers. It was not surprising that

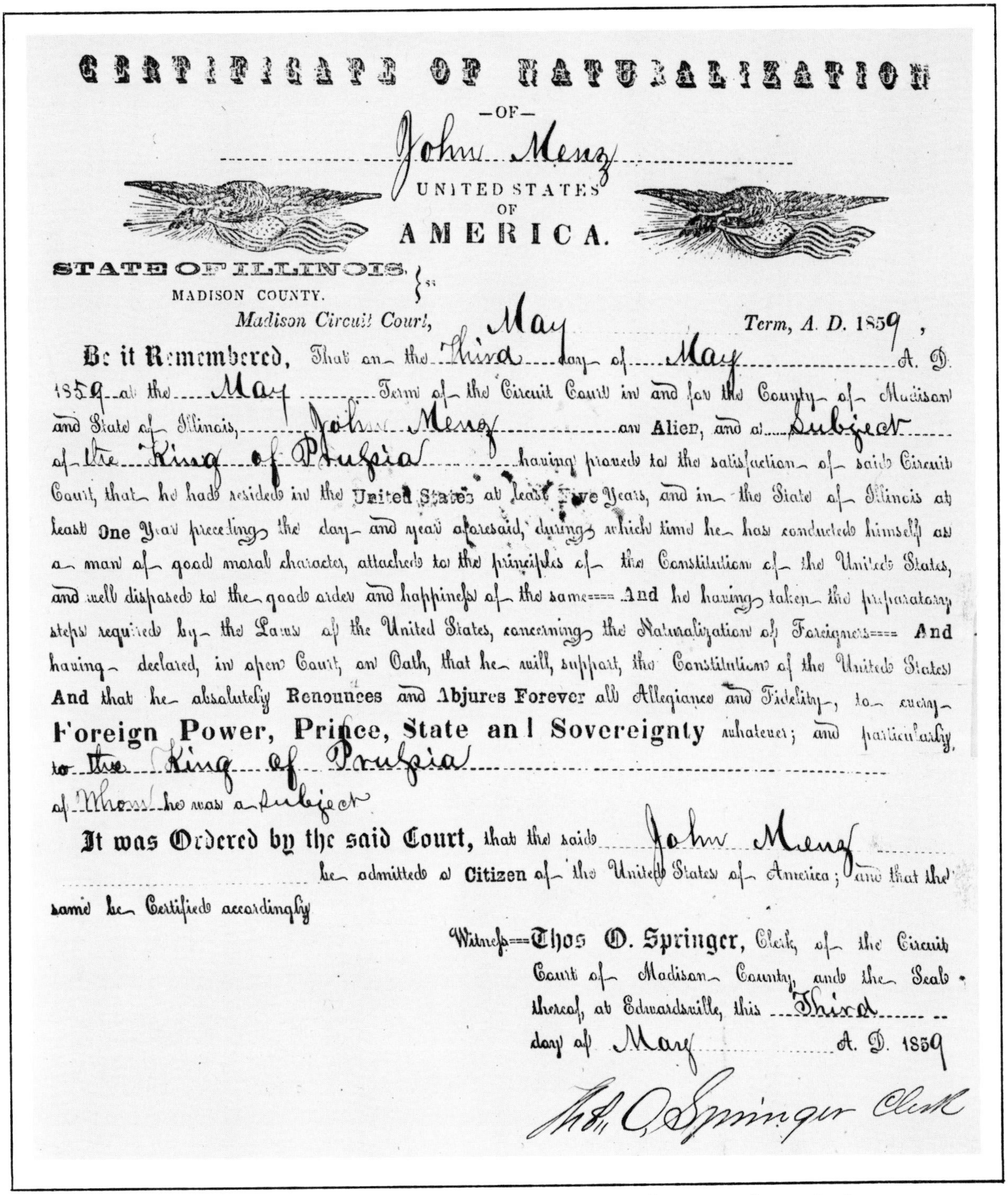

CERTIFICATE OF NATURALIZATION

— OF —

John Menz

UNITED STATES
OF
AMERICA.

STATE OF ILLINOIS,

MADISON COUNTY.

Madison Circuit Court, May Term, A. D. 1859,

Be it Remembered, That on the Third day of May A. D. 1859 at the May Term of the Circuit Court in and for the County of Madison and State of Illinois, John Menz an Alien, and a Subject of the King of Prussia having proved to the satisfaction of said Circuit Court, that he had resided in the United States at least Five Years, and in the State of Illinois at least One Year preceding the day and year aforesaid, during which time he has conducted himself as a man of good moral character, attached to the principles of the Constitution of the United States, and well disposed to the good order and happiness of the same===== And he having taken the preparatory steps required by the Laws of the United States, concerning the Naturalization of Foreigners==== And having declared, in open Court, an Oath, that he will support the Constitution of the United States And that he absolutely Renounces and Abjures Forever all Allegiance and Fidelity, to every **Foreign Power, Prince, State and Sovereignty** whatever; and particularly to the King of Prussia of Whom he was a Subject

It was Ordered by the said Court, that the said John Menz be admitted a Citizen of the United States of America; and that the same be Certified accordingly

Witness===Thos O. Springer, Clerk of the Circuit Court of Madison County, and the Seal thereof, at Edwardsville, this Third day of May A. D. 1859

Thos O Springer Clerk

A certificate of naturalization issued, 1859, in Madison County, Illinois, to a German immigrant born in Prussia. (Smithsonian Collection of Business Americana)

German emigrants arrive at Castle Garden, New York, on their way to Salt Lake City, 1879. (New York Public Library)

An Amish farmer prepares his field in Illinois for corn planting. This picture taken in 1968 shows the extent to which the descendants of early German immigrants clung to the methods of a previous century. (United Press International)

Baking bread in Pennsylvania, using the old oven, 1905. (Library of Congress)

there was little uniformity in their adjustment or indeed much capacity for cooperation.

Those who possessed funds to take them directly to farms in the West settled immediately as landowners. The ideals of independent proprietorship and of agriculture as a way of life were attractive; even those who had never themselves tilled the soil at home felt a romantic desire for closeness to nature. In Belleville, St. Clair County, Illinois, for instance, a cluster of university graduates, disillusioned with the failures of liberals in Europe, settled down to the plow and, from their habit of reading, became known among curious neighbors as the Latin farmers.

The peasants attempted to apply to the New World the agricultural traditions they brought with them. Cautious by habit, they looked for traces of limestone and for heavily wooded tracts, which they regarded as measures of the richness of the soil. As a result, they avoided the prairies and low-lying meadows. Nor did they have a taste for the frontier; their skills were not those of the hunter or woodsman, but rather of the stable tiller of the earth. They were likely to buy out cleared farms and to settle near people like themselves.

It seemed plausible therefore to expect that joint efforts would help the migrants find their way to destinations where they could prosper together. The idea was

Farmers in a cattle yard. (*Frank Leslie's Illustrated Newspaper,* April 29, 1876, New York Public Library)

particularly attractive to nationalists who feared that the Germans, dispersed throughout the vast American continent, would lose their strength as a group. Such people believed that it would be much better to concentrate the immigrants in a few places where they could preserve their language, religion, and culture. Thus, Paul Follenius and Friedrich Münch, idealistic young men who despaired of events in Europe in 1830, conceived of a free Germany in the New World where their transplanted countrymen could enjoy the liberty denied them at home. In 1834, they led a group that took up farms in Warren County, Missouri, and formed a nucleus that attracted other Germans. A little later, some noblemen in Hesse formed the Mainzer Adelsverein in order to settle a colony in the Republic of Texas. For a fixed sum, they offered to provide any family with transportation, a log house, and a 160-acre tract. In 1845, the first detachment created the town of New Braunfels. The settlement grew thereafter, despite the mismanagement of the company.

These were exceptional instances. Most immigrants made their way to farms in individual families. Nevertheless, their preference for being together produced a natural clustering along the routes they traveled out of the ports to the interior. From New York, Philadelphia, and Baltimore, they moved into the Ohio Valley and, after 1850, to Iowa and Wisconsin. From New Orleans, by way of Saint Louis, they advanced into Missouri and southern Illinois.

Everywhere the German farmers exhibited common traits that earned them a reputation for tightfistedness and industry; not for them the wasteful practices of the native American pioneer. Thrifty, hard-working, and disciplined, the Germans preferred to exhaust their own bodies rather than the soil. The women and children toiled long hours, as did the men; and more effort went into the construction of barns and the care of animals than on comforts for the home or on the fripperies of dress. Prudence was the watchword. At least for the first generation, the memory of what they had escaped was too frightening to permit the risk of a decline back into dependence.

A substantial number of Germans also settled in the cities. Many remained in the great ports of arrival, notably New York, Philadelphia, and Baltimore, which handled most of the shipping from Germany. They were less likely to settle in New Orleans, where Negro slaves were the labor force. In the interior, the most important settlements were at Cincinnati, Saint Louis, Chicago, and Milwaukee. These newcomers to the cities developed their own institutions and social organizations.

Although many were laborers, there were more artisans among the Germans than among the Irish. The German butcher and baker, for instance, became familiar figures in many towns. From these shops, it was a short step to extensive businesses, at least for the most fortunate. Two grocers from Hanover set the example. Ferdinand Schumacher arrived in 1850 at the age of twenty-eight. He tired of farming and opened a store in Akron, Ohio, where in 1856 he began to sell rolled oats, introducing Americans to a novel breakfast food. Claus Spreckels was even younger when he opened his grocery in Charleston, South Carolina. Determined to do better, he moved first to New York and then to California. In San Francisco he decided to operate a brewery and that experience led him into sugar refining, from which he gained enormous wealth.

Some among the German Jews advanced from the

A view of New Braunfels, Texas, late nineteenth century. (Lithograph, Library of Congress)

German immigrants on the way to New Braunfels. (Rudolf Cronau, *Drei Jahrhunderte Deutschen Lebens in Amerika*, Berlin, 1909)

The office of the *Staats-Zeitung*, a German-language daily in New York. (Brown Brothers)

Unloading oyster luggers in Baltimore. (Detroit Collection, Library of Congress)

The Goodrich docks, Chicago, at the end of the nineteenth century. (Library of Congress)

German saloon types — the waiter, the sausage man, and the wienerwurst man. (*Kenny's Cincinnati Illustrated*, 1880, Smithsonian Collection of Business Americana)

Workers in a meat-packing plant. (Peter Roberts, *The New Immigration*, New York, 1912)

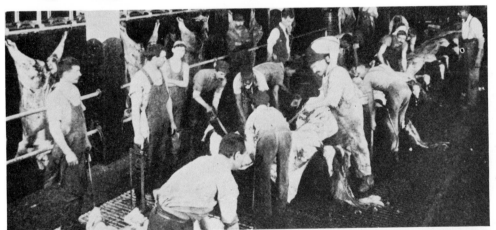

A butcher shop on South Canal Street, Chicago, 1901. (Library of Congress)

peddler's pack to the country store and then to the merchant's emporium. The three Seligman brothers, Joseph, Jesse, and Henry, had each operated a dry goods or general store in Alabama, New York, and California after they arrived from Bavaria in 1837. In 1857 they became partners in New York City and opened a brokerage house. Five years later, they went into banking, and in 1880 the firm had branches in London, Paris, and Frankfurt.

Such men were as exceptional as Heinrich Schliemann who came from Pomerania to California in 1851, made a fortune in the gold rush and later went off to excavate ancient Troy. Most tradespeople however, did not rise but spent their lives in their little shops, earning enough to elevate themselves above the level of laborers. Retailers formed a significant middle-class element among the more numerous working people with whom they migrated.

In the large cities, German neighborhoods were easily recognizable. In Cincinnati, for instance, the area known as "Over the Rhine" was solidly Teutonic; English was almost a foreign language, and distinctive shops and beer gardens reflected the tastes of the immigrants. Everywhere, too, newspapers in their own language served their needs.

Social life was active but variegated and decentralized. Hundreds of singing societies enlisted immigrants and their children, and they supported musical organiza-

tions, which had an impact upon American culture. In some cities there was also a German theatre, which had less influence on outsiders because of the language barrier, but which nevertheless was important to the group.

Internal divisions, however, made it difficult to organize the group politically or socially. While the Irish swiftly learned to use political power, the Germans, who were at least as numerous, made little headway. Unfamiliarity with the predominant language was, no doubt, a discouraging factor, but not the decisive one. Educated leaders like Carl Schurz and the resources of a substantial middle-class population did not offset the handicap because the group as a whole lacked the cohesion of common interests or viewpoints.

The effort, led by some ideologists, to form a German-American community came to naught; the social foundations were lacking. Thus, ideological elements inevitably crept into the activities of the *Turnvereine*, gymnastic organizations that originated among the liberals in Germany. The suspicion that these groups might be vehicles for radical activity kept many immigrants from joining, and reflected a deep division between radicals, especially Forty-eighters, and conservatives. Although rising nationalist sentiment after the establishment of the empire in 1870 tended to submerge these differences, they long impeded efforts at collaboration.

Religious action was more effective because the distinctions among various groups of immigrants were clear

Left to right:
Ferdinand Schumacher. (*National Cyclopedia of American Biography*)
Claus Spreckels, the "Sugar King." (Drawn by T. V. Chominski, New York Public Library)
Joseph Seligman. (*National Cyclopedia of American Biography*)

Festival of the German singing societies, Chicago. (Sketch by W. B. Baird, *Harper's Weekly*, July 4, 1868, New York Public Library)

Heinrich Schliemann (1822–1890). (New York Public Library)

Reception of the German singing societies in New York City Hall Park. (Sketch by A. R. Waud, *Harper's Weekly*, August 5, 1865, New York Public Library)

Sunday evening in a New York German beer garden. (*Harper's Weekly*, October 15, 1859, New York Public Library)

A German beer garden. (*Illustrated London News*, December 3, 1864, New York Public Library)

The German Stadt Theatre in New York. (*Harper's Weekly*, October 22, 1859, New York Public Library)

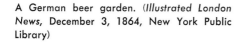

Conried's Deutsches Theater. (Brown Brothers)

and because sectarianism was already a recognized pattern in the United States. German Lutherans, Catholics, and Jews developed effective organizations to meet their particular needs for worship. The Lutheran churches formed in the eighteenth century were too Americanized for the tastes of the newcomers of the 1830s and 1840s. From their strongholds—the Missouri Synod and the Concordia Theological Seminary in Saint Louis—their spokesman, C. F. W. Walther, insisted that pastors and communicants remain faithful to traditional doctrines. Catholics who recognized the central authority of Rome could not break away from the preponderantly Irish-American church; but separate German-speaking parishes served the immigrants in most cities. And Isaac

Mayer Wise directed a nascent reform movement in which German Jews were active; his efforts led to the establishment of the Union of American Hebrew Congregations in 1873 and the Hebrew Union College in 1875.

The German migrations of the nineteenth century thus brought to the United States groups diverse in background and experience. They entered into American life in ways that emphasized the differences among them, rather than unifying them. They therefore were less likely as a group to express their identity in a coherent centralized form than in the local activities through which they participated in their communities.

C. F. W. Walther. (A photograph of 1881, Library of Congress)

Top left: A *turnverein* festival in Milwaukee, 1894. (New York Public Library)

Three thousand *turner* participate in a wand exercise, Milwaukee, 1894. (New York Public Library)

Meeting room of the German
Lutheran home for immigrants,
New York, 1905. (Photoworld)

German immigrant home, New
York. (Photoworld)

Fluctuations in immigration from
Germany, Netherlands, and Switzerland. (E. A. Ross, *The Old
World in the New*, New York,
1914)

A German apothecary on West
Fourth Street, New York, about
1900. (Brown Brothers)

Period	Number	Note
1826-30	8000	
1831-35	49000	
1836-40	109300	
1841-45	110000	
1846-50	337800	
1851-55	672400	POLITICAL REACTION IN GERMANY
1856-60	316100	HARD TIMES IN UNITED STATES
1861-65	242500	CIVIL WAR IN UNITED STATES
1866-70	577600	
1871-75	532700	
1876-80	220200	HARD TIMES IN UNITED STATES
1881-85	1031500	MILITARISM AND OVERPOPULATION
1886-90	548200	IN
1891-95	432600	GERMANY
1896-1900	120100	HARD TIMES IN UNITED STATES
1901-05	214300	
1906-10	211400	

Emigrants leaving England. (Drawing in *The Graphic*, December 18, 1869, New York Public Library)

6
From the North

The immigrants who came from the countries of northern Europe after 1820 had a good deal in common. England, the Netherlands, and Scandinavia were already well launched in the process of modernization, and many of their people were equipped by experience to deal with the problems of the New World. As a result their adjustment to America followed a course different from that of the Irish or German newcomers.

A variety of immigrant types left the British Isles for the United States. The number of displaced peasants was smaller after 1820 than earlier; the most disturbing changes in agriculture were complete by then and, in any case, new factories close at hand provided an outlet for much surplus labor.

But the nineteenth-century English, Welsh, and Scottish migrants were not the sort to be satisfied to sink into or remain in the ranks of the wage earners engaged in manufacturing. Some farmers, squeezed by the rise in rents and in the value of land, felt the attraction of the abundant space across the ocean. Artisans, worried about their ability to compete with the machines, sought a fresh start in the New World. And, occasionally, laborers judged that opportunities were more attractive abroad than at home.

The British government long wished to prevent skilled artisans from leaving. But, if its people were to depart, it desired to direct the flow to its colonies, particularly to Canada, Australia, and New Zealand. It failed in both efforts. Despite substantial inducements, these Eng-

lishmen preferred to come to the United States. Neither the wars of 1776 and 1812 nor independence had made such men resentful of the Republic. Once trade had been reestablished, a steady stream flowed westward. In all, about a million Englishmen came to the United States between 1820 and 1880.

The unskilled laborers among these immigrants did not fare much better than their Irish or German counterparts. But men with a skill could move directly into industries like those they left, and on better terms than at home. Textile and ironworkers thus found a place in the cotton and woolen mills of New England and in the foundries of Pennsylvania. Silk weavers from Macclesfield established themselves in Paterson, New Jersey, in 1840, and were followed by thousands of others after 1860 when England ceased to protect its silk industry. Familiarity with the language and the ability to read and write also enabled many Englishmen to find positions as clerks and to open small businesses.

Those who wished to be farmers could prosper if they brought some capital with them. The persistent publicity devoted to the settlement established by Morris Birkbeck and George Flower at Albion, Illinois, after 1817 attracted hundreds of their countrymen to the vicinity. It was not unusual for a group of neighbors to move together, as did the Sussex people who went to Lyon County, Kansas, or those from Cornwall, who gathered in Grass Valley, California. Others made their way across as individuals.

Dockyard workmen embark as emigrants at Portsmouth, England. (*Illustrated London News,* May 8, 1869, New York Public Library)

A nineteenth-century factory in northern England. (Brown Brothers)

Bell time in a New England factory. (Drawing by Winslow Homer, *Harper's Weekly,* July 25, 1868, Library of Congress)

Tenement house tobacco strippers. Children work, despite the laws against their employment. (*Frank Leslie's Illustrated Newspaper*, January 28, 1888, Library of Congress)

A New York sweatshop and its victims. Above, the boss drives his female employees. Below right, women carry bundles home to work; below left, the end of a working girl. (*Frank Leslie's Illustrated Newspaper*, November 3, 1888, Library of Congress)

The foundry department of a steel mill in the early twentieth century. (Library of Congress)

Scene in a stamping mill, 1888. (Library of Congress)

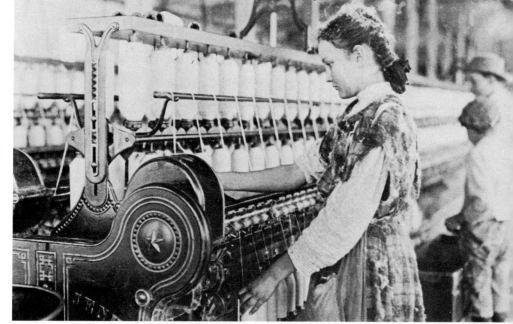

Young textile workers, 1909. In the North Carolina mills native Americans were as bad off as the immigrants. (Photograph by Lewis W. Hine, New York Public Library)

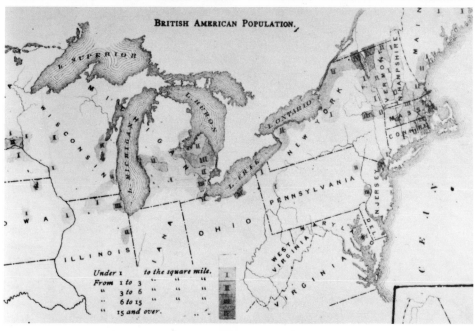

The distribution of British-American population, 1870. (*Indiana Atlas*, Library of Congress)

Immigrants pulling their handcarts on the Oregon trail. (Watercolor by Jackson, Library of Congress)

E. C. ("Teddy Blue") Abbott (left) with Charles Russell. (Montana Historical Society, Helena)

Occasional young men felt a romantic pull to the West. E. C. ("Teddy Blue") Abbott came with his father from Norfolk in England to a farm in Nebraska, but was not content to spend his life behind a plow. As soon as he could, he made off to a cowboy's life in Montana. For somewhat related reasons, a few Victorian gentlemen, persuaded that the West could make a man of anyone, sent their wayward sons to rural America; there were clusters of these young people in places like Victoria, Kansas.

The Scots were less likely to be farmers than artisans or craftsmen. Andrew Carnegie was typical in origin if not in achievement. His father was a damask weaver in Dunfermline who did well at his trade until the introduction of steam made his hand looms useless. In 1848, when Andrew was thirteen and his father forty-three, the family sold its meager possessions and left home. Years later the boy recalled his father's sweet voice singing:

To the West, to the West, to the land of the free,
Where the mighty Missouri rolls down to the sea;
Where a man is a man even though he must toil
And the poorest may gather the fruits of the soil.

The Carnegies never got to the soil, and for years their days were full of toil; Andrew worked as a bobbin boy in a cotton mill to add his mite to the support of the household. But there was at least a chance for an able, aggressive, and ambitious young man to push ahead. And although very few enjoyed his good fortune, the glimmer of hope that they might drew many more on. About two hundred thousand Scots joined the movement to America between 1820 and 1880.

In the same period, migration out of Wales brought about thirty thousand people to the New World. Religious zeal and economic discontent drove them from home. Industrialization had unsettled their communities, and periodic revivals left them emotionally stirred and ready for change. In the United States, they played a prominent part in the Pennsylvania coal-mining industry. After 1830, Welsh miners helped develop the anthracite fields of the Schuylkill and Susquehanna valleys and later the bituminous mines between Scranton and Wilkes-Barre.

Finally, a new source of immigrants appeared in Canada. The number to cross the border was difficult to count; here, American entry requirements were much

The homes of coal miners in Pennsylvania. (Sketch by Joseph Becker, *Frank Leslie's Illustrated Newspaper*, December 12, 1874, New York Public Library)

Andrew Carnegie. (*National Cyclopedia of American Biography*, 1899)

A group of miners in Scranton in 1906. (Library of Congress)

less stringent and formal than by sea. Perhaps as many as five hundred thousand immigrants came south, mostly British by origin, although there were some French among them. The movement reflected both the dissatisfaction with Canada's colonial status and economic prospects and the continuing lure of the United States.

Mormon missionary activity after 1837 generated a distinctive current within the general stream of British immigration. The recruitment of converts was a religious duty of Latter-Day Saints, and zealous emissaries moved through the distressed regions of England, offering the poor aid in making a new life in the New World. About thirty thousand Britons moved under Mormon auspices, first to Nauvoo, Illinois, and then to Utah.

Except for the Welsh, the British immigrants came from a society very much like that of the United States and were spared some of the difficulties that bothered the Irish and Germans. Familiarity with the language

Boys were not too young to work in the coal pits. (Photograph by Lewis
W. Hine, 1908, Library of Congress)

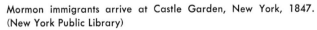

Boys picking slate in an anthracite mine, 1913. (Library of Congress)

Mormon immigrants arrive at Castle Garden, New York, 1847.
(New York Public Library)

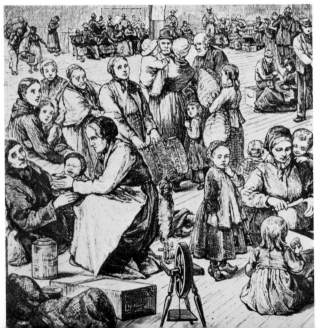

Church leaders read an order to a Mormon settlement. (Drawing by Frenzeny and Tavernier, *Harper's Weekly*, February 6, 1875, New York Public Library)

Mormon immigrants on the way to Utah aboard ship draw lots for vans across the desert. (*Illustrated London News*, April 18, 1857, New York Public Library)

The Mormon temple at Nauvoo, 1854. (New York Public Library)

and institutions of the United States eased some of the shock of making their way in the New World. Characteristically, for instance, an unusually high proportion of these newcomers did not feel it necessary to become American citizens. So, too, the pressure to form churches of their own was not as intense as among other groups. Most of the English were Anglicans or Methodists and could find places in existing churches.

Yet there was some desire to preserve local religious and cultural institutions. The Welsh were particularly sensitive to their separateness. Even those who knew English felt that the language used in business and in earthly bargains of all kinds was hardly fit for church and chapel on Sunday; many considered no sermon convincing unless delivered in the *hwyl*, the peculiar intonation of the Old Country. They subscribed to *Y Drych*,

Mormons crossing the plains. (*Ballou's Pictorial*, September 20, 1856, New-York Historical Society)

published in New York from 1851 onward, and to other, smaller newspapers; and they participated in the *eisteddfods,* or singing competitions.

So too, although there were no theological grounds why the Scots in New England should not have worshiped with the Congregationalists, these immigrants insisted upon setting up Presbyterian churches of their own. They also joined Caledonian clubs, which provided the games, food, and conviviality with which they were familiar. When numbers permitted, the natives of smaller districts formed associations of their own; the people from Cornwall set up societies in Chicago, Boston, and New York, as did those from the Isle of Man. Other more comprehensive organizations and newspapers served Britons in general.

After the middle of the century, British immigrants brought with them the traditions of trade unionism. American labor by contrast was still unorganized, and the newcomers provided a stimulus and, sometimes, leadership in starting workers' associations. George Gunton, for instance, arrived in Fall River in 1874, after which the local newspaper he edited urged the employees of the mills to take steps to improve their conditions.

The Netherlands generally was able to contain its own growing population, and, in addition, its extensive colonial possessions in Asia and America absorbed the more venturesome people who wished to leave home. Yet under special circumstances some groups preferred to go to the United States. About fifty thousand people arrived between 1820 and 1880.

Many responded to a religious impulse in migrating. Considering the problem in 1845, Henrik P. Scholte, for instance, recognized that those who sought temporal advantages alone had better stay home. Scholte was one of a group of Seceders who objected to the moderniza-

tion of the Church in the Netherlands and sought a new place where they could escape these tendencies. In 1847, some nine hundred of them, organized as the Christian Association for Emigration, made their way to Pella, Iowa. Theirs was not a communal settlement; each family owned and worked its own land. But religion and nationality provided strict means of discipline and Scholte was a powerful leader—minister, publisher of the local newspaper, banker, notary public, real-estate agent, and representative of the life insurance company.

Similar clusters appeared in Holland, Groningen, Vriesland, and Zeeland, in Michigan. These were substantial agricultural communities where men dedicated to life on the soil planted deep roots. To them came other Hollanders who could not possibly dream of owning farms at home and who were attracted by the combination of economic opportunity and a familiar culture. The Netherlanders, who found it a hard penance to be silent when they did not understand the English of strangers, long considered it desirable to dwell by themselves in communities compatible with their own national character. In addition, small groups of Catholic Walloons and Flemings came with their priests from Holland and Belgium to Wisconsin.

The migrants from Scandinavia were more numerous, although the movement was not yet in full swing in 1880. By that date, about four hundred thousand had reached the United States.

The pioneers left in response to religious motives. The first Norwegian immigrants in 1825 were Quakers. A revival in Småland in the 1840s touched off the Swedish movement, and Mormons in the 1850s recruited several thousand Danes. The first comers started settlements, organized religious and cultural institutions, and sent home word of the prospects for success.

The Scottish Rite Temple, Oakland, California. (United Press International)

Dancing the Highland fling—the fondness for Scottish customs and costumes survives through the nineteenth century. (*Harper's Weekly*, July 5, 1890, Nostalgia Press, Inc.)

A sack race at the Caledonian games. (*Harper's Weekly*, July 5, 1890, Nostalgia Press, Inc.)

Scottish-Americans playing at curling. (*Harper's Weekly*, July 5, 1890, Nostalgia Press, Inc.)

A Labor Day parade, early twentieth century. (Brown Brothers)

A procession of workmen in the Bowery agitating on behalf of the eight-hour day. Laborers then were eager to demonstrate their respectability and peaceable intentions. (Wood engraving by M. Morgan in *Frank Leslie's Illustrated Newspaper*, June 29, 1872, Library of Congress)

An official of the Working-Women's Protective Union hears complaints from some of the members. (Drawing by Robert Lewis, *Harper's Weekly*, February 21, 1874, New York Public Library)

A poster of the Brotherhood of Locomotive Firemen emphasizing its concern for sobriety, benevolence, and industry, 1885. (Smithsonian Collection of Business Americana)

The effects of strike—the capitalist takes his ease, the workingman suffers. (Harper's Monthly, April, 1852, New York Public Library)

Immigrant Dutch children. (Brown Brothers)

Landing of the early Dutch settlers in the New World. Like other immigrants, the Hollanders were eager to demonstrate their place in the building of the nation by reverence to their ancestors. (New York Public Library)

A party of Dutchmen, coming to settle in Albany in the colonial period. (New York Public Library)

Social and economic changes induced many others to follow. A rising birth rate and increasing population put a strain on the meager resources of Norway. The *husmänd* or landless peasants found life more and more difficult, and a growing number left their homes to sail for the New World. The tide increased rapidly after the Civil War. Some went into the interior to settle on farms. There were also substantial groups of seamen and laborers in Chicago, Minneapolis, Brooklyn, and other cities, and not a few worked in the forests of Michigan.

Somewhat later, the desire to migrate spread across the Norwegian border to Sweden. The general cause was similar—the pressure of population operating in a changing economic system incapable of providing a place for the peasant. The movement out of Denmark, Iceland, and Finland was much smaller in these years than from other parts of Scandinavia. By 1880, how-

Norwegian immigrants at Castle Garden. (Nostalgia Press, Inc.)

The Quaker meetinghouse in Newport, Rhode Island, 1857, shows the continuing prosperity of the American Friends; which attracted their coreligionists from Norway. (Drawn by John Collins, Library of Congress)

A party of Swedish immigrants passes through Boston on the way to the West. (Wood engraving from *Gleason's Pictorial Drawing-Room Companion*, October 30, 1852, Library of Congress)

ever, all these people had made a start in forming New World institutions. Newspapers, Lutheran churches, and cultural societies established their roots in American soil.

The immigrants from northern Europe thus left societies that had already advanced toward modernization. Many had the benefit of some education, which gave them preparation of a kind for their new experience and imbued them with hope and a conviction that success was possible.

Not all did well. Many labored in factories, as did other immigrants, and even those who got to the farms encountered difficulties. Yet, the relative prosperity of some was an indication of the quality of the training they brought with them.

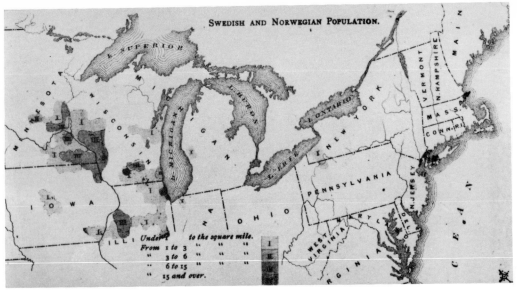

Distribution of the Norwegian and Swedish immigrant population of the United States, 1870. (*Indiana Atlas*, Library of Congress)

Gustavus Adolphus Lutheran Church, serving Swedish immigrants. (Nostalgia Press, Inc.)

A Swedish folk festival. (Drawing by W. A. Rogers for *Harper's Weekly*, Nostalgia Press, Inc.)

A shipping advertisement for immigrants from Scandinavia to America. (Smithsonian Collection of Business Americana)

The San Dolores mission in San Francisco, 1849.
(New York Public Library)

Immigrants on the way to California by way of Cape
Horn, 1849. (New York Public Library)

7

The Chinese

California was a special case from the start, for it faced the Pacific rather than the Atlantic Ocean and its immigrants came from the west as well as from the east. Settlement there did not proceed as it did in every other region—step by step through the pressure of population on the frontier. It came in a great spurt. California until 1846 was a Mexican province, with its important connections to the south. Though separated from the United States by mountains and the fear of a great desert reputed to block all travel, California received occasional visits from Americans, who generally arrived by sea, but it became home to only a few of them.

Two sudden events ended California's isolation. The Mexican War (1846–1848) transferred possession to the United States, and the discovery of gold in 1848 brought a host of fortune seekers to the interior. Yet California's orientation remained with the Pacific Ocean, which offered the most convenient route for the carriage of its goods and passengers. The western coast had long been a station for trade with Asia, and even California's connections with Europe or the Atlantic coastal cities were easier by way of the Strait of Magellan or the Isthmus of Panama than overland.

During the gold rush, thousands of easterners, Europeans, and Australians rushed into the territory. The adventurers crowded the diggings and quickly made San Francisco a cosmopolitan metropolis. But the men who came were unwilling to spend their time in the humdrum tasks of building cities or supplying others with goods and services. Instead their presence increased the demand for an already scarce labor supply. Wages went up astronomically, along with all the costs of existence.

It was vain to expect relief from European immigrants. The poor peasants of Ireland and Germany rarely had the means to get beyond the eastern cities, and those who did arrive in California usually hastened to join the gold hunters. Under these circumstances, Californians looked westward for a remedy for their labor shortage.

In the eighteenth century, an extensive trade in Chinese peasants had developed in southeast Asia. Kwangtung Province and, in particular, the Pearl River delta around Canton suffered from excess population. People in abundance were available there for export under indenture. In return for passage they agreed to work until they had paid off their debts with interest in the hope that they could then retain their future earnings. In addition, some coolies simply were seized and forced into service. Various Chinese companies arranged the business, sending thousands of laborers to Indonesia, Indochina, Siam, Malaya, and Burma. In the middle of the nineteenth century, the trade extended into South America and the West Indies.

It was also to supply California. Chinese entrepreneurs in Hong Kong arranged for shipments to San Francisco, using English and American sailing vessels

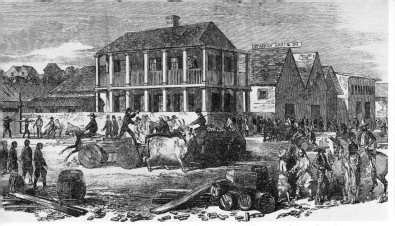

A street view of San Francisco. (*Illustrated London News*, December 28, 1850, Library of Congress)

Emigrants leave Strasbourg for California. (*L'Illustration*, Paris, January 28, 1854, New York Public Library)

A view of Cunningham Wharf, San Francisco, showing a steamer discharging passengers. (New York Public Library)

Sold for debt—a Chinese family disposes of its children. (Russell H. Conwell, *Why and How*, Boston, 1871)

The Chinese in San Francisco—street types. (*Illustrated London News*, January 23, 1875, New York Public Library)

An alley in the Chinese district of San Francisco, 1875. (New York Public Library)

The Chinese quarter in Bakersfield, California, 1882. (New York Public Library)

In San Francisco the Chinese lived much as they had at home. (Photograph by Arnold Genthe, National Park Service)

The corner of Jackson and DuPont streets in San Francisco, showing Chinese homes. (*Harper's Monthly*, May, 1883, New York Public Library)

Chinese immigrants at the San Francisco customs house. (Drawing by P. Frenzeny, *Harper's Weekly*, February 3, 1877, Nostalgia Press, Inc.)

for the two-month journey. Hundreds of Chinese crowded in the holds, suffered in patience while they made their way to the New Golden Mountain—California.

Their number mounted steadily. By 1870, some one hundred thousand had arrived. The coolies worked in mining camps in a variety of menial jobs, and they accumulated in a quarter of their own in San Francisco. Because of the nature of their migration, they did not tend to stay permanently. As in the migration to southeast Asia, the expectation was to return ultimately to their homeland.

The Chinese therefore lacked the European immigrant's commitment to the New World. Regarding themselves as temporary sojourners, the Asians were not prepared to make a permanent adjustment to the society

The Chinese fishing quarter in Monterey, California. (*Harper's Monthly*, 1882, New York Public Library)

Chinese dry fish in Monterey. (*Harper's Monthly*, September, 1882, New York Public Library)

A traditional Chinese school in America. (Russell H. Conwell, *Why and How*, Boston, 1871)

A Chinese Methodist chapel in San Francisco. (*Frank Leslie's Illustrated Newspaper*, November 27, 1875, New York Public Library)

Altar in a Chinese joss house, San Francisco. (*Harper's Weekly*, March 25, 1871, New York Public Library)

A Chinese theatre. (New York Public Library)

about them and preferred as far as possible to retain their old ways. The culture developed in Chinatown was self-contained and remote from that of the Americans. There was no family life; fewer than 5 percent of the Chinese immigrants in 1880 were women. Clan loyalties tied the individual to those who had originated in the same place. The five companies, which corresponded to districts in Kwangtung, controlled the life of each worker and shielded him from contact with any external influences. Later, secret societies, or tongs, which managed gambling, prostitution, and drugs, assumed even greater power over the laborers.

These unusual features of Chinese immigration created a sense of uneasiness among Californians though the labor of the Orientals was considered valuable. Gangs efficiently managed by their own bosses and overseers made possible the laying of tracks of the Central Pacific Railroad across the mountains to Utah. The docility and low cost of such workers even tempted factory owners from as far away as Massachusetts and New Jersey to experiment with their use. But there was some concern throughout the country about these Chinese not being free and their strange and possibly vicious or sinister habits.

That concern was intensified when competition with the Orientals became a threat to the wage standards of other laborers. In the booming first decade after the discovery of gold, the Chinese had taken the jobs no one else wanted, and it seemed their own business if they accepted miserably low pay. But the situation changed after 1870. Hasty exploitation by then had depleted the

mines and well-paying positions for non-Orientals were no longer easy to get. When the depression of 1872 caused hardship throughout the state, many Californians came to believe that the "rice-eaters" were a threat to the welfare of free wage earners and their families.

On the streets of San Francisco, Denis Kearney, an Irish-American spokesman for the Caucasians, denounced the rich and threatened to burn down their elegant homes on Nob Hill. His fiery oratory also exposed the menace of the Chinese. By manipulating prejudice he recruited supporters for the Workingmen's party he helped organize in 1877. Fear of the Orientals spread throughout the country, fed by doubts about whether they would ever be assimilated. Some of the anxiety was racist in origin; some arose from suspicion of any type of labor that was not entirely unfettered. In 1880, this agitation had not yet borne fruit in laws to exclude or deport Orientals. But popular animosity and a slackening demand had reduced the annual number of arrivals and stabilized the Chinese population.

The hostility to this exceptional group of newcomers clearly revealed the values Americans attached to immigration. They expected the movement of people to be free, undertaken by individuals who made a permanent commitment to the country and were ready to participate fully in its life. But the unusual features of the Chinese migration had produced doubts that it met these tests and whipped up prejudice against this element of the population.

Chinese coolies employed by the Central Pacific in the Sierra Nevada had to fight winter snow drifts to get the railroad built. (Sketch by Joseph Becker, Association of American Railroads)

The Chinese must go—Denis Kearney addresses the workingmen of San Francisco. (Drawing by G. W. Peters, New York Public Library)

An anti-Chinese riot in Seattle, Washington. (Drawn by W. P. Snyder, *Harper's Weekly*, March 6, 1886, New York Public Library)

Denis Kearney is applauded by his followers. (Painting by Howard Pyle, New York Public Library)

A Word of Caution to Our Friends, the Cigar-makers. The anti-Chinese movement appealed for support to eastern workingmen, using the threat of hordes of cheap yellow laborers who would take away the jobs of whites. (*Frank Leslie's Illustrated Newspaper*, November 10, 1877, New York Public Library)

A meeting of the anti-Chinese Workingmen's party on the sandlots of San Francisco. (*Frank Leslie's Illustrated Newspaper,* Brown Brothers)

Chinese immigrants in class being prepared for naturalization, San Francisco, late nineteenth century. (Photoworld)

The lure of American wages, c. 1855. This woodcut contrasts the British surplus population with the need for manpower in the United States, just beyond Castle Garden. (Museum of the City of New York)

8

The Frontiers of Farm and City

Nineteenth-century immigration, from whatever source, operated within a common environment that influenced its results. Each group of newcomers brought a distinctive heritage to America. But all entered a rapidly expanding society that used them on its frontiers—of farm and of city. All immigrants had to adjust their habits and ideas to the novel, changing conditions of the New World. The process had important economic, social, and cultural effects on the nation; and it exacted a heavy toll from the participants.

The flow of people into the United States had a direct, stimulating effect upon the economy. It provided both the labor and the capital which the expanding nation needed. Thousands of persons eager to work added to the supply of manpower at a time when the growth of agriculture, industry, and transportation all made demands on it. The accretion of capital was also important. The little stores of savings which some immigrants brought with them added up to substantial totals. In addition, the immigrants were not evenly distributed by age groups—a high percentage were in the prime of life and capable of immediate employment. Relatively few

were so old as to be dependent or so young as to be unproductive charges upon society.

Immigration provided a reserve of laborers flexible enough to adapt to violent fluctuations in employment then afflicting the expanding economy of the United States. Since the movement of people across the Atlantic ebbed and flowed in response to the business cycle, the supply of workers adjusted itself freely to the demand. Immigrants were available when needed, but they postponed their departure or decided not to come at all when employment slackened. Furthermore, those already in America did not add to the costs of the native communities. The foreigners were expected to provide for their jobless countrymen, and did. Industrialists were therefore in an enviable position; they could hire and fire as they wished, knowing that plenty of workers would always be waiting at the factory gates.

Many other established Americans also gained from the effects of immigration. The newcomers of the nineteenth century took the lowest jobs and therefore sank to the bottom of the social order. Everyone already in the country rose in consequence. Moreover, the presence

Advertisement of the American Emigrant Company about 1865, offering to arrange employment in advance for European immigrants. Actually, relatively few arrivals had made such arrangements in advance. (Smithsonian Collection of Business Americana)

A street peddler on the East Side of New York. (Library of Congress, Bain Collection)

Pushcart and delivery wagon, c. 1895. (Smithsonian Institution)

Railroad construction workers in 1860. (Library of Congress)

Advertisement of land in New York State, 1837. (New-York Historical Society)

Advertisement of land in Minnesota, 1858. (United States Department of Agriculture)

On the Road

Crossing a River

Scenes of farm life in America, 1878. The family made its way across the prairie, crossed the river, broke the soil, and built fences. By the second year (above right) it had a prospering home. (New York Public Library)

of an abundance of willing workers, by forcing down wages, made servants available to many people of moderate income. Furthermore, the newcomers required services; they were ministered by doctors, lawyers, and shopkeepers. Rarely equipped on arrival to fill these middle-class roles themselves, the immigrants created new opportunities for Americans.

Both agriculture and industry felt the expansive effects. The immigrant farmer played an important part in the cycle by which the frontier advanced. The Europeans characteristically moved in just behind the American pioneers who opened the wilderness and made the first clearings. The newly arrived peasants, unfamiliar with gun and ax, preferred to buy land ready for the plow; their purchases permitted the more restless natives to go ever farther west, while the immigrants settled down to the hard work of making the farms productive. The division of labor was advantageous to all concerned: speculative Americans received stakes to carry them to fresh opportunities, and immigrants acquired holdings ready for stable agriculture.

There was also little rivalry between native and foreign-born for work in the cities. Mostly the newcomers took the jobs more skilled Americans did not want. The carriers, diggers, and sweepers, far from competing with the craftsmen and clerks, eased the work and lowered the costs of all middle-class people. Until the Civil War, industrialization did not substantially alter the situation. The textile mills and other factories represented relatively new industries and displaced very few artisans.

The immigrants, whether on the farms or in the cities, paid a heavy price in their adjustment to America. Apart from the thousands who died on the way and the many others who failed after arrival, even those who succeeded and became prosperous landowners never forgot the hardships through which they had passed. The pride of ownership could not obliterate the memory of being alone and helpless when an unknown ache or fever struck or when the unfamiliar, seemingly endless winter settled down on the family.

A homestead in Michigan. (Library of Congress)

Farmer plowing, 1835. (Woodcut in *Davey Crockett Almanac*, Library of Congress)

162

Settlers clearing the land, 1880. (United States Department of Agriculture)

Pioneer settlers in western New York. (O. Turner, *Pioneer History of the Holland Purchase*, Buffalo, 1850, New-York Historical Society)

View of a Maryland farm. Note the broad fields, the isolated houses, and the lack of a village of the European type. (Engraving from *Columbian Magazine*, July 20, 1788, Library of Congress)

A mower on an Ohio farm, 1864. (*Harper's Weekly*, Library of Congress)

The farms were different from those of Europe—in environment, size, and layout. The Cornishman who had never seen snow had much to learn in Michigan; so did the Scandinavian in the treeless prairies. Certain wild animals, scarcely known in Europe, were ever-threatening pests in the United States. The deer and raccoons nibbled away at the tender shoots, while the squirrels dug the corn and potatoes out of the ground as they were planted. To peasants accustomed to the cramped quarters and tight spaces of the Old Country village, a homestead pitched within an 80- or 160-acre farm might at first have seemed attractive. But they soon learned that the greater the size, the harder they had to work, and that with space came isolation and loneliness.

In the initial years of settlement, even the food was strange. In the absence of stoves in which to bake bread, Dutch farmers cooked pancakes of bran over a fire, and they had to learn from the Indians how to soften corn in wood ashes and water before using it. Tools once taken for granted were sorely missed. When water left standing overnight froze and cracked the family's one iron pot, someone had to make a two-day journey on foot to replace it. Even the domesticated animals were alien. One farmer, having finally bought a pair of oxen, found that they would obey only commands in English and ignominiously had to leave their management to his children.

Breaking the prairie. The strength of several teams of oxen was needed to cut through the hard topsoil. (*Harper's Monthly*, March, 1858, New York Public Library)

Emigrants moving into the Great Plains. (*Harper's Monthly*, March, 1858, New York Public Library)

Tools used by American farmers in 1790. (Smithsonian Institution)

The Great West. This lithograph by Currier & Ives, 1870, conveys the impression of immense distances and strange landscape that struck the foreign-born in the American countryside. (Association of American Railroads)

The peasants discovered more subtle problems when they began to deal in the American money and market economy. Some, after decades of cautious thrift, were tempted to imitate the Yankees about them in buying additional land or machinery on credit. Then a poor crop or, as in 1874, a plague of locusts swept everything away. An English farmer in Kansas felt like a king when he surveyed the broad acres unimaginable at home. Then, after a succession of drought years, he heard his wife complain: "We would have more pleasure of our life if we lived in old England." Perhaps in England he would have remained a day laborer all his life; but then at least he would have got his day's pay for a day's work. Whereas on the prairie, the whole family toiled for many a month with no reward at all. Many farmers, broken by their miseries, dreamed of a return to their former homes, as present failures blurred the recollection of the difficulties of European village life.

The city had its own problems for it was utterly strange to people who had spent their previous lives in a rural environment. The dense crowds, the makeshift

A young woman perceives the utter strangeness of America upon her arrival at Ellis Island, 1920. (United Press International)

A Granger meeting in the woods in Illinois. (Sketch by Joseph B. Beale, *Frank Leslie's Illustrated Newspaper,* August 30, 1873, Library of Congress)

The spirit of the Granger movement, 1882. The picture portrays the ideals of the American farmers —abundant fields, good transportation, a healthy home life, and the church. (New York Public Library)

housing, the impersonal jobs, even marketing were perilous traps for the unwary. Those who survived were generally exhausted by the strain of learning to cope.

Yet throughout this period Americans assumed that
each family was on its own. Neither the state nor existing
philanthropic or educational associations did much to
help. Each individual had to devise his own way of reach-
ing out to his neighbors.

In the rural regions, population was often so dispersed that social organization was hardly possible.
Neighbors who lived miles apart from each other met in-
frequently. Some foreign-born farmers participated in the
activities of the Granges and similar groups, but could
hardly feel a sense of belonging among strangers.

The immigrants therefore sought, where possible, at
least to make homes among people of their own kind.
The newly arrived German or Englishman tried to settle
among his own countrymen to whom common language
and common worship provided unifying links. Though
there were no public houses as at home where men
could meet and chat, they could visit of an evening and
on Sunday and amuse themselves by reading and singing.
The strongest communities developed in such clusters of
settlement.

In the cities also, the immigrants learned to form
communities precisely because they were strangers, separated from others by religious, cultural, and linguistic
differences. The newcomers had to develop the means of
clinging together. No one else took responsibility for

The National Grange convention in St. Louis. A group
of delegates discussing the program. (*Frank Leslie's
Illustrated Newspaper,* February 21, 1874, New York
Public Library)

Russian immigrant home, 1913.
The protective association helped
the newcomers meet the problems of urban existence. (Library
of Congress)

A Hungarian newspaper published in New York, 1907. The
immigrant press remained the
most important medium of communication into the twentieth
century.

The Hebrew immigrants' home, New York, 1913. The picture shows the arrival of survivors of the S.S. *Volturno*. (United Press International)

A community meeting, drawing together representatives of twenty nationalities. (Peter Roberts, *The New Immigration*, New York, 1913)

them. In most groups the church served a central function; often it was the only institution transplanted intact and American practice tolerated sectarian differences.

But the immigrants were also able to form totally new institutions when the need arose. In the closed circle of the Old World village, word of mouth was adequate to convey all the news the peasants required. Many men and women were illiterate not only because of the lack of schooling but because the ability to read or write was not very useful to them. By contrast, the strange world of America created a demand for some medium of communication, a demand which the immigrant press satisfied.

Those who by departure lost the other resources of the Old World village or town also had to devise other communal means of protecting themselves against illness or poverty and of furnishing themselves with entertainment and fellowship. In the American cities they developed a multitude of voluntary associations to do so. The needs of migration thus laid a basis for meeting the problems of urban existence. Many of these institutions survived beyond the period of their first establishment and performed an important function in the later life of the great cities.

Black and white slaves, a cartoon published in New York about 1846. Some immigrants resented the sympathy abolitionists lavished on the black slaves and the simultaneous disregard of the oppression of the Irish in their homeland. On the right, the scene is England where the father exclaims, "O heaven! in this boasted land of freedom to be starving for want of employment! No relief from the purse-proud aristocracy whose bloated fortunes have been made by our blood and toil!" the callous capitalist responds, "Come pack off to the workhouse! that's the only fit asylum for you!" (Smithsonian Institution, Peters Collection)

9

The Civil War and Its Aftermath

The great conflict that opened at Fort Sumter in 1861 had profound consequences; the United States would never be the same again. Although immigration was not directly involved in the controversy between North and South, it felt the indirect results of that struggle. The war momentarily slowed the flow of newcomers to the United States and then helped shape conditions that would make room for many millions more.

While the outbreak of fighting interrupted the movement of people across the Atlantic, the long-term consequences were quite different. The war revealed the importance of immigrant manpower, reaffirmed the American sense of nationality, and encouraged industrial development that depended upon a continuing growth in population.

The war enlisted the services of a great many immigrants, North and South. The largest number had made their homes above the Mason-Dixon line and therefore

served in the Union Army. The bounty system, which rewarded volunteers with cash, and the draft, from which the well-to-do could escape by hiring substitutes, drew heavily upon the laborers, mostly foreign-born. In addition, in the haste to recruit men, the War Department gave commissions to almost any prominent individual able to enlist his followers. Immigrant leaders therefore assembled regiments composed entirely of troops of a single nationality. New York's "fighting 69th," led by Colonel Michael Corcoran, was but the best known of thirty-eight Irish regiments. T. F. Meagher and Carl Schurz also were among the foreign-born officers. The Confederacy likewise drew upon the services of the immigrants within its borders. Although the number of men of alien birth was smaller in the South than in the North, companies of Germans, regiments of Irish, and a cosmopolitan European brigade were evidence of the willingness of these adopted citi-

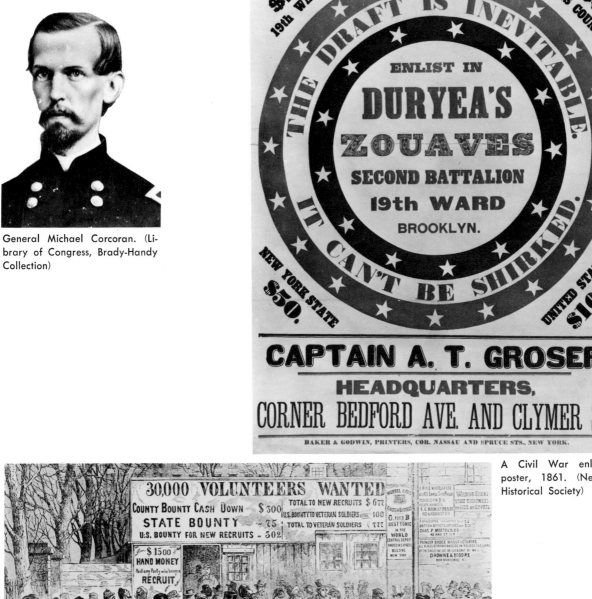

General Michael Corcoran. (Library of Congress, Brady-Handy Collection)

A Civil War enlistment poster, 1861. (New-York Historical Society)

The recruiting office in New York City Hall Park. (New York Public Library)

Recruiting for the New York Zouaves. (New York Public Library)

Recruiting for the Irish Zouaves in New York. (*Illustrated London News*, December 27, 1862, New York Public Library)

zens to enlist in the Confederate army. The Irish Major General Patrick R. Cleburne, the German Brigadier General John A. Wegener, and the Scottish Brigadier General Peter A. S. McGlashen were among those who advanced to the higher ranks of the Confederate officer corps.

Immigrants were involved in outbursts of dissent on both sides. Irishmen were the leading participants in the New York City riots of 1863. Directed at the unfair operations of the draft law and sparked by hatred of the Negroes, these disorders led to a heavy loss of life. More serious still was the opposition of antislavery Germans in Texas who remained loyal to the United States and refused to fight for the Confederacy. In June, 1862, Germans from Gillespie, Kendall, and Kerr counties in the Lone Star State formed a Union Loyal League to protect themselves against vigilante committees and the secret Knights of the Golden Circle which harrassed them. A massacre on the Nueces River on August 10 destroyed the power of the Germans, who were thereafter exposed to lynching and expropriation.

The most important sources of dissent, however, were native—the anti-war Copperheads in the North and the anti-Confederate Unionists in the South. Distracting as the Irish and German incidents were, they were treated as the exception by other Americans. In both North and South, the loyalty and dependability of the newcomers reassured Americans at whose side they fought.

The conflict that had begun in a dispute over the country's unity ended by reaffirming it. Once peace returned, the belligerents on both sides turned to nationalism to justify the sacrifices of the war. The affirmation that the United States was one nation, indivisible, with liberty and justice for all, cast a new light upon old quarrels and passions and also discredited earlier suspicions of the foreign-born. For example, before the war, the arrival of the Irish had stirred latent anti-Catholicism; an unruly mob in 1831 had burned a convent in Charlestown, near Boston, and for a long time thereafter apprehensive citizens read of the frightening disclosures of a "Maria Monk," who pretended to reveal a plot of priests and pope to subvert free institutions. Also, beer-

Recruiting for the 2nd Regiment, New York. (New York Public Library)

Anti-slavery Germans leave Texas for Mexico rather than support the Confederacy during the Civil War. (*Pictorial War Record*, New York, 1883, Nostalgia Press, Inc.)

The great riot in New York City, 1863, expressed resentment of the draft, of the Negroes, and of the abolitionists. Here the mob attacks *The Tribune*, Horace Greeley's newspaper identified with the Negro and with abolition. (New York Public Library)

The lynching of a Negro on Clarkson Street during the draft riots. (*Illustrated London News*, August 8, 1863, New York Public Library)

Rioters marching down Second Avenue. (New York Public Library)

Rioters burning and sacking the colored orphan asylum. (*Harper's Weekly*, August 1, 1863, New York Public Library)

Hard times increased the number of recruits for the army. (Sketch by Thomas Worth, *Frank Leslie's Illustrated Newspaper,* February 21, 1874, New York Public Library)

drinking and Sabbath-breaking Germans attracted unfavorable attention among native advocates of temperance and reform.

Concern about the foreigners had not yet produced a demand to end immigration; the needs of the country for manpower were too great. But for a few years after 1854, fear of the newcomers had sparked a movement to limit their political rights. The Know-Nothings—so called because of their secrecy—wished to extend the period of naturalization and to restrict the privileges of voting and holding office. They had gained control of several states, and, for a while, held the balance of power in the House of Representatives. Their influence had waned before 1860, and the war, which proved the loyalty of the foreign-born, quieted the fears that had nurtured the nativism of the previous decades.

A song dedicated to the Know-Nothings, 1854. (Smithsonian Institution)

An anti-Catholic riot in Philadelphia, 1844. The "native Americans" in the tall beaver hats attack the militia, which protects the Catholic church. (New York Public Library)

The outcome of the conflict also created a subtle assumption that all parts of the country would thereafter follow the same line of development. Even Southerners who retained a sentimental attachment to an idyllic vision of plantation society recognized that the cause was lost. The war had demonstrated the superior worth or, at least, the irresistible force of the victor's institutions, and the New South was destined to industrialization, like the North. In any case, slavery had disappeared; some former masters preferred to hope that free white workers would supply the South's labor force of the future, and the southern states embarked upon a long effort to recruit immigrants.

Indirectly, too, the war had stimulated industrial growth. The political and economic institutions further stabilized by the war encouraged the growth of manu-

facturing. In the meantime, the dominance of the Republican party, committed to a protective tariff, a national banking system, and a liberal land policy, had created conditions conducive to growth and thus generated a steady demand for labor. Immigration only partially offset the shortages that resulted from mobilization, and new factories everywhere needed larger pools of workers. The contract labor law enacted in 1864 was intended to stimulate migration by authorizing American firms to sign up workers abroad. But it did not prove necessary. By the time it went into effect, the flow had resumed, and, after 1880, would reach higher levels than ever before. Immigration was to be as much a part of the America that emerged from the Civil War as of that which had come out of the Revolution.

Freed Negroes leave the South to find new homes in the North. (Sketch by W. L. Sheppard, New York Public Library)

Other freed men move north by land. (New York Public Library)

Threats of the contract-labor law. The drawing, which is hostile to the law, shows hordes of immigrants arriving in the United States. Actually, relatively few entered under the terms of the contract-labor law, and most of those who did were skilled laborers. (Library of Congress)

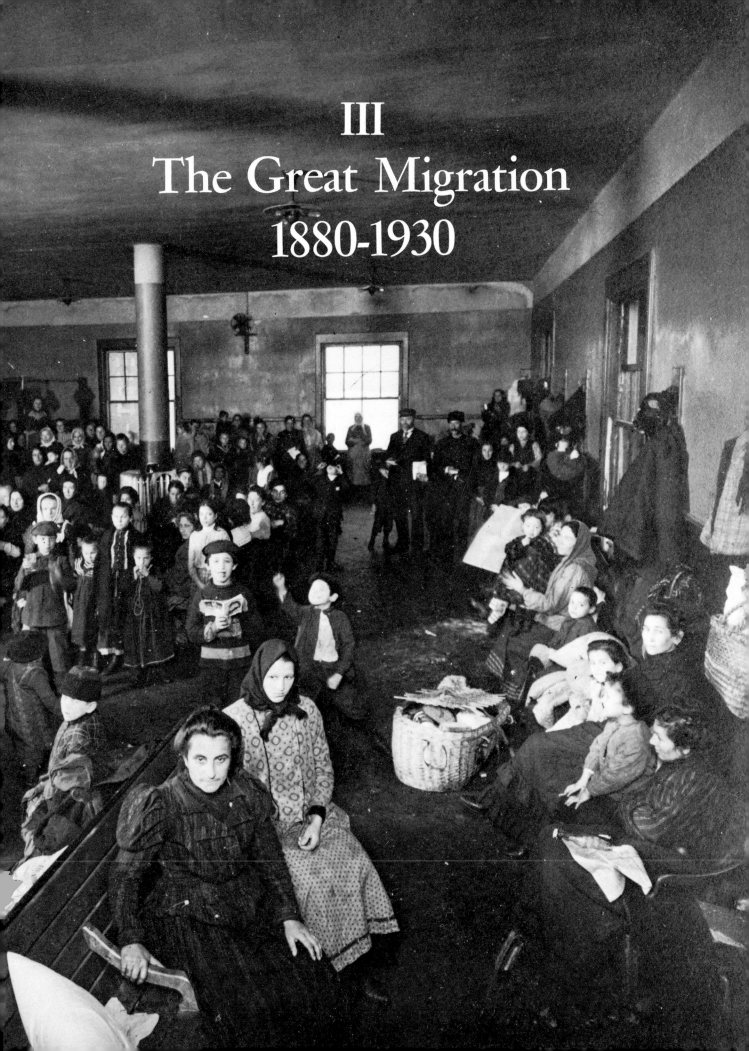

III
The Great Migration
1880-1930

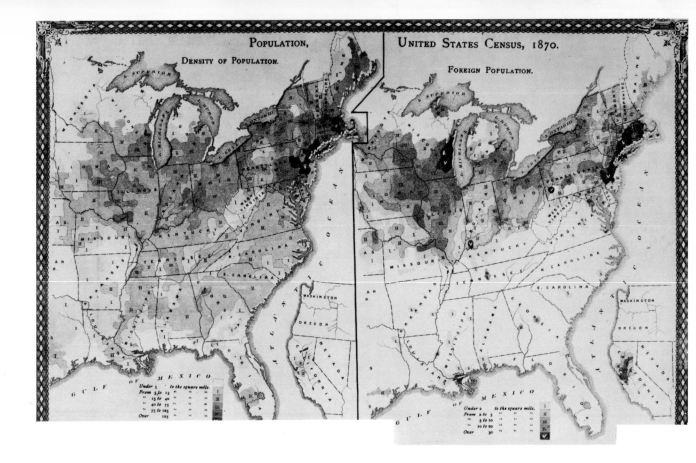

Density of population in the United States, 1870. The map at the left shows total population, the map at the right, the foreign-born. (*Indiana Atlas*, Library of Congress)

1
Old Streams in New Channels

The immigrants who reached the United States after 1880 came from a much wider geographical area than earlier. Among them were passengers from Western and Northern Europe, who were by now familiar, but also migrants from Eastern Europe and the Mediterranean, who brought with them languages and customs theretofore scarcely known in the New World.

The numbers admitted rose between 1880 and 1930 to an order of magnitude completely different from that of the previous sixty years. In 1880, the United States and the world economy, of which it was a part, had recovered from the depression of the 1870s. Thereafter, immigration mounted steadily, except for brief setbacks during the depressions of 1893 and 1907. The number of immigrants who entered annually rose from about two hundred thousand in 1880 to seven hundred thousand in 1884, and passed the million mark in 1905. In six of the ten years after 1905, immigration remained above the million level.

Only the great war of 1914 seriously interrupted the flow. Four years of fighting and the dislocation of international trade blocked departures from Europe. Peace permitted a brief resumption of travel after 1918, and admissions climbed back, exceeding eight hundred thousand in 1921. But nationalistic policies in the United States and in Europe put an end to the movement. In all, between 1880 and 1930, 25 million immigrants entered the United States. They contributed significantly to a population increase of from 40 to 130 million during those years.

The population movements of the half century after 1880, from whatever geographical source, were the products of an economy geared to operate across national boundaries. The forces of modernization that industrialized Europe and displaced its peasantry continued to spread with effects similar to those before 1880. But the process now operated on a far vaster scale.

In the decades after 1880, efficient communications drew together the most distant parts of the globe. Each country and indeed each region and city still sought to protect its own interests. But until 1914 the assumption prevailed that goods, capital, and people would move relatively freely through the world economy. Trade

176

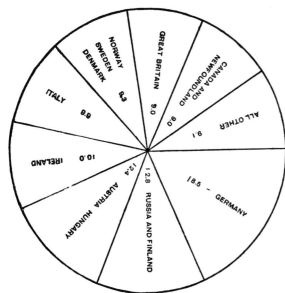

TOTAL FOREIGN BORN, 1910: 13,515,886

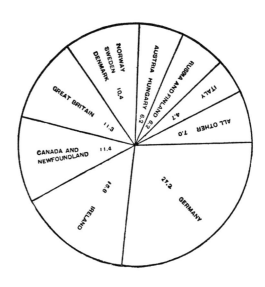

TOTAL FOREIGN BORN, 1900: 10,341,276

Foreign-born population by countries of birth, 1910 and 1900. (E. A. Ross, *The Old World in the New*, New York, 1914)

Immigrants arriving in Ellis Island, 1920. (United Press International)

would carry manufactures and raw materials to the best markets; investment would put funds to the most profitable use; and immigration would carry labor to its most advantageous employment.

Thousands of miles of new railroad tracks and shipping routes supplied the means of moving commodities and migrants during these years. After 1880, the great maritime powers engaged in strenuous competition for supremacy on the seas. Britain, Germany, Italy, and France were among the rivals who subsidized their carriers for prestige and for the potential use of steamers in wartime. The practice severely damaged the American merchant marine, which received no such aid, but indirectly helped the immigrants get to the United States. The subsidized steamship firms, less interested in passenger profit than in capturing and retaining control of shipping routes, could afford to build ever larger vessels. The steamers of the 1850s had not been much above 2,000 tons; the White Star Line *Oceanic* in 1871 had been exceptional in its 3,700 tons. After 1880 the scale changed. The Inman Line's *City of Paris* launched in 1888 seemed grand with its 11,000 tons, but was out-

distanced after the turn of the century by the Cunarders *Caronia* (19,000 tons, 1904) and *Mauretania* (31,000 tons, 1906), and by the still greater floating palaces of the Hamburg-American Line, *Imperator* (51,969 tons, 1912) and *Vaterland* (54,000 tons, 1913). And the greater space of these ships not only diminished the pressure of overcrowding, but also reduced the cost to the immigrant. In 1900, twenty dollars could bring a steerage passenger from Finland or Sicily to New York, in an ocean voyage which had lost much of its terror. Quarters were still cramped, and seasickness still plunged the landsmen into misery. But steam had mercifully reduced the length of the journey, and vessels were large enough to provide decent accommodations to the lowliest passengers.

Furthermore, the spread of railroads brought most parts of Europe into direct connection with some port and through lines knit together the whole United States. The long train ride was still an exciting and exacting experience, but travelers now were at least spared the uncertainty and the physical exhaustion of the past. Many indeed bought, or received from America, pre-

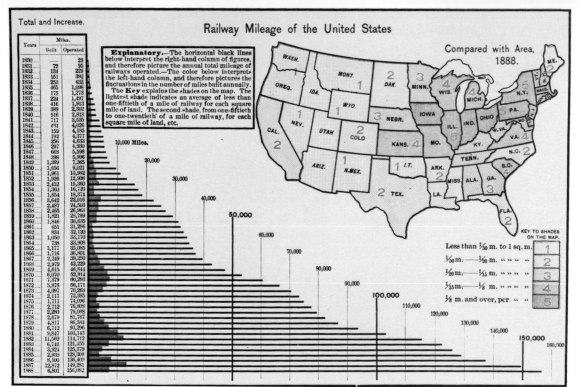

Railway Mileage of the United States

Total and Increase.

Years	Miles Built	Miles Operated
1830	——	23
1831	72	95
1832	134	229
1833	151	380
1834	253	633
1835	465	1,098
1836	175	1,273
1837	224	1,497
1838	416	1,913
1839	389	2,302
1840	516	2,818
1841	717	3,535
1842	491	4,026
1843	159	4,185
1844	192	4,377
1845	256	4,633
1846	297	4,930
1847	668	5,598
1848	398	5,996
1849	1,369	7,365
1850	1,656	9,021
1851	1,961	10,982
1852	1,926	12,908
1853	2,452	15,360
1854	1,360	16,720
1855	1,654	18,374
1856	3,642	22,016
1857	2,487	24,503
1858	2,465	26,968
1859	1,821	28,789
1860	1,846	30,635
1861	651	31,286
1862	834	32,120
1863	1,050	33,170
1864	738	33,908
1865	1,177	35,085
1866	1,716	36,801
1867	2,349	39,250
1868	2,979	42,229
1869	4,615	46,844
1870	6,070	52,914
1871	7,379	60,293
1872	5,878	66,171
1873	4,097	70,268
1874	2,117	72,385
1875	1,711	74,096
1876	2,712	76,808
1877	2,280	79,088
1878	2,679	81,767
1879	4,817	86,584
1880	6,712	93,296
1881	9,847	103,143
1882	11,569	114,712
1883	6,743	121,455
1884	3,924	125,379
1885	2,930	128,309
1886	8,100	136,409
1887	12,872	149,281
1888	6,801	156,082

Explanatory.—The horizontal black lines below interpret the right-hand column of figures, and therefore picture the annual total mileage of railways operated.—The color below interprets the left-hand column, and therefore pictures the fluctuations in the number of miles built annually. The **Key** explains the shades on the map. The lightest shade indicates an average of less than one-fiftieth of a mile of railway for each square mile of land. The second shade, from one-fiftieth to one-twentieth of a mile of railway, for each square mile of land, etc.

Compared with Area, 1888.

KEY TO SHADES ON THE MAP.

Less than 1/50 m. to 1 sq. m.	1
1/50 m. — 1/20 m. " " " "	2
1/20 m. — 1/15 m. " " " "	3
1/15 m. — 1/8 m. " " " "	4
1/8 m. and over, per	5

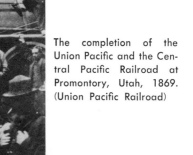

Railway mileage of the United States, 1888. The table gives the miles built and operated, and the chart portrays the growth graphically. The map shows the relationship between mileage and area in each state. (Smithsonian Institution)

A construction gang near Greenville, Pennsylvania, 1891. (Bessemer and Lake Erie Railroad)

The completion of the Union Pacific and the Central Pacific Railroad at Promontory, Utah, 1869. (Union Pacific Railroad)

A transatlantic steamship. (*Illustrated London News,* December 19, 1857, New York Public Library)

A steamer of 1872. The vessel was still a side-wheeler and still used sail to take advantage of the wind. (New York Public Library)

The *Caronia,* 1904. By then, the steamers had grown in size, were driven by screw propellers, and had shed their sails. (Cunard Line)

The *Imperator* of the Hamburg-American line leaves New York harbor, 1913. (Library of Congress)

The *Mauretania,* 1904—a mammoth vessel of 31,000 tons. (Cunard Line)

"Never before so close together"—a shipboard scene. (E. A. Steiner, *The Broken Wall,* New York, 1911)

Immigrants lining up for water on the S.S. *Prince Frederick Wilhelm*, 1915. (United Press International)

Immigrants boarding the cars in Europe. (E. A. Steiner, *From Alien to Citizen*, New York, 1914)

Immigrants crowd the deck of an Atlantic liner. (Photograph by Edwin Levick, 1906, Library of Congress)

◄

Every inch of deck space was precious for the fresh air it offered. (Photograph by William H. Raw, 1902, Library of Congress)

Immigrant train on the Baltimore and Ohio Railroad, 1910. (Smithsonian Institution)

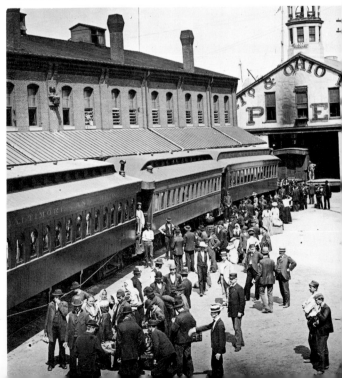

Advertisement offering through tickets on the Union Pacific connecting the Atlantic to the Pacific, 1869. (Smithsonian Institution)

sand people a day and house six hundred in dormitories. These accommodations—and their counterparts in Liverpool and lesser cities—were decent and well supervised, thus eliminating some of the hazards of the past.

The Hamburg-American Line did most for the steerage passengers at its home port. Its immigrant station on the outskirts of the city of Hamburg was a model village or city, walled and guarded, where the new arrivals were examined, ticketed, washed, fumigated, and fed. If they passed muster, they were permitted to enter the inner quarter, a large and beautiful enclosure with a Protestant and a Roman Catholic church, as well as a synagogue. A hotel offered accommodations at various price levels; and a brass band played the tunes of different fatherlands every afternoon.

After 1880, the immigrants were more likely to encounter bureaucratic than physical problems. The law in Europe and America was complex and confusing. Each country established its own requirements for departure, transit, and arrival. Bewildered travelers fearfully clutched bits of paper that vouched for their identity, that enabled them to leave their old homes, and that secured them admittance to the promised land. After 1918, the regulations grew still more difficult when passports, visas, and exit permits put serious barriers in the way of international travel.

To offset their difficulties, the immigrants of these decades enjoyed more detailed, more reliable, information than had their predecessors. The printed newspaper, the scrawled letter home, and anecdotes passed along by word of mouth made the stages of the journey familiar in the remote villages of Russia, Italy, and the Balkans. Communications were swift enough so that prospective immigrants knew when jobs were available, and where and what conditions they would find on arrival.

For a time, employers in the United States could recruit workers abroad, according to the terms of the contract labor law. But few firms made use of the privilege and none mourned its repeal in 1884. Some railroads and state governments tried to lure immigrants to their territory. The Northern Pacific, for instance, sent hundreds of agents to inform Europeans of the virtues of its land. But these efforts had little effect upon the flow of population. Each individual and family made its own decision to come, and chose its destination according to the ease of communication—in terms of preferences shaped by friends, relatives, and reputation. Even the schemes of the federal government and of philanthropic organizations to relocate newcomers outside the crowded cities came to nothing.

Although they mingled after 1880 in a vast stream fed by numerous nations, newcomers continued to arrive in the United States from Western and Northern Europe. The old sources had not dried up. The continued rise of population and industrialization still set people in motion in the countries that had earlier sent off vanguards.

paid tickets that carried them from their homes all the way to their destinations.

Residence in the ports, whether on the European or the American side of the ocean, was also less demoralizing than formerly. Stopovers were now relatively brief because regular sailing schedules permitted travelers to plan their journeys efficiently. Furthermore, organized private societies or government agencies met the newcomers on arrival and helped arrange transfers.

New York was now the greatest receiving port. Castle Garden, much too inadequate as an immigrant station, closed its doors in 1891 when an act of Congress gave the new federal Immigrant Bureau exclusive control over the reception of immigrants. The Bureau operated first in the Barge Office at the Battery and then on Ellis Island where the disembarking aliens were numbered, inspected, and either admitted or deported. Although the bureau station suffered from a fire in 1897, the new buildings that opened in 1900 could process eight thou-

First sight of New York Bay. The passengers on this European steamer were the fortunates, able to pay the full fare, unlike the immigrants who arrived in steerage. (*Harper's Weekly*, June 2, 1877, New York Public Library)

Dining room in the Hamburg-American model village. (E. A. Steiner, *From Alien to Citizen*, New York, 1914)

The Barge Office. This building on the Battery in New York City was the center of operation of the federal Immigrant Bureau until the opening of Ellis Island. (*Harper's Monthly*, June, 1884, New York Public Library)

A ferry operated by the immigration service conveyed immigrants from Ellis Island to shore. (National Park Service, Sherman Collection)

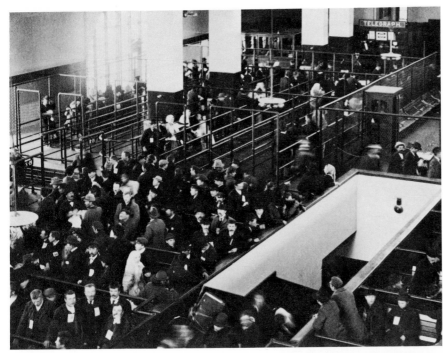

A portion of the great examination hall in Ellis Island, 1904. Here the immigrants passed on the way to inspection that would determine whether they could enter the United States or not. (Library of Congress)

The detention room of Ellis Island, 1903. (Drawn by G. W. Peters, engraved by R. C. Collins, *The Century*, March, 1903, New York Public Library)

The main building of Ellis Island. (W. Evans-Gordon, *The Alien Immigrant*, New York, 1903)

Immigrants passing through the depot at Ellis Island, 1907. (United Press International)

Part of the dining room on Ellis Island where immigrants awaiting admission were fed, 1907. Note the sign in various languages on the right. (Library of Congress)

The money exchange on Ellis Island, 1921. The immigrants admitted could turn in their old currency for dollars and also use the post office (on the left) if they wished. (The National Archives)

The admitted immigrants and their friends wait for the ferry to take them to shore, 1910. (The National Archives)

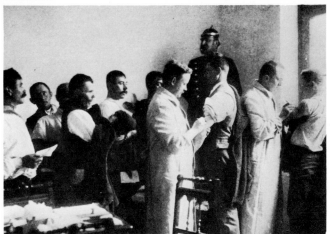

The medical examination before departure in a German port. (E. A. Steiner, *The Broken Wall*, New York, 1911)

An advertisement offering farmland for sale in Kansas, 1893. (Smithsonian Collection of Business Americana)

At Ellis Island, a Board of Special Inquiry considered the special cases of immigrants who were not immediately admitted and might be subject to deportation. (E. A. Ross, *The Old World in the New*, New York, 1914)

HEM FÖR SKANDINAVER

— I —

CENTRALSTATEN KANSAS.

Ett ovanligt anbud!

Vi undertecknade erbjuda till salu cirka 1,200 hemman (farmar), de flesta å en fjerdedels section eller 160 acres hvardera; men många äro blott hälften så stora, andra 8 á 10 gånger större. De äro belägna i 61 Countier (Härader) af de 106, som finnas i Kansas. De äro förnämligast belägna i *södra hälften af staten*, från östra till vestra gränsen.

Omkring hälften äro uppodlade, en del mer, en del mindre. Hus, åbyggnader och stängsel hör till en stor mängd. Läget af hvar och en af alla dessa farmar är fullt beskrifvet med deras nummer, gränslinier, m. m.

PRISERNA ÄRO BETYDLIGT LÄGRE

än på kringliggande egendomar och kunna i medelpris beräknas till 10 dollars per acre, med uppodling och byggnader.

I vestra delarna af staten är priset lägst; varierande från $2,25 till 5 á 6 dollars per acre, då deremot i mellersta delen af staten, såsom i McPherson och Marion County, priset är från 12 till 25 dollars per acre. Endast i tre Countier är priset så högt.

MÅNGA SKANDINAVER BOSATTA

i alla dessa trakter gör det tilldragande för deras landsmän. Aldrig förr har Skandinaver haft ett tillfälle som detta, att i en hel stat, — och denna stat med de bästa framtida utsigter för allmän välmåga, — kunna göra ett sådant urval af egendomar, till så lågt pris, som nu erbjudes.

EN ÖSTERNS BANKIR,

HOMES FOR THE INDUSTRIOUS
(Advertising cut widely used by the Illinois Central Railroad in 1860 and 1861)

An advertisement used by the Illinois Central Railroad in 1860 and 1861. (United States Department of Agriculture)

A German stone worker. (Photograph by Titzenthaler, Harvard University Social Ethics Collection) ▶

A German boilermaker. (Photograph by Titzenthaler, Harvard University Social Ethics Collection)

Britain and Germany, as earlier, provided substantial numbers of immigrants. Within fifty years after 1880 more than 2 million people arrived from England, Scotland, and Wales, and more than 2.5 million from the German Empire. The familiar sources were thus far from depleted. These newcomers, however, differed significantly from those who had crossed in earlier decades. They now left industrial societies, there were few peasants among them, and the majority had no intention of making careers in agriculture. Many had already done factory work or held other kinds of urban employment before they left home, and they generally expected to move from a plant, mine, shop, or office in the Old Country to one very much like it in the New Country. Sometimes, indeed, a whole group shifted as a unit, as did the Cornish tinplate workers in 1893.

Familiarity with the economic system eased the adjustment of these later immigrants and communities of their countrymen, already in existence, were available for help. The English and Scots were often indistinguishable from native Americans and, though retaining a sentimental and cultural attachment to their homelands, rarely sought to separate themselves in their place of residence or in social organization.

Differences in language and culture were more important among the Welsh and the Germans. Although the Welsh continued to use their own tongue, most of them also knew English. In addition, the fewness of their numbers, combined with their great mobility, had a disruptive effect upon their communities.

The Germans were more likely to remain apart. In New York, Chicago, and other large cities, German

A German cooper. (Photograph by Titzenthaler, Harvard University Social Ethics Collection)

A family of English immigrants arrive in the New World, 1908. (National Park Service, Sherman Collection)

A German blacksmith. (Photograph by Titzenthaler, Harvard University Social Ethics Collection)

A Yorkshire collier, on his way to work, 1886. (Brown Brothers)

A group of English boys arrives in New York. (*The Graphic,* January 8, 1870, New York Public Library)

A Scottish family on the way to Alabama, 1905. (National Park Service, Sherman Collection)

Employment office for German servants, early twentieth century. (Photoworld)

German beer hall in Yorkville, New York City. (Photoworld)

German aliens being fingerprinted at the 88th Street police station, New York, 1918. Popular suspicion during the First World War led to this precautionary measure. (United Press International)

Notice to enemy aliens, 1917. The sign posted on the waterfront street warns Germans against trespassing. (United Press International)

neighborhoods retained their identity until after World War I; only a few wealthy individuals before then had begun to follow the general trend to the suburbs. Until 1900, when the second and third generations increased in importance, Lutheran churches rarely used English, and the German-language press retained a hold on its readers.

World War I was therefore a shock. Popular hatred found its target not only in the Kaiser and in Prussian militarism, but in the Hunnish German people and culture. When superpatriots demanded the banning of Beethoven and the transformation of sauerkraut into "liberty cabbage," loyal Americans of German birth and antecedents also felt the wound. The sense of difference did not disappear; indeed it may have grown more in-

Enemy aliens being rounded up at Gloucester, New Jersey, 1918. (United Press International)

Police, fearful of spies, seize enemy aliens in the New York municipal lodging house, 1917. (United Press International)

tense, and it was associated with a defensiveness that persisted throughout the 1920s. The pain of rejection was all the more acute because until 1914 most German immigrants made the transition from the Old to the New World with little hardship.

Emigration also continued from Ireland after 1880, despite the fact that the pressure of overpopulation was no longer severe. Although rent wars continued to erupt through the nineteenth century, the great outflow of the 1840s and 1850s had opened the way to the gradual solution of the land problem, and the cottiers had almost disappeared as a group. Nevertheless the half century before 1930 saw the arrival of 1.6 million Irish, some of them after having first tried their luck in England or Canada. The movement was far different from the ex-

odus of the 1840s and 1850s. The newcomers after 1880 knew their destinations. Friends, relatives, and jobs awaited them. And they arrived in communities in which the Irish were no longer strangers.

Migration from Scandinavia also followed well-established lines. Departures from Norway reached new highs in the 1880s and 1890s and then again just after the turn of the century. The Norwegian communities were now stable and well organized, as Knute Nelson's election to the governorship of Minnesota showed in 1892. The harsh realistic novels of Ole Rölvaag, who had himself been involved, preserved the recollection of the bitter experience of migration and the conquest of the prairies. But by 1900, the most difficult part of that resettlement was over.

190

Irish immigrants reach Boston, 1921. (United Press International)

Armed peasants guarding the house of one of their leaders in County Donegal, Ireland. (*Illustrated London News,* February 25, 1888, New York Public Library)

Burning the houses of evicted tenants in County Kerry, Ireland, during the rent war. (*Illustrated London News,* January 29, 1887, New York Public Library)

Knute Nelson of Minnesota. (Photograph by Harris & Ewing, 1909, New York Public Library)

Vilhjalmur Stefansson and Dr. R. H. Anderson, arctic explorers. (Photoworld)

Finn Morterud's store. The shop was located in the heart of the Norwegian section of Bay Ridge in Brooklyn, New York. Although many Scandinavians went to the Middle West, Brooklyn contained a very large concentration of Norwegians. (United Press International)

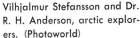

1841-45	4900	
1846-50	9500	
1851-55	15900	
1856-60	9200	
1861-65	16700	
1866-70	108800	
1871-75	119600	
1876-80	123300	HARD TIMES IN U.S.
1881-85	352300	INTRODUCTION OF MACHINE POWER
1886-90	304200	ON SCANDINAVIAN
1891-95	244600	FARMS
1896-1900	127000	HARD TIMES IN U.S.
1901-05	291600	HYDRO-ELECTRIC INDUSTRIES
1906-10	213700	IN SCANDINAVIA

Changes in the rate of Scandinavian immigration, 1841–1910. (E. A. Ross, *The Old World in the New*, New York, 1914)

Scandinavians in a Minnesota lumber camp. (Brown Brothers)

More Swedes came to the United States than formerly, and also a good many Danes. But many seamen, industrial workers, and miners were now moving along with the peasants.

The Scandinavians were joined toward the end of the century by smaller groups of kindred origin. The parents of Vilhjalmur Stefansson, the anthropologist and explorer, were north-coast Icelanders who had moved to Manitoba in 1887. Three years later disastrous floods swept away the products of all their labor, and they fled south to settle in Dakota Territory among their countrymen. The growing Vilhjalmur learned to read from the Icelandic weekly newspaper, and in the evenings heard his elders repeat the old sagas.

Men of the forest. Foreign-born workers in Minnesota take time to learn English. (Peter Roberts, *The New Immigration*, New York, 1912)

Finnish lumberjacks in Wisconsin, 1904. (Pinchot Collection, Library of Congress)

The immigrants from Finland were also Scandinavian by culture, although subjects of the Russian czar. In the 1880s and 1890s, a few thousand were arriving each year, mostly from the northern provinces. Then in 1899 the number climbed to more than twelve thousand, and to more than twenty-three thousand in 1902, as the emigration fever spread to the south. The flow continued until the First World War, by which time there were about two hundred thousand Finns in the United States.

Some two-thirds of the Finnish immigrants were tenants or landless laborers whose motives for emigrating were similar to those of other agricultural migrants—too many people, too little land, and no opportunity at home. Terrible famines in 1892 and 1903 made the peasants aware of their plight. In addition, compulsory military service and the Russification of their country also spurred them to leave. Yet many of them came with the intention of accumulating enough to return home as landowners, and, indeed, about 10 percent of those who arrived managed to go back.

The majority, however, neither returned to Finland nor found farms in America, but entered the industrial and mining labor force. The great metropolitan cities had no attractions for these people who feared the sense of being totally lost there, for their own language was utterly strange to Americans as well as to other Europe-

Logging in Minnesota. (Library of Congress)

Minnesota iron miners ready for work, 1906. (Library of Congress)

Skidding logs in the state of Washington. (Library of Congress)

ans. The Finns therefore sought out smaller towns like Maynard, Massachusetts, or Montreal, Wisconsin. There they found work in the mills, mines, quarries, and forests. Although the life of the wage earners was hard in these places as elsewhere, it offered some the hope that they might ultimately go on to farming. Meanwhile the communities were small enough to give the group cohesion and permit it to organize effectively. The Finns formed clubs and supported newspapers, as well as indulged in their distinctive sauna. Churches affiliated with the Apostolic Lutheran, the National Lutheran, or the Suomi Synod served the immigrants, who developed thriving temperance and cooperative movements.

The struggle to preserve Finnish identity against pressure from Russia gave political overtones to the nationalist movement on both sides of the ocean. Any enemy of the czar was a friend of the Finns. That sentiment had encouraged an alliance with socialism in the Old Country, and the same favorable attitude carried over to the United States. The American Finns were enthusiastic supporters of Eugene V. Debs. To a considerable extent, this was "Hall Socialism"; people came to the meetings for conviviality and for the dances, rather than out of ideological commitment. Some Finns for the same reasons were receptive to the recruiting efforts of the International Workers of the World and, after 1917, the Communists. The radicals not only struck a blow at the czar, but also provided the comradeship not readily available in the New World.

Other small groups from Northern and Western Europe also preserved their identity. Dutch Catholics, for instance, established a colony at Butler, Minnesota, as late as 1910; and there was a steady if tiny movement of Swiss from the Ticino, and of Russian-German Mennonites through these years. Despite their small size, these clusters insisted on maintaining their respective characters.

All these people considered themselves quite different from the immigrants from Eastern and Southern Europe. In many a mining town, the Cornish Methodists and the Catholic Irish, who had been feuding for years, for the first time discovered how much they had in common when they met the competition of Slavic and Italian workers. Important cultural differences divided the men of the old stocks from those of the new; but, in addition, they were separated by the fact that the former had already been prepared for American life, while the latter had still to discover the meaning of the factory and the city.

Industrialization thus created a context for immigration radically different from that of the decades before 1880. New conditions on both sides of the Atlantic made the factory more important than the farm, even among people from countries which had long been the sources of immigration. But the change would be more evident among those who were now, for the first time, joining the stream of immigrants.

A Finnish woman by her log cabin in northern Wisconsin near Lake Superior. (E. A. Ross, *The Old World in the New*, New York, 1914)

News of the end of the war with Russia reaches the Finnish Educational Association in New York, 1940. National sentiment was still strong in America when the Soviet Union attacked Finland. (United Press International)

Eugene V. Debs, 1909. (Library of Congress)

An I.W.W. meeting in Union Square, New York, 1914. (United Press International)

A Dutch mother and her eleven children on the way
to Minnesota, 1908. (National Park Service, Sherman
Collection)

Dutch immigrants arriving on the S.S. *Vedic*, 1921.
(United Press International)

Mennonites in Kansas, 1875. (Kansas State Historical Society, Topeka)

MENNONITES AT WORSHIP ON THE PRAIRIE.

GNADENAU, LOOKING EAST.

Mennonite life on the prairie, 1875. The picture above shows this group at worship, the lower pictures show the settlement at Gnadenau. (Kansas State Historical Society, Topeka)

The Russian-German settlement at Eureka, North Dakota. The pictures show: 1. a typical peasant; 2. the church; 3. the market center on a busy day; 4 and 5, children and women; 6. the home of one of the most prosperous farmers; and 7. a sod house and stable built of clay and straw. (Nostalgia Press, Inc.)

Workers in the McCormick factory, Chicago, about 1900. (Harvard University Social Ethics Collection)

The country peddler, a familiar figure in American rural life. (Drawn by E. W. Kemble, New York Public Library)

2
The East
European Jews

The number of Jews in the United States in 1880 was still small, although the immigration of the preceding sixty years had raised it to about three hundred thousand. These well-established people were apparently far along on the way to assimilation. Reform Judaism had offered them a means by which to adjust ancient traditions to American conditions. Increasingly the Jews regarded themselves as one in culture with their fellow citizens, while their distinctive faith became but another of the numerous sects characteristic of the country's religious life.

German influences among them were strong not only because many Jews had ties to that country through birth or antecedents, but also because the kaiser's empire seemed a model for the future. Its progressive civilization and its science were impressive, and it too was willing to treat Jews as equals in citizenship though different in forms of worship. The German experience was regarded as proof that Jews could adjust to modern society and justified their Americanization in the United States. In that spirit, the Central Conference of American Rabbis at Pittsburgh in 1885 affirmed that Jews formed a religious, not a national, community, and that the United States was their home. The conference therefore rejected, even as an ideal, the concept of a messianic return to Palestine.

Social forces confirmed these tendencies. The Jewish population was by no means concentrated in the cities but rather was widely dispersed in every region of the country and in many small towns. This pattern was not the result of any plan but reflected the dependence of the loosely organized American economy on many widely dispersed traders. Jews, like Yankees, served as peddlers and shopkeepers in every part of the country.

The great migrations that had transformed the prosperous, optimistic communities of American Jews originated in Eastern Europe. Some Jews still arrived from Germany after 1880, but these were a tiny minority among the 2 million of their coreligionists who came to the United States in the next half century. Most of these newcomers were Russians and Poles who left an environment, and brought with them a culture, totally different from those of Germany and the United States. They therefore experienced serious strains not only in their contacts with other Americans, but also in their relationships with German Jews.

Eastern Europe in the second half of the nineteenth century was on the threshold of momentous change. Though the political grip of the great empires—Russian, Austrian, Ottoman, and German—was still unshaken, the forces of modernization were undermining the economic and social foundations of an old order, which

Russian Jews at Ellis Island. (Photograph by Lewis W. Hine, in E. A. Ross, *The Old World in the New*, New York, 1914)

The Jewish quarter in Amsterdam, 1886. (Painting by Andreas Achenbach, New York Public Library)

Immigrants at Ellis Island. The man is Jewish, the woman Slovak. (Photograph by Lewis W. Hine in E. A. Ross, *The Old World in the New*, New York, 1914)

Jewish immigrants from Russia arrive in New York. (Sketch by S. F. Yeager, Nostalgia Press, Inc.)

Russian Jews on the way to America. (E. A. Steiner, *On the Trail of the Immigrant*, New York, 1906)

Immigrants in the waiting room at Ellis Island, 1907. (Library of Congress)

would not endure long after the end of the century. The Jews who were confined to a limited and anachronistic social role in the area felt the consequences more rapidly than other groups.

The increase in population was a dramatic warning of the radical challenge the Jews were about to face. From about 2 million in 1800, the number of Jews in Eastern Europe mounted to more than 8 million in 1900. That growth created difficulties because these people were not free to take advantage of the opportunities within the economy. Such restrictions were a result of their relationship to peasant society.

For centuries, the great majority of Jews in Eastern Europe had been middlemen. Typically, they lived in the *shtetl,* or little village, close by the peasants with whom they traded. A few acted as agents of the landlords or as innkeepers, and there were some artisans in the ur-

ban ghettos. But the vast majority, forbidden to hold land and excluded from agriculture, eked out a livelihood by buying and selling within the narrow confines of their small towns. The incessant growth of Jewish population left many of them with nothing to do. By 1900, in Galicia, where the situation was extreme, for every ten peasants, there was a Jewish trader trying desperately and hopelessly to make a living.

In the parts of Poland that had fallen to Austria and Germany in the partitions of the eighteenth century, there was some hope for the most enterprising Jews. If the *shtetl* could not sustain them, they could move to Berlin, Vienna, Prague, and the other growing cities where employment and education were available. But in Russia, the decisions of the czar confined the Jews to the Pale of Settlement, the densest area of the remainder of Poland and the Ukraine, and forbade them access to

The Jewish market in Cracow, 1880. (Engraving by Unger of a drawing by A. Schönn, New York Public Library)

such cities as Moscow and Saint Petersburg, except by special permits always subject to revocation. There also, they were denied opportunities for education and for entry into the professions and some branches of business.

Modernization of the economy made matters worse. The large landed estates, producing for distant markets, did not need the services of local middlemen. Also, the peasant population, depressed by the choice between remaining where it was, in poverty, or migrating to the cities, regarded all traders with suspicion and made poor customers. Everyone felt cramped, the Jews most of all, and the only escape was in departure.

Prejudice and persecution prodded the Jews on their way. To the traditional religious dislike of the people held responsible for the rejection of Christ, the nineteenth century added scientific anti-Semitism, which spread the doctrine that the Jews were racially different— unproductive and dangerous parasites. Hatred of the de- spised minority offered an emotional outlet to frustrated people in every social class.

Religious and political discrimination therefore further limited the ability of Jews to survive. The effects were rather mild in Turkey, Germany, and Austria, where the inequality existed mostly in obtaining access to political office and to some professions. In Russia and Rumania, the restrictions were more severe and subjected the Jews to heavy economic, social, and political disabilities. In those countries also, the outbreaks of unrestrained violence during pogroms were actual threats to personal security. In 1870, 1881, 1899, and 1905, the peasants took to the ax and the torch—if not encouraged, at least not restrained, by the authorities. The massacres at Kishinev and elsewhere shocked the conscience of the world, but there was no relief for the surviving victims other than in flight.

Yet in these same decades the effects of the Enlight-

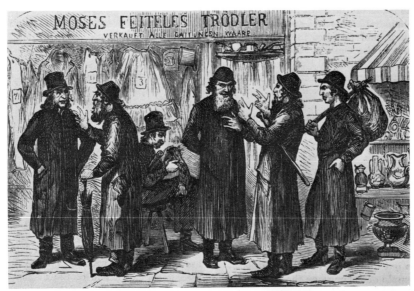

A Jewish street in Vienna, 1879. (New York Public Library)

The Jewish bread market in Polotsk, Poland, about 1900. (Mary Antin, *The Promised Land,* Boston, 1912)

Students at a Jewish school in St. Petersburg, privileged youngsters whose parents received the right to live outside the Pale of Settlement. (W. Evans-Gordon, *The Alien Immigrant,* New York, 1903)

Polish Jews in Czestochowa, 1914. (United Press International)

Early anti-Semitism in Germany—the Jewish witness is compelled to take an oath standing barefoot on a pigskin.

English Jews arriving in America. (National Park Service, Sherman Collection)

A Jewish agent solicits immigrants for a steamship company. (E. A. Ross, *The Old World in the New,* New York, 1914)

enment were beginning to disturb traditional Jewish communities also. New ideas led some young Jews to radicalism. More general was a willingness to pursue secular knowledge and to accept the values of the outside world. Increasingly Jews ventured away from the ghetto and the *shtetl.* They shaved off their side curls and exchanged their conventional gabardines for western frock coats. Above all, they considered new thoughts. For generations on end they had learned that until the coming of the Messiah, in God's good time, man could do little to alter his lot on earth. Now to risk action seemed more plausible than simply to acquiesce to a divinely ordained fate.

The migration of East European Jews to the United States began in the late 1870s. It climbed steadily year by year until after the turn of the century, and it reached its height in 1906 when more than 150,000 arrived.

The development of communication eased their movement, as did the assistance of various philanthropic organizations on both sides of the ocean. Protective societies were at work in various American cities in the 1880s, and these local efforts culminated in the formation of the Hebrew Immigrant Aid Society (HIAS) in 1902. From the European side, the Baron de Hirsch Fund tried to direct migration into constructive channels.

Jews already well established in the United States be-

Immigrants await the arrival of relatives in New York. The Hebrew Immigrant Aid Society continued its work after the peak of immigration and was prepared to assist the displaced persons of 1948. (Photoworld)

Poor Jews carry home free matzoth, 1900. (Library of Congress, Bain Collection)

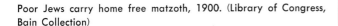

fore 1880 were by no means eager to stimulate immigration. Fearful of anti-Semitic reactions, they would have preferred the East Europeans to stay at home. Yet, once the migration started, the German and American Jews felt obligated to aid their coreligionists; also, they were anxious lest the newcomers create a social problem. The older communities therefore remained intimately involved in the fate of the newer ones.

Both their cultural heritage and the character of the new society they entered influenced the settlement of the East European Jews. They left the *shtetl* and the ghetto for the industrial metropolis; the transition set the terms of their lives.

Few became farmers. Some of the romantic young people in Russia had dreamed of work on the soil that would enable them to enjoy the produce of their own vines and fig trees. They made their way to such remote places as Sicily Island, Louisiana; Crémieux, South Dakota; and New Odessa, Oregon. American philanthropists helped others settle in Alliance, Vineland, Woodbine, and Carmel, New Jersey. Indeed, HIAS and similar organizations, for a time, tried to divert the main flow

Jewish girl in a Chicago sweatshop, about 1900. (E. A. Ross, *The Old World in the New*, New York, 1914)

The Jewish agricultural school in Woodbine, New Jersey, about 1900. (Harvard University Social Ethics Collection)

Jewish farmers at work in Woodbine, New Jersey, about 1900. (Harvard University Social Ethics Collection)

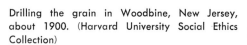

Drilling the grain in Woodbine, New Jersey, about 1900. (Harvard University Social Ethics Collection)

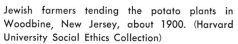

Jewish farmers tending the potato plants in Woodbine, New Jersey, about 1900. (Harvard University Social Ethics Collection)

Jewish farmers at home, about 1900. (Harvard University Social Ethics Collection)

A group of well-to-do Jewish farmers in Woodbine, New Jersey, about 1900. (Harvard University Social Ethics Collection)

Friends from the city come to visit the Woodbine, New Jersey, farmers, about 1900. (Harvard University Social Ethics Collection)

The old samovar is central to a Woodbine, New Jersey, tea party, about 1900. (Harvard University Social Ethics Collection)

The young people dress up at Woodbine, New Jersey, about 1900. (Harvard University Social Ethics Collection)

The older folk celebrate Simchas Torah, the holiday for rejoicing in the law. (Harvard University Social Ethics Collection)

Peddlers in the Jewish district of New York, about 1890. (Drawing by W. Bengough, Nostalgia Press, Inc.)

of migration from the Atlantic coast cities to Galveston, Texas, hoping thus to bring the newcomers closer to the agricultural heartland of the nation, but these efforts were unavailing. In 1912, there were fewer than four thousand Jewish families on the land. The failure was not surprising. This was a period when native Americans were leaving the farm for the city; immigrants had no reason to run counter to the trend.

There was plenty of space in the prairies. But the immigrant Jews concentrated in the great cities. New York, Chicago, Philadelphia, and Boston became the homes of 70 percent of them. These places were large enough to support the whole range of communal institutions and activities—synagogues and charities, newspapers and schools, theatres and fraternal societies, all magnets attracting still more immigrants.

An area of primary settlement in each city offered low rental accommodations to the families just off the ship. In 1916, some seven hundred thousand Jews crammed New York's lower East Side and Boston's North End, and the density of population was almost as high in Chicago's West Side. Poverty and the miserable sanitary conditions of the slums took their toll on these as on other immigrants. Families suffered from desertion by husbands, from the obligation of women and children to work, from the presence of boarders, and from the inability of parents and children to understand each other.

But in these neighborhoods at least people were not alone among strangers. These districts were near the job and therefore economical in terms of carfare; and the synagogue and the ritual bath, the Jewish theatre, and the kosher butcher were all close at hand. Even when the more successful immigrants were able to move, it was to contiguous areas like Williamsburg or Harlem in New York or the West End or South Side in Chicago, or, later still, farther out to Brownsville, the Bronx, Dorchester, or Chelsea, where they could take their familiar institutions with them.

Almost all the newcomers who settled in the great cities became laborers, having brought to the economy only their willingness to work. They found jobs in light

A Jewish immigrant home in New York, 1907. The Americanized clothing of the couple is an indication of progress in adjustment. But the window still opens on an airshaft. (Brown Brothers)

The summer heat forces the Chicago poor to sleep out-of-doors. (Brown Brothers)

Hester Street, the heart of New York's East Side, throbs with life, 1900. (The National Archives) ▶

The Jewish quarter of Boston. (Watercolor by W. A. Rogers, *Harper's Magazine*, November, 1899, Library of Congress)

The center of Chicago's Jewish district in the 1890s. (Harvard University Social Ethics Collection)

The mother is central to the Jewish family in America. (Harvard University Social Ethics Collection)

A group of Philadelphia Jews in the first decade of the twentieth century. (Harvard University Social Ethics Collection)

A Philadelphia Jewish family, about 1910. (Harvard University
Social Ethics Collection)

Worshipers leave the synagogue on Rivington Street, New York, on the Jewish New Year, 1911. (Library of Congress, Bain Collection)

manufacturing and in the building trades, where the demand and the opportunities were. Mass-production methods were transforming the ready-made-garment industry as the fabrication of coats, cloaks, shirts, blouses, hats, and caps shifted from the consumer's home or the artisan's shop to the factory and the machine. Jews, who had previously been strangers to these occupations, taught one another to use the shears and the sewing machine, and they learned to support themselves through long hours of low-paid labor. In some branches of the trade the whole family could work together in its crowded tenement home, where a few of the most fortunate could save enough to become contractors or small businessmen.

The habit of generations in Eastern Europe persuaded many Jews that peddling and retail trades offered the readiest escape from the life of unremunerative toil. It took effort, frugality, and calculation to accumulate enough capital to take to the road or open a store, and as many failed as succeeded. Opportunities were best in the neighborhoods where they could serve immigrants still unfamiliar with American buying habits or in the small cities of the interior, where the great chain and department stores had not yet penetrated. But progress was slow and in 1930 the majority of Jewish immigrants were still wage laborers.

Their institutional life reflected their poverty and their concentration in the cities. The Orthodox community that had centered in the synagogue changed in the transplantation from the *shtetl* to the metropolitan center. Efforts to form a *kehillah,* or overall unifying organization, failed. Instead, each group of *landsmen,* people from the same European district or town, provided for its own needs. Little places of worship, fraternal and philanthropic societies, and religious schools sprouted spontaneously as the immigrants struggled to preserve their traditions in the strange environment.

They also developed altogether new associations. A nucleus of intellectuals with experience in Russian *bunds* or the English trade unions led the immigrants into the labor movement. The United Hebrew Trades, formed in 1888, stimulated organization in the various crafts. The International Ladies Garment Workers Union gained steadily in strength; from the great strike of 1910 emerged a protocol with the manufacturers providing for collective bargaining. The I.L.G.W.U. and the Amalgamated Clothing Workers supported a broad range of activities in an effort to improve not only wages and working conditions, but also to help members adjust to the New World. The immigrant press and the Yiddish stage played a somewhat similar role. The *Jewish Daily Forward* of New York, which first appeared in 1897, was the most important Jewish newspaper. Edited for many years by Abraham Cahan, it had affiliations with the labor unions and the Socialist party. Like the other journals, it rendered many services to readers, communicating the news and providing information and advice about the problems of adjustment to the New World.

This was also the function of the plays presented in the Yiddish theatre.

Gradually, these developing institutions created unique East European communities in the large cities, existing side by side with those of the German Jews. Philanthropy and the defense against anti-Semitism occasionally united them. But until 1930, the newer immigrants were almost as far removed from their coreligionists who had come earlier as they were from native Americans of other faiths.

The greatest point of contact between newcomers and natives was through the educational system. The rapid expansion of urban school facilities opened up attractive opportunities, to which East European Jews responded because of their own tradition of learning. Many were willing to make painful sacrifices to send their children to the public schools and on to college. As a result, within decades of their arrival some of these immigrants and their children were able to move into the professions, particularly into medicine and law. Thus, their experience was hard, but not devoid of promise.

The advertisement summons the audience to a Yiddish adaptation of *Thrilby.* (*Harper's Monthly,* December, 1898, New York Public Library)

Street merchants in the Jewish market of New York, 1890. (Drawing by W. A. Rogers, Nostalgia Press, Inc.)

Jewish workers in a machine shop, about 1900. (Harvard University Social Ethics Collection)

A Jewish laborer and his family, about 1900. Harvard University Social Ethics Collection)

A sweatshop in a Ludlow Street tenement, 1889. (Photograph by Jacob A. Riis, Library of Congress)

A twelve-year-old boy works pulling thread in a sweatshop, 1889. (Photograph by Jacob A. Riis, Library of Congress)

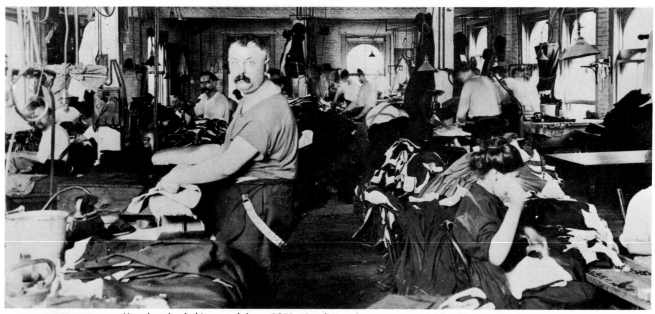

Moe Levy's clothing workshop, 1912. Conditions here are a considerable improvement over those in the early sweatshops. (The Byron Collection, Museum of the City of New York)

◄ Jewish wage earners—left, the dressmaker, below, the fruit vendor. (Drawing by W. A. Rogers, *Harper's Weekly*, December, 1889, Nostalgia Press, Inc.)

Pushcart peddlers on New York's East Side. (Library of Congress, Detroit Collection) ►

Father, mother, and daughter work together sewing clothing at home. (Photograph by Lewis W. Hine, Library of Congress)

Jewish street-level shops in a New York City tenement district, 1905. (Library of Congress)

A makeshift synagogue, 1912. On the Jewish high holidays, synagogues were so crowded that theatres were used for overflow congregations. (Bain Collection, Library of Congress)

A yeshiva, a house of study, in New York. (*Munsey's,* August, 1900, New York Public Library)

Jewish and Italian garment workers unite in a strike, 1913. (Brown Brothers)

Jewish garment workers on strike, 1913. The sign in Yiddish announces that all the workers of Boss Shishansky's Shop at 117 Hester Street will go back only under union conditions—a fifty-hour week. (United Press International)

220

The Grand Theatre offers Jacob P. Adler in the Yiddish drama *Elischa*. (Brown Brothers)

Abraham Cahan, 1913. (New York Public Library)

The tradition of learning—a school in Polotsk, Poland. (Mary Antin, *The Promised Land,* Boston, 1912)

Pupils—mostly Jewish—in a public school, Chelsea, Massachusetts. (Mary Antin, *The Promised Land,* Boston, 1912)

An evening school for newsboys. (*Harper's Weekly,* May 18, 1867, New York Public Library)

The beggars of Naples. (John Russell Young,
Around the World with General Grant,
New York, 1879)

3

The Italians

Reference to Italy had mixed connotations for nineteenth-century Americans. On the one hand, Italy was associated with the ideals of culture: from there ancient Rome had spread civilization to the world and, there, in a later period, the great personages of the medieval and Renaissance civilizations had made their homes. Every schoolchild had learned to value Italy's contribution the the Western heritage, and artists and writers from the United States flocked to Rome and Florence, hoping these hallowed sites would stimulate their own creativity.

But travelers who passed through the peninsula on one of those continental tours considered obligatory for the well-brought-up also observed other, less admirable, features of Italian society. They commented on the hosts of beggars in the streets, the pervasive poverty, and the firm grip of the Catholic Church on the minds of the people. Furthermore, they noticed the political instability, matched only by the chaos and disorder of the cities. Italy boasted a glorious past, but in the nineteenth century it seemed deplorably backward. A remote area, without close associations with the United States, its fate seemed to have no apparent relevance for the New World. Yet, between 1880 and 1930 millions of Italians came to share the American experience.

Italy in the middle of the nineteenth century was divided, some of its provinces still subject to Spanish and Austrian rulers and some governed as independent, feudal principalities. Its regions differed markedly in culture and in the level of economic development. Poverty and backwardness existed everywhere, but to a lesser degree in the north than in the south. The northern areas had more advanced political and economic institutions, and by the time of the unification of the country in 1870 were experiencing some industrialization. Important Austrian influence in Lombardy and Venetia, and French influence in Piedmont gave a cosmopolitan tone to the whole region, orienting it toward Western and Central Europe. By contrast, the south, a vague designation that covered Naples, Sicily, and the provinces between Abruzzi and Calabria, was cut off from the modernizing economic and cultural currents of the time.

North or south, the peasant's lot was unenviable. Extreme fragmentation of holdings in the north and the preemption, in the south, of most of the land by the *latifundia,* or great estates, reduced the agriculturists to tenancy and day labor. Everywhere, the rapid growth of population made it impossible for villages to sustain their members, even those on the coast who could supplement their incomes by fishing. Famine, flood, and drought increasingly set men in search of work wherever they could find it. The destinations within easiest reach were the cities of the north and of France, Switzerland, and Germany.

The movement overseas started in northern Italy and at first affected the relatively prosperous, who could exercise some choice about where they would go. Similarities of language, religion, and culture drew many Italians to South America, and proximity drew others to Tunis and North Africa. The few who came to the United States before 1880 were mostly professionals or workers with skills.

In the last two decades of the nineteenth century, however, economic dislocations grew more severe and

Adjusting to the New World—the drawing to the left shows Italian beggars trying their old trade in America; the drawing at the right shows Italians working with pick and shovel. (Drawn by Paul Frenzeny, *Harper's Weekly*, February 1, 1873, New-York Historical Society)

1866-70	8300
1871-75	27100
1876-80	28700
1881-85	109500
1886-90	197800
1891-95	289200
1896-1900	369300
1901-05	959800
1906-10	1186100

Fluctuations in Italian immigration, 1866–1910. (E. A. Ross, *The Old World in the New*, New York, 1914)

A village lane in northern Italy, 1905. (Harvard University Social Ethics Collection)

Street scene, Como, Italy, 1905. (Harvard University Social Ethics Collection)

The burdens of Italian women, 1905. (Harvard University Social Ethics Collection)

Italian woman. (Photograph by Lewis W. Hine, in E. A. Ross, *The Old World in the New*, New York, 1914)

Italian gypsy mother and her child. (Photograph by Lewis W. Hine, in E. A. Ross, *The Old World in the New*, New York, 1914)

The courtyard, setting for Italian family life in San Remo, 1905. (Harvard University Social Ethics Collection)

An Italian Swiss town, 1905. (Harvard University Social Ethics Collection)

The countryside is not far from the city streets in San Remo, 1905. (Harvard University Social Ethics Collection)

Italian immigrants satisfy their hunger in the Ellis Island waiting room. (Photograph by Lewis W. Hine, in E. A. Ross, *The Old World in the New*, New York, 1914)

A skilled Italian stonecutter at work, early twentieth century. (Peter Roberts, *The New Immigration*, New York, 1912)

news of New World opportunities spread to the remotest villages. Emigration then became a mass movement. Its source shifted to the south, and the people it carried along were predominantly peasants. Several Mediterranean shipping lines provided rapid service from Genoa, Naples, and Palermo to New York and Boston and permitted the migration of very large numbers. The flow quickly gained momentum. There were five hundred thousand arrivals in the 1890s and some 3 million more by 1914.

Italian immigration aroused suspicion; it seemed largely transient and dominated by avaricious bosses. Many peasants arrived each spring to work for a season or a year, with the full expectation of returning to their homes. They thus extended to the United States the pattern of migratory labor with which they were already familiar. Some Americans, however, considered the "birds of passage"—single men who lived under disorderly conditions and without families—undesirable. The Italians seemed to be coming to withdraw the riches of the United States rather than to share its life. Although in time many immigrants brought their wives and children and settled more permanently, the movement back and forth across the ocean caused mistrust.

There was mistrust also of the padrone system, which seemed to have many characteristics of involuntary servitude. The padrone, or boss, was a contractor, usually Italian, who recruited and controlled the migrants. He took on jobs for a flat fee, out of which he supported the men dependent upon him. Interested in making a profit on the laborers, this middleman sometimes ruthlessly exploited his countrymen. Yet the boss was also an essential intermediary in the process by which foreigners who lacked even a few words of English could find employment in the New World.

The distinctive features of Italian immigration were shaped by the role that awaited these newcomers in the American economy. Almost all became laborers; the pick and the shovel were their assigned instruments. In that respect, they were the successors of the Irish of a previous generation. The Italians became railroad maintenance-of-way workers; they built the streets and subways; they laid the pipes and wires essential to the modern city. They also filtered into the building trades, in which the contracting system prevailed. Those with experience found employment as masons or plasterers; others simply carried hods or pushed the wheelbarrows loaded in the endless process of excavation and building.

The expanding mines and factories likewise found uses for the labor of Italian immigrants despite the handicaps of unfamiliar language and customs. These jobs at least had some degree of permanence, and they brought the worker indoors—considerations of some importance for those immigrants who settled down permanently and brought families with them. The desire for stability led others to develop skills in service occupations for which there was a demand in the New World —as barbers, waiters, peddlers, icemen, ragpickers, bootblacks. And although tradition frowned on the employment of women, need often forced the family to make use of the earning power of all its members.

Only a tiny but fortunate minority supported itself by agriculture, and it did so by seizing an opportunity native Americans overlooked. The growth of great cities created a demand for fruits and vegetables that could be raised on truck farms in the nearby suburbs. Industrious Italians applied themselves to the task in Connecticut, New Jersey, and California.

Italian sculptors at work in a studio in New York. (*Harper's Weekly*, February 27, 1869, New-York Historical Society)

The boss, one of the padrone. (E. A. Steiner, *On the Trail of the Immigrant*, New York, 1906)

Italians playing cards in Columbia Hall, New York. (Drawn by Matthew Morgan, *Frank Leslie's Illustrated Newspaper*, March 29, 1873, New-York Historical Society)

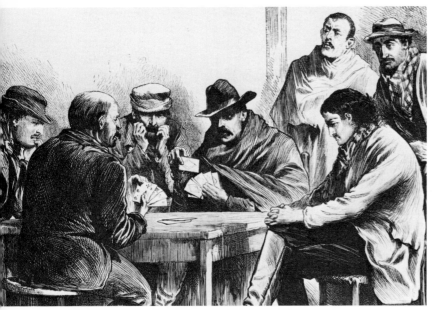

Mulberry Bend, the center of the Italian district of New York, 1895. (Drawing by W. Bengough, Museum of the City of New York)

Street scene in a village near Palermo, Sicily. The sign over the shop at No. 8 reveals that its proprietor has been to the United States and returned. (Photoworld)

Italian workingmen laying the street railroad line at Union Square, New York. (Drawn by Hughson Hawley, *Harper's Weekly*, September 26, 1891, Library of Congress)

Italian laborers working on the tracks. (Peter Roberts, *The New Immigration*, New York, 1912)

Workers paving Fourth Avenue, New York City. (Drawn by A. Castaigne, New York Public Library)

Italian women sell fish on Hester Street, New York. (The National Archives)

Construction workers on a Broadway skyscraper. (Drawn by G. W. Peters, *Frank Leslie's Illustrated Newspaper*, April 25, 1895, Library of Congress)

The ice-cream man—a scene on the streets of New York, 1885. (New York Public Library)

Italian bread peddlers on Mulberry Street, New York. (Library of Congress, Detroit Collection)

A street peddler on a feast day. (Library of Congress, Bain Collection)

Italian peddlers selling fruits and vegetables, 1894. (New York Public Library)

Tenement homework. An Italian family of five bunches flowers in its New York City home, 1908. (Photograph by Lewis W. Hine, Library of Congress)

Peddling fruit in Philadelphia, about 1900. (Harvard University Social Ethics Collection)

An Old World skill—Italian bonnet makers. (Harper's Monthly, September, 1863, New York Public Library)

An Italian truck-farming district in Tennessee, early twentieth century. (E. Lord, J. J. D. Trenor, and S. J. Barrows, *The Italian in America*, New York, 1905)

The fire escape of an Italian tenement is an extension of the flat, c. 1890. (Photograph by Jacob A. Riis, Library of Congress)

The kind of community the immigrants developed depended on the setting. In New York, Boston, Philadelphia, and Chicago, density of settlement was the dominant influence. Almost every family took in boarders; a typical three-room apartment at the turn of the century was home to fourteen people, who slept four to a bed, as well as on the kitchen floor and the dining-room table. The costs of such crowding were painfully clear when illness struck, and were reflected also in the delinquency of children, the defiance of the law, and the outbreaks of violence. Here was the breeding ground of the gang life that would make Al Capone notorious in the 1920s.

On the other hand, the same circumstances often forced people to cooperate. Since there was no room within, children and adults spent much of their time outdoors, on the street, and learned to help, or at least not to hurt, one another. The neighborhood consisted entirely of countrymen, familiar, devoted to the same customs, guided by the same habits, and able to cooperate in supporting social and cultural institutions. By 1920, for instance, the Italians of Chicago maintained 110 mutual-aid societies.

Smaller areas escaped both the advantages and the disadvantages of the big city. Housing in the mill and

The yard of a Jersey Street tenement in New York, 1888. The rent was only $1 a month, but the immigrants paid a high price in discomfort. (Photograph by Jacob A. Riis, Library of Congress)

A gambling den in Baxter Street, c. 1868. (New York Public Library)

The children of an East Side tenement, early twentieth century. (United Press International)

Italians are displacing Swedes on this Chicago street, about 1900. (Harvard University Social Ethics Collection)

The Italian Men's Civic Club, Rochester, New York, early twentieth century. (E. A. Ross, *The Old World in the New*, New York, 1914)

Market day in an Italian settlement in Louisiana. (E. Lord, J. J. D. Trenor, and S. J. Barrows, *The Italian in America*, New York, 1905)

mining towns was less crowded, if not more sanitary, than in the metropolitan centers, and the open countryside was not altogether out of reach. But here it was difficult to develop a community. Numbers were fewer, and generally the Italians lived scattered in clusters among native Americans and immigrants from other countries. It was not feasible under these conditions to preserve cultural distinctiveness or ties based upon common antecedents.

In both environments Italianization was the initial step in Americanization. At their first arrival, the immigrants identified themselves, as they had at home, by their locality or province. People from Apulia spoke the same dialect, celebrated the same *festa* in honor of the same patron saint, tried to live on the same block, and often took up the same occupation. They had little in common with the newcomers from Salerno or Palermo; and the sense of local loyalty, or *campanilismo*, persisted for a surprisingly long time.

Yet adjustment to life in the United States revealed their common identity as Italians. Here regional variations in language became less important than the total strangeness of English. As the immigrants listened to speakers or attended the opera or read their newspapers, they discovered that Italian, despite its local variations, was an easier medium of communication than English.

Religious developments pointed in the same direction. The Italians were mostly Catholic; yet the churches they found in existence at their arrival were not like those

Progressive Italian-Americans. The upper picture shows the Lincoln Civic Club, New York City; the lower picture a night school in Indianapolis. (William P. Shriver, *Immigrant Forces,* New York, 1913)

Protestant efforts among Italians. The upper picture shows a tent service at the Church of the Ascension, New York; the lower picture shows a daily vacation Bible school. (William P. Shriver, *Immigrant Forces,* New York, 1913)

An Italian kindergarten in Pennsylvania, early twentieth century. (John R. Henry, *Some Immigrant Neighbors,* New York, 1912)

An Italian on Bleecker Street, New York. (Drawing by W. A. Rogers, *Harper's Weekly,* October 18, 1890, Nostalgia Press, Inc.)

they had left at home. Worshipers, priests, and saints were Irish or German in derivation. The missionary activity of Protestant sects and the agitation of freethinking radicals created the genuine danger that the Italians might drift away from their ancestral faith; indeed, an occasional group did so.

Yet the great mass of immigrants increasingly looked to the church for assistance, as Maria Francesca Cabrini discovered. As a sickly girl in her village in Lombardy, Maria Francesca had known the pinch of poverty and had taken as her task the service of the helpless people about her. Decades of labor for the Missionary Sisters of the Sacred Heart forged a chain of schools and orphanages throughout Italy. In 1889 she carried her work to the New World immigrants. She remained in the United States until her death in 1917, having become an American citizen in 1909. Her efforts built seventy schools,

231

Italian-Americans on parade, 1938—a procession by the members of twenty-five Italian Catholic parishes in Brooklyn, Queens, and Long Island. (United Press International)

An Italian concert hall and restaurant. (Brown Brothers)

Saint Frances Xavier Cabrini. (Library of Congress)

Children praying before the shrine of the Mother Cabrini School in New York, 1946. (United Press International)

hospitals, and orphanages, and enlisted four thousand nuns to succor the dependent. In time, Mother Cabrini, beatified and canonized, became the first American saint, and through her the Catholic tradition of charity became part of the general pattern of American philanthropy.

The Italian immigrants had been accustomed to finding aid of this sort through their churches and it confirmed their loyalty. In time, a compromise permitted the formation of national parishes where communicants could use their own tongue. But the emphasis was on Italian rather than on the local or regional character of the affiliation.

A similar though slower transformation occurred in voluntary organizations. The first mutual-aid societies consisted of people from a single locality of Italy. Later organizations like the Unione Siciliana drew upon a whole region for their membership. Finally, the Order of the Sons of Italy in America, founded in 1905, was open

to natives of the whole peninsula, including their children. The Italian labor movement ultimately rested on just as broad a base.

The fact that the peasants lacked leaders of their own left the Italian community open to a struggle for control that lasted throughout the 1920s. In each city a cluster of *prominenti* claimed the right to speak for all. Among them were contractors who had earned some wealth, doctors or pharmacists who practiced among their *paesani,* and local politicians with a following. Often the local consul, who represented the Italian government, was the ally of the *prominenti.* The latter could communicate with the laborers and yet also deal with municipal officials and other agents of the outside world.

Generoso Pope, for instance, came to New York from Arpaise, Benevento, in 1904 at the age of thirteen. His first job was as a water boy. He climbed up through the ranks of labor, and ten years later was superintendent

Columbus Day in New York City, 1932. Mayor O'Brien, speech in hand, looks up at the statue of the discoverer. At the left is Generoso Pope, Italian-American publisher. (United Press International)

Carlo Tresca addresses a crowd in New York, 1927. (United Press International)

IL PROCRESSO ITALO-AMERICANO

PRIMO GIORNALE QUOTIDIANO ITALIANO FOND

ANNO VII. N. 10   BARSOTTI & POLIDORI, Editori-Proprietari.   NEW YORK, MERCOLEDI' 13 GENNAIO 1886

An early edition of *Il Progresso Italo-Americano*, 1886.

◄ Advertisements from *Il Progresso Italo-Americano*, 1886.

Nicola Sacco (right) and Bartolomeo Vanzetti (left). (United Press International)

Benito Mussolini (Il Duce) in full voice, about 1927. (Photoworld)

of the Colonial Sand Company, which distributed building materials through the fast-growing city. In 1917 he became president of the enterprise and established connections with the dominant Democratic party. His interests spread to include two newspapers, *Il Corriere d' America* and *Il Progresso Italo-Americano;* awards from the Order of the Crown of Italy and the Order of the Holy Sepulchre testified to his importance among his countrymen.

Against the *prominenti* was arrayed a rival set of aspirants to leadership, one that was radical in political orientation and secular in its point of view. Carlo Tresca, who arrived in America in the same year as Pope, came from a quite different background. Son of a prominent landowning family in Sulmona, Abruzzi, Tresca became a socialist as a youth, edited a radical newspaper, and was secretary of the Italian Railroad Workers Union. Political enemies harried him, and he sought refuge in the United States where he took up the

Portuguese whale-men at Monterey, California, 1882. (New York Public Library)

Women sorting cranberries on Cape Cod, 1876. (New York Public Library)

Cranberry pickers. (Brown Brothers)

cause of immigrant laborers. He had well-to-do relatives in Brooklyn and Boston, but his intimate associates were radicals in the coalfields and the textile mills; his newspaper, *Il Martello,* fought every form of oppression, opposing both the Fascists and the Communists in his effort to organize the Italian-Americans within the labor movement.

The conflict between the *prominenti* and the radicals reached a crisis in the 1920s. The radicals exhausted their strength in the unsuccessful struggle to save Nicola Sacco and Bartolomeo Vanzetti, convicted of robbery and murder in a trial prejudiced by their immigrant origins and their anarchist views. Their execution in 1927 disheartened their supporters. Moreover, the labor movement was then in retreat, and factional divisions left a multitude of little cliques bickering with one another. Meanwhile, Benito Mussolini had seized power in Italy, and his blustering rhetoric seemed to command the respect of the Catholic Church and of the great powers of Europe. The nationalistic sentiments he whipped up had overtones in the United States; and the renewed pride in being Italian buttressed the position of the *prominenti.* Down to World War II the influence of men like Pope grew, that of Tresca and the radicals waned.

Those Americans who considered all Latins of a

kind sometimes confused the Italians with a smaller and different group, the Portuguese. Actually, the 150,000 or so Portuguese-speaking immigrants came from three distinct sources—the Azores, Portugal proper, and the Cape Verde islands. The Azoreans were the first to arrive, for American fishing and whaling vessels had long been accustomed to picking up crewmen in the islands, and a nucleus of settlement already existed in New England before 1880. After 1880 there was a moderate increase in numbers. The little communities thus established later attracted additional members from Portugal and some dark-skinned Bravas from Cape Verde; a few thousand recruits emigrated to Hawaii between 1911 and 1914 to work on the sugar plantations.

By 1920, two big Portuguese concentrations of settlement around New Bedford, Massachusetts, and Oakland, California, were well established. These immigrants took jobs in the textile mills, in agriculture, and in the fisheries, and steadily improved their status. Such specialized crops as cranberries and asparagus depended largely on their labor. They formed mutual-aid societies to protect the living and bury the dead, and established newspapers in their own language. They also managed to assert their national character in their own Catholic parishes. On a small scale, the Portuguese thus met and resolved the problems other immigrants had encountered in the New World.

234

A group of Ruthenian peasants from the Carpathian mountains. (E. A. Steiner, *The Immigrant Tide,* New York, 1909)

4

The Slavic Peoples

Few Americans in 1880 knew much about the lands or the peoples of Eastern Europe. The area beyond Germany was not a favored destination of travelers, and its cultural and economic links with the New World were fragile. The arrival of millions of immigrants from that remote region was therefore a considerable cultural shock.

In the United States, the strangers seemed all of a kind, whether they were Poles or Ruthenians, Slovaks or Slovenes. All were identified as Slavs because of the common assumption that they spoke variants of the same tongue. The description was not altogether accurate, for the Hungarians and the Rumanians differed from the others in origin as well as in language. However, something more important held these people together: the kind of society they left and the situation they encountered in the United States.

The whole of Eastern Europe was subservient to the great empires of Russia, Germany, and Austria. Even the independent states of Serbia and Rumania lived under the shadow of their imperial neighbors. Everywhere a small landowning class dominated society; town life was ill developed; and the mass of the population consisted of peasants. The effects of economic change were therefore drastic, particularly after 1860 when the last legal traces of serfdom vanished. The increase in

population and the modernization of agriculture combined to displace millions of husbandmen, who took refuge either in the growing industrial cities or in emigration. Also, the railroads in the last quarter of the nineteenth century opened the channels for a substantial movement to America.

Precise numbers are unattainable since the immigration statistics were kept by the country of departure—an arrival listed in 1890 as a native of Austria might have been a Pole from Galicia or a Czech from Bohemia. But the trend was clear. Migration from the entire area mounted steadily in the two decades after 1890. In 1910, about 2.5 million foreign-born Americans identified themselves to the census takers as Poles, Czechs, and Magyars, and by other designations that revealed their East European origins. Since a good many were transients who returned after spending a year or two in the United States, the total number of arrivals must have been well over 3 million.

Whatever their place of birth, almost all these people found employment in industry after their arrival in America. Little clusters of Czechs took up farms in Nebraska, and some Russian-Germans settled in Kansas and North Dakota. The Wends—Slavs from Lausitz, Germany—wandered into Texas, and occasional Polish families raised vegetables on Long Island or tobacco in

Peasant women from Slovakia. They wear tags fastened around their necks to give their names and destinations. (National Park Service, Sherman Collection)

Gypsies from Slovenia, about 1900. (National Park Service, Sherman Collection)

A substantial family of Russian Germans arrives in New York in 1905 on their way to North Dakota. (National Park Service, Sherman Collection)

Czech women and children arrive in Ellis Island, 1920. (United Press International)

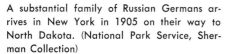

A young Magyar woman. (National Park Service, Sherman Collection)

Two peasants from the Black mountains of Montenegro. (E. A. Steiner, On the Trail of the Immigrant, New York, 1906)

The home of the Kovarik brothers, Saline County, Nebraska. The first home of such immigrants was sometimes a dugout, easy to construct and relatively secure in the winter. A more commodious house followed after the first tasks of settlement were finished. (Nebraska State Historical Society)

Displaced Serbian peasants on the move, driven by war and economic change. (*Illustrated London News*, September 9, 1876, New York Public Library)

The Nesba family farm in Howard County, Nebraska, 1880. (Nebraska State Historical Society)

A threshing scene on a Czech farm near Schuyler, Nebraska, 1893. (Nebraska State Historical Society)

The Kucera family, Czech pioneers in Cheyenne County, Nebraska. (Nebraska State Historical Society)

Connecticut. But the great majority of these newcomers earned a livelihood in the mills and the mines.

They therefore pitched their homes in the industrial heartland of the nation. A great chain of factories, including their related mines and railroads, reached from Buffalo and Pittsburgh in the east through Cleveland and Detroit, continuing to Chicago and on to Milwaukee. Here was the heaviest demand for labor in the production of metals and machines, and here the East Europeans were most densely settled. The low wages they commanded and the harsh conditions they toiled under dictated the circumstances of their lives. And the problems of existence, whether in the shanties of the mill towns or the tenements of the urban slums, took their usual heavy toll, as it had of other immigrants. In one of these towns "run wide open," a perceptive observer in 1910 noted that civilization had broken down. The people could not help themselves individually as they could back home in their villages; nor did they know how to help themselves collectively.

Unaccustomed to acting outside the familiar modes of their ancestral villages, these newcomers were slow to learn how to cooperate under the new conditions. They desired places of worship and facilities for mutual aid, but did not at first know how to provide for them. One priest sadly pointed out that his flock lacked the habits of orderly life and also the leaders to show them the way.

Polish gardeners on Long Island, New York, early twentieth century: The top left picture shows a load on its way to market. Below left and above, the men and women work separately. (William P. Shriver, *Immigrant Forces*, New York, 1913)

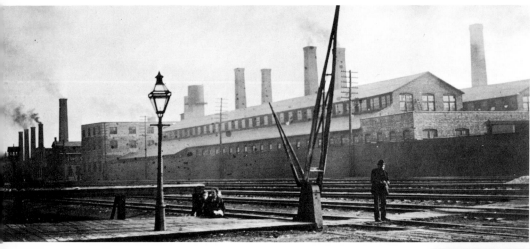

Polish women come to work in the early morning at the union stockyards in Chicago. (Photograph by Burke & Atwell, E. A. Ross, *The Old World in the New*, New York, 1914)

Workers pouring copper at Hancock, Michigan, early twentieth century. (Library of Congress, Detroit Collection)

The ironworks dominate the horizon of this section of Chicago. (Harvard University Social Ethics Collection)

Sunday scene among the Rumanian steelworkers in Youngstown, Ohio. (E. A. Ross, *The Old World in the New*, New York, 1914)

A group of Slovenians curiously observes the operations of democracy at a visit to a session of the Cleveland city council. (E. A. Ross, *The Old World in the New*, New York, 1914)

Women workers study English in a Cleveland, Ohio, factory twice a week in the afternoon. (E. A. Ross, *The Old World in the New*, New York, 1914)

A long-anticipated dream of the Serbian-Americans comes true. The Right Reverend William T. Manning, Bishop of the Protestant Episcopal Diocese of New York, presents a solid silver cross to the Very Reverend D. J. Shoukletovich (left), dean of the newly dedicated cathedral of St. Sava, 1944. (United Press International)

There were frequent efforts to draw the various Slavic groups together. On one such occasion, Mayor Fiorello La Guardia of New York receives a formal invitation to the unity festival sponsored by the American Slav Congress, 1943. (United Press International)

Each of the numerous groups that joined in the migration met the crisis of resettlement in its own fashion. The success of adjustment depended somewhat on the size of the population involved, on the length of time it had to plant roots, and on the degree to which its members held together out of a consciousness of their cultural and social distinctiveness.

Estimates of Polish immigration range above 2 million, much of it concentrated in Chicago, New York, and Buffalo. Furthermore, a small number of intellectuals and political refugees had preceded the heavy flow of peasants and had begun to organize communal institutions before 1880. Yet the experience of these newcomers was turbulent and marked by frequent internal conflicts.

Although the immigrants' immediate problems were internal, springing from poorly paid jobs and wretched housing, the impulse toward unity emanated from abroad. The long struggle for independence in Poland, which did not succeed until 1918, deeply influenced them all. The spread of the Order of the Falcons from the Old World to the New, and the frequent lecture tours of the famous pianist Ignace Paderewski stimulated nationalistic sentiment.

Deep divisions arose over concrete questions about how to preserve Polish identity in America. Some Poles insisted that the important element in their heritage was national and secular; others wished to emphasize loyalty to their Catholic faith. The divergence in attitudes long divided the group.

The national, secular viewpoint dominated the thinking of the men who in 1880 founded the Polish National Alliance of North America. The organization thereafter absorbed many local benevolent societies and by 1909 had more than a thousand branches. It strove to preserve the ancestral language and culture and, to help do so, in 1912 set up Alliance College in Pennsylvania. The newspaper *Zgoda* generally expressed its point of view. Some extremists went so far as to create the schismatic Polish National Church.

Other Polish-Americans were, however, more concerned with preserving their traditional affiliation with the Catholic Church, although they had no desire to be absorbed into existing Irish, German, or Italian parishes. They therefore struggled to unite national and religious forces; their mutual-aid societies were dedicated to St. Michael the Archangel or to St. Casimir, and they contributed their bitterly earned wages to establish churches, schools, and orphanages that would be both Polish and Catholic. The Polish Roman Catholic Union in America was the central organization of these people and *Narod Polski* their journal. Whether they belonged to one faction or another, the Poles at least had the advantage of consciousness of their national identity, a sentiment heightened by the fact that for almost a century they had lived under the suzerainty of alien monarchs.

The lines that defined other groups became clear only with the passage of time and with the accretion of experience. The immigrant who arrived from Bohemia or Moravia in the 1880s, for instance, found himself pulled in a variety of directions. He might continue to consider himself a subject of the Austrian emperor and join German-speaking societies or churches. Or, he might subscribe to a newspaper edited by freethinking intellectuals who stressed his Slavonic culture and Czech language.

An early Polish market in New York City, 1884. (New York Public Library)

Violence in the course of a strike by Polish miners, Shenandoah, Pennsylvania, February, 1888. (Brown Brothers)

Milwaukee Avenue and Division Street, center of Polish Chicago, 1927. (United Press International)

Polish churchgoers in Northampton, 1910. (New York Public Library)

Site of the first Polish church in America at Panna Maria, Texas, 1854. (Painting by A. Szyk)

Ignace Paderewski, first premier of the Polish republic. (Painting by A. Szyk)

Karol Blaszkowicz, an eighteenth-century cartographer. (Painting by A. Szyk)

Olbracht Zaborowski, a Polish settler of the colonial period. Like other immigrants, the Poles sought to establish their connections with the history of the United States by locating their roots in the colonial period. (Painting by A. Szyk)

Jakub Sadowski, a Polish frontiersman in America. (Painting by A. Szyk)

Vladimir Krzyzanowski at the battle of Cross Keys. (Painting by A. Szyk)

Polish pioneers in Virginia in the seventeenth century. (Painting by A. Szyk)

Houses occupied by Polish immigrants in a New England mill town, about 1900. (Harvard University Social Ethics Collection)

Polish immigrants at the doors of their homes, Lowell, Massachusetts, about 1900. (Harvard University Social Ethics Collection)

The wooden three-deckers and the flapping lines of laundry are life's setting for the children of Polish immigrants. (Harvard University Social Ethics Collection)

The mill town is small enough so that Polish children play with children from Irish and Turkish families. (Harvard University Social Ethics Collection)

The dwellings of Polish immigrants lie in the shadows of the factories. (Harvard University Social Ethics Collection)

The mastheads of some Slavic newspapers published in the United States, 1910. (New York Public Library)

Or yet, he might respond to the pull of traditional faith and organize his life within the activities of the Catholic parish. By the same token, a newcomer from the northern districts of Hungary might equally well count himself a Slovak or a Pole.

Events in Europe clarified some of these questions. The Bohemian National Alliance, formed in Chicago in 1914 to collect relief funds for war victims, allied with the leaders of the movement for autonomy in Prague. In the next four years, the Slovaks and the Czech nationalists and Catholics learned to cooperate with one another in support of the new state of Czechoslovakia created in 1918. Smaller groups like the Bulgarians, Lithuanians, and Latvians passed through similar processes of self-discovery.

But diversity of origins complicated developments among southern Slavs. Down to World War I, Croatia and Slovenia were parts of the Austrian empire. Serbia was an independent monarchy, and other provinces occupied an uncertain status in the vacuum left by the slow crumbling of the Turkish empire, of which they had once been a part.

The bulk of the immigrants from these areas were poor peasants, ill prepared for American life. They left tiny farms, cultivated by primitive methods, and plunged directly into an urban industrial world.

A few Dalmatian seamen and Croat peddlers had turned up in the New World before 1880. But the mass migration came after. The decline of the Adriatic fisheries, the spread of phylloxera—a disease that ruined the vineyards—and the prohibition of the raising of goats in order to protect the forests, all combined to diminish peasant incomes. In addition, the requirement of three years' compulsory military service aggrieved the subjects of the Austrian emperor.

Those immigrants able to get to the land did well. Pajaro Valley or New Dalmatia in California was an agricultural paradise. In that state, Mark Rabasa introduced the apple and Steve Mitrovich, the fig. There were also scattered rural settlements in Illinois, Michigan, and

A Bohemian cigarmaker at work in his tenement, 1889. The wife and children help, of course. (Photograph by Jacob A. Riis, Library of Congress)

Poles and Slovaks at Ellis Island. They are looking at tracts distributed by missionaries. (Brown Brothers)

Dalmatian peasant girls. (United Press International)

A young Dalmatian woman in her Sunday best. (United Press International)

Iowa. In California, too, some of these people participated in the tuna and oyster fisheries.

Most South Slavs, however, found employment in the mines and the factories. Since many of the laborers came with the intention of returning to their former homes, there were far more males than females in this migration. As a result, the Slavs were slow to develop a stable family life. Frequently, they lodged in boarding-houses, which they organized on the model of the Zadruga, or communal household, of the Old Country. These lonely, hardworking men, who lacked the company of their own women, too often sought solace in wine and in the transient feminine pleasures available in the red-light districts. Outbursts of rowdyism and disorder earned these immigrants an unfavorable reputation among Americans and reflected the absence of group discipline.

Yet internal divisions prevented the appearance of supporting institutions. The Croats and Slovenes were Catholic; the Serbs, Greek Orthodox; and the Bosnians, Muslims; and each little cluster struggled with its own

Croatian copper miners at Calumet, Michigan. (Emily Balch, *Our Slavic Fellow Citizens*, New York, 1910)

A Croatian saloon in Hibbing, Minnesota. (Emily Balch, *Our Slavic Fellow Citizens,* New York, 1910)

A celebration by a group of Croatians who intend to return to the old country. (E. A. Ross, *The Old World in the New,* New York, 1914)

These three scenes are of a Croatian *zadruga* near Agram, now Zagreb. This communal household consisted of nine men, seven women, and numerous children who worked on the twenty-one-acre farm they held in common. (William P. Shriver, *Immigrant Forces,* New York, 1913)

A Slavic boardinghouse. The men live in crowded quarters while waiting to return or to bring families. (Peter Roberts, *The New Immigration,* New York, 1912)

A Croatian Sokol, or gymnastic society, in Gary, Indiana, where many worked in the steel mills. (William P. Shriver, *Immigrant Forces,* New York, 1913)

A group of marriageable girls arrives in the United States on the S.S. *Baltic,* 1907. (Photograph by Bain, Library of Congress)

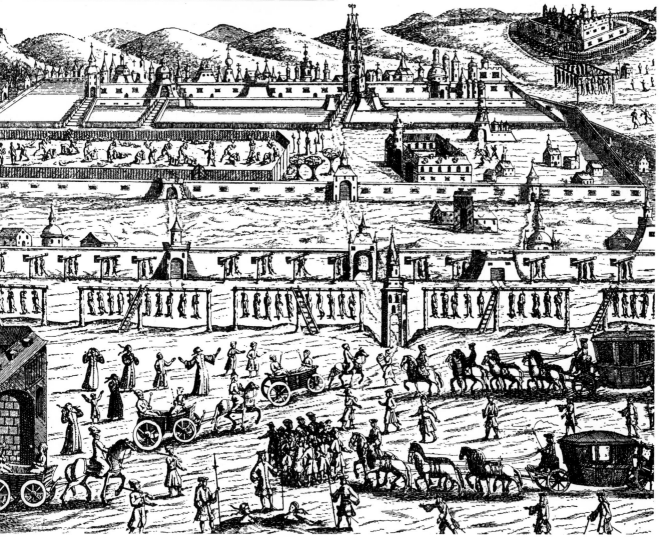

A mass execution under Peter the Great. Some of the dissidents are being hung from the scaffolds in the center and background. Others, as in the foreground, are buried up to their heads, to be trampled by horses. The history of brutality under the czars helps explain the repressive conditions that lasted through the nineteenth century. (J. G. Korb, *Diarium Itineris in Moscoviam,* Vienna, 1700)

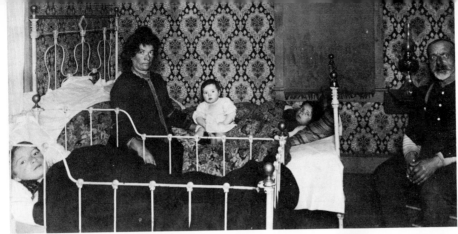

Close quarters—a Russian immigrant family, about 1900. (Harvard University Social Ethics Collection)

A Russian peasant family. The picture to the left shows the home and the spinning wheel; to the right are the children in the field. (John R. Henry, *Some Immigrant Neighbors*, New York, 1912)

parochial problems. Collaboration among them was difficult for smoldering animosities, the origin of which had long since been forgotten, continued to set these people off against one another.

As among the Poles and Czechs, therefore, the process of organization was slow. In 1894 the Croatian Society of the United States established its first branches, and the Slovenians followed a little later. Local benevolent and cultural societies also sprouted, and *Slavenska Sloga* was the first of numerous newspapers. Efforts at union reflected events in Europe. In 1912, the Croats and Serbs of Allegheny City, Pennsylvania, began to meet to protest Austrian and Hungarian oppression, and out of that collaboration grew the Jugo-Slav Republican Alliance, which gave its support to the state that was created at the 1919 Paris Peace Conference. But the patriotic emotions inspired by the war and its aftermath did little to give coherence to the lives of the immigrants.

The Great Russian, White Russian, and Ukrainian immigrants arrived too late to move very far in the process of organization. The czar had not abolished serfdom until the 1860s, and communication with the West remained difficult through the end of the century. Furthermore, the Russian government, while tolerating the departure of Jews, was reluctant to permit the loss of any part of the dominant stock. Movement was consequently difficult. Not until after the failure of the revolution of 1905 did economic modernization and the liberalization of politics produce any substantial current of emigration. Between three hundred thousand and five hundred thousand people arrived in the next decade. Then the war and a successful revolution put an end to the movement. However, some three hundred thousand Russian immigrants remained in the United States in the 1920s, employed in industry, and were just taking the first steps toward organizing their religious and communal life.

Some small groups achieved a high degree of organi-

Immigrant inspection card issued in Russia, 1907. (New York Public Library)

246

Eight Russian orphans arrive in New York, having lost their mothers in a massacre, 1908. (National Park Service, Sherman Collection)

◄

Rumanians dress in their Sunday best, Youngstown, Ohio. (E. A. Ross, *The Old World in the New*, New York, 1914)

►

Three Rumanians arrive in New York, early twentieth century. (National Park Service, Sherman Collection)

A Hungarian family arrives in the United States. (National Park Service, Sherman Collection)

zation more promptly because their previous experience had already armed them with the techniques of self-preservation. The three hundred thousand or so immigrants from the eastern districts of Hungary, on the Russian border, jealously guarded their identity in the Old as in the New World. These Carpatho-Ruthenians were Uniate by religion. They adhered to the Roman Catholic Church and therein differed from the Russians; yet they followed the Greek rite, and their priests were allowed to marry, and here they differed also from the Hungarians. Once in America, the Ruthenians bent every effort to keep their heritage alive.

Distinctive languages and cultures were responsible for the self-awareness of the Hungarians and Rumanians. In Europe, these two groups were already conscious of the differences that separated them from the Slavic peoples around them. They remained so in America, and therefore were relatively quick to organize for their own protection.

Many of the Slavic immigrants in the United States thus varied considerably. The great majority, peasants at home, became industrial laborers after their arrival, though on both sides of the Atlantic they all shared the hardships of earning a bare livelihood. But the extent to which they could absorb the shock of migration depended upon their cultural and social traits, which governed the speed of their adjustment to new conditions.

Immigrants from a Persian region of Turkey, 1907. (Brown Brothers)

5

Out of the Old Ottoman Empire

Through most of the nineteenth century, Turkey was the sick man of Europe. Intrusions by westerners in the Napoleonic era had loosened the sultan's hold over his far-flung territories. Economic, intellectual, and political influences emanating from England, France, Italy, and Germany steadily eroded the basis of his authority; one by one his outlying possessions in Europe and Africa broke away to establish their own national identity. World War I completed the process of contraction. Its conclusion left Turkey with little more than the Anatolian peninsula and the hinterland of Constantinople.

The change unsettled scores of national groups which until then had adjusted to an uncomfortable but tolerable coexistence under the suzerainty of the sultan. The heightened sense of nationalism and the need to locate within the new boundaries forced many families to move. At the same time, the increase in population and economic modernization, as elsewhere, displaced thousands of peasants. Some of the hordes thus thrown in motion found homes in the United States.

The immigrants from Turkey were extraordinarily diverse. The cultural tastes they shared—styles of cooking and music, patterns of leisure, and habits of trade—did not offset the deep divisions between Greeks and Albanians, Turks and Armenians, Syrians and Assyrians. The adjustment each group made depended on its peculiar heritage, the reception it encountered in the New World, and its ability to unite to deal with common problems.

The Greek war for independence (1821–1832) captured the imagination of Americans. The people of that little country who centuries ago had given birth to democracy were now struggling for liberty against a great Oriental despotism. Fervent young men like Samuel Gridley Howe of Boston went off to join the fighting; many others contributed funds. Once free, Greece continued to hold the interest of American missionary societies anxious to spread education and preserve Christianity in the Balkans and the Near East. These attachments created an initial sense of sympathy for immigrants from the region.

Actually, at the end of the nineteenth century, a majority of the Greeks lived not in Greece but were dispersed throughout Asia Minor. The rise of nationalism in the Near East affected them adversely. Many of them, accustomed to operating freely as traders throughout the Turkish empire, now were regarded as aliens in language and religion. Their opportunities shrank, and ultimately they were crowded out of cities like Smyrna, where they had lived for centuries, and driven back to the kingdom of Greece.

But the first to leave Europe were the peasants of Epirus and the Peloponnesus, whose stony fields were incapable of yielding a livelihood to the growing num-

248

Refugees in a Serbian province of Turkey. (*Illustrated London News*, November 25, 1876, New York Public Library)

A Greek and two Turks in Syracuse, New York. (E. A. Ross, *The Old World in the New*, New York, 1914)

A Turk on the streets of New York, 1898. (Photo by E. A. Austin, Library of Congress)

Samuel Gridley Howe. (Engraving by H. W. Smith, Library of Congress)

Greek fugitives. (Painting by Charles L. Eastlake, New York Public Library)

Greek peasants forced out of their ancestral homes in Asia Minor by the hostility of the Turks after the First World War. (Photoworld)

bers dependent on them. More than 80 percent of the population of Greece in 1880 was rural, and was not thriving. Indeed, the situation deteriorated as the century drew to a close. War with Turkey in 1897 led to a burdensome rise in taxes; and the loss of the market for currants, an important cash crop, drove some families to desperation.

The outward movement had started in the 1870s, gaining steadily in momentum thereafter. The opening of direct steamship communications with America by the Hamburg-American and Levant lines after 1900 increased the flow. In all, perhaps five hundred thousand arrived by the time American law restricted their entry in the 1920s.

Some Greeks found employment in the California fisheries, and one group settled down as sponge divers in Tarpon Springs, Florida. But these were exceptions. Nor did many enter agriculture. The times were unpropitious for farmers, and, in any case, most of these immigrants arrived as single men, intending to work for a time and then return to their old homes. Generally, it was only after some period of residence in America that many changed their minds, decided to stay, and sent for their families. Such people were less likely to dream of farms in the West than to seek quick earnings as laborers in the cities.

The largest settlements of Greeks were in New York, Chicago, and Boston, although there were some in almost every large city. A variant of the Italians' padrone system aided their adjustment. Greek immigrants occasionally took construction work or entered the building trades. More often they entered various service occupations, which they soon made their own. They became peddlers, bootblacks, and restaurant workers. The industrious and the lucky saved up the little sums that enabled them to open shops of their own and thus to lift themselves above the ranks of the workers.

A few were extraordinarily successful. Solon Vlasto, for instance, came to New York in 1873 at the age of twenty-one. His first job was in a candy factory, then he became a steamship agent, and finally he moved into the import-export business; the wealth he gained made him a leader among his countrymen. Charles Skouras arrived in Saint Louis just after the turn of the century and held jobs as a newsboy, waiter, and bartender. He sent for his two brothers, and the three of them bought a nickelodeon. By 1926 they were the proud owners of thirty-seven theatres.

The immigrants clung together as a matter of course. They settled in neighborhoods composed of compatriots from their home town or region. There they could congregate sociably in coffeehouses, as they had in the Old Country, learn about job opportunities, and provide a buffer for one another against the strange New World. The first organizations to develop therefore drew their membership from among those already related—by geography, at least—before they left home. Only years of experience in the New World revealed to people of Laconia and Arcadia, of Patras and Tripolis, their common identity as Greeks.

Religion was one tie that drew these people together, for they had struggled for centuries to retain their faith in a Muslim world. In the United States, the Greek Orthodox Church not only preserved the familiar ritual and calendar, but through its afternoon schools communicated the ancestral language to the children. Resources of both money and priests were meager so that the faithful of various provinces had to cooperate, at least in their religious institutions.

Recollection of the long history of struggle against the Turks also tended to stimulate nationalistic emotions. The outbreak of the Balkan Wars in 1912 released a flood of patriotism among the Greek immigrants. Between four and five thousand of them returned home to take up arms. They were encouraged to do so by the Pan Hellenic Union formed in 1907 to draw together all people of Greek antecedents.

Most immigrant institutions stressed national over local ties. Such newspapers as *Neos Kosmos* (Boston) and Vlasto's *Atlantis* (New York) were particularly important in shaping a sense of Greek identity. They conveyed information about the activities of the whole group, regardless of place of origin, and emphasized common cultural and social interests.

The desire to counteract the effects of occasional outbreaks of anti-Greek sentiment also drew the group together. The Greeks were the targets of frequent riots in towns as far apart as Boise, Idaho, and Roanoke, Virginia. The most serious incident occurred in South Omaha, Nebraska, after the murder of a policeman on February 19, 1909. A mass meeting blamed the killing on the Greeks, whereupon a mob descended on the little foreign community in an orgy of vandalism and terror, causing $250,000 in damages and driving a thousand victims out of town. The antipathy toward these immigrants persisted into the 1920s and in time led to the formation of two defensive organizations—the American Hellenic Educational Progressive Association (AHEPA) in 1922 and the Greek American Progressive Association (GAPA) in 1923. Both devoted themselves to the tasks of assimilation and of educating their members in the nature of American democracy. Their growth was evidence that the Greeks had become Greek-Americans, permanently at home in the United States.

Two forceful individuals helped several thousand immigrants from the southern shore of the Adriatic discover that they were a distinctive group—neither Greek nor Slavic, but Albanian. Most of these people were mill workers in eastern Massachusetts; they lived in crowded communal tenements, as some Serbs had, and formed fraternal societies of their own. Then in 1908 Faik Bey Konitza arrived to study at Harvard and established a newspaper, *Dielli*, to serve his countrymen in their own language. At about the same time Fan Sylian Noli came to Boston and was installed as the first bishop of the Autocephalous Albanian Orthodox Church. Together they drew the local groups into a national Pan-Albanian federation. When their homeland became an independent

Greek farmers in California. (Thomas Burgess, *Greeks in America*, Boston, 1913)

Greek slaughterhouse workers in Somerville, Massachusetts. (Thomas Burgess, *Greeks in America*, Boston, 1913)

Greek railway laborers in the West. (Thomas Burgess, *Greeks in America*, Boston, 1913)

A Greek construction gang. (Thomas Burgess, *Greeks in America*, Boston, 1913)

Greek girls arrive to marry husbands, most of whom they have never met, 1921. Courtships were carried on by mail and by an exchange of photographs. (United Press International)

Young Greeks Educational Association, Chicago. (Thomas Burgess, *Greeks in America*, Boston, 1913)

The track team of the Greek-American Athletic Club, New York. (Thomas Burgess, *Greeks in America*, Boston, 1913)

Patriotic Greeks apply for passports to go back to serve their country during the Balkan War, 1912. (Photoworld)

A group of immigrants poses before a Greek restaurant. (Brown Brothers)

A Greek wedding party in Newark, New Jersey. (Thomas Burgess, *Greeks in America*, Boston, 1913)

The dedication of the Greek Orthodox Cemetery in Waterbury, Connecticut. (Peter Roberts, *The New Immigration*, New York, 1912)

The council of the Pan-Hellenic Union. (Thomas Burgess, *Greeks in America*, Boston, 1913)

Advertisements in *Atlantis*, 1895.

Albanian weekly published in Boston, 1906.

Members of the Order of AHEPA call on President Harry S. Truman, 1945. Solon J. Vlasto is at the President's left. (United Press International)

Two Albanian immigrants. (National Park Service, Sherman Collection)

Bishop Fan S. Noli of the Albanian Orthodox Church of America prays for help for his native land on the invasion by Italy in 1939. (United Press International)

Armenians in their clubroom in New York, early twentieth century. (Photoworld)

Rival Armenian factions battle one another in Boston, 1934. (United Press International)

In New York, an Armenian girl busy at traditional embroidery, about 1915. (Photoworld)

Armenian silk weavers in a modern mill in the United States. (Library of Congress)

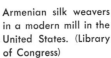

country after the First World War, several thousand residents of Massachusetts returned home to take part in its government. But enough remained to perpetuate the group in the United States. Like the Macedonians, Turks, and Assyrians, they formed little enclaves, permanently situated in their new homes.

The Armenians and Syrians were more numerous, each group numbering about one hundred thousand. The Armenian provinces had long been divided between Russia and Turkey, yet a common language and a common religion united the Armenian people. Toward the end of the nineteenth century, a movement for national independence gained considerable support. The nationalists did not shrink from violence and evoked a ruthless response from the Turks, which culminated in the massacre of some three hundred thousand victims in 1894. Subsequent persecution induced many terrorized families to flee.

In the United States most of the Armenians became laborers who worked in the mills of the eastern cities and lived in communal tenements until their women joined them. A few brought skilled crafts in silk and rug weaving with them, and there was a notable group of farmers around Fresno, California, who introduced the casaba melon to the New World. But it was the number of business people who participated in the migration that distinguished the Armenians from other arrivals in the United States. Commercial skills previously acquired and an exceptionally high literacy rate enabled many to prosper.

Their status as a minority in the Old Country had accentuated in these people a consciousness of their separate identity. Like the Greeks in Asia Minor, they had been interspersed among other peoples. Only strong communal institutions and solid family, business, and religious ties had kept them from being assimilated into the societies around them. Some of the protective habits they developed in the Old World proved useful in their adjustment to the New. *Hairenik,* an influential paper published from 1899 on, first in New York and then in Boston, repeatedly stressed the need for cohesiveness. Yet the impact of nationalism for a long time deflected the Armenian immigrants from unifying in America. The benevolent societies they joined were branches of organizations with headquarters in Paris or Cairo, dedicated to achieving an Armenian state and not very sensitive to American problems. And conflicts between the representatives of the Dashnag and Hunchagist parties, each with its own platform for Armenian aspirations abroad, kept communities in the United States in turmoil long after 1930.

The Syrians in America were also divided, but for religious rather than for political reasons. Among the arrivals from that Turkish province after 1890 were peasants, laborers, and traders who took jobs in the mills or traveled about as peddlers of dry goods and notions. A bit of capital enabled some of them to open shops in which they sold groceries, candy, linens, and lace. Washington Street in New York became known as Little Syria, and there were smaller communities in Boston, Philadelphia, Fall River, Toledo, and Detroit.

The Syrians brought with them a variety of faiths, all equally strange to the United States. Melkite and Maronite Catholics, Moslems, Druzes, and communicants of the Orthodox churches as well as Protestants found themselves associated in the process of migration. The Arabic language was the common element among these people, but it was not a force strong enough to draw them together. Significantly, such newspapers as *Al-Hoda* and *Meraat-ul Gharb* remained connected with one religious group or another. The United Syrian Organization, which attempted to bring together all these people, did not approach in importance the local societies named after the particular towns of origin.

Thus, the Syrians reflected the nature of the Ottoman society they had left—internally divided and unable to meet the challenges of modernization without strain. In the United States the former subjects of the Turkish empire tended to fly apart and to depend upon local and family ties. They were therefore slow to discover the methods of group action unless stimulated to do so—as were the Greeks and Armenians—by recollections of having been minorities in the Old World.

An Armenian from Turkey dispenses orange drinks from the tank over his shoulder in the Turkish fashion on Orchard Street, New York. (Photoworld)

A tenement occupied by Syrians in Chicago, about 1900. (Harvard University Social Ethics Collection)

Street scene in the Syrian, Turkish, and Armenian section of New York City at Washington and Rector streets, 1930. (The National Archives)

◄

A Syrian woman arrives in the United States about 1910. (Brown Brothers)

A narrow alley leads away from the street to the home of Syrians in Lowell, Massachusetts. (Harvard University Social Ethics Collection) ►

Wooden Syrian dwellings, about 1900. (Harvard University Social Ethics Collection)

Syrian food vendors in New York City, early twentieth century. (Library of Congress)

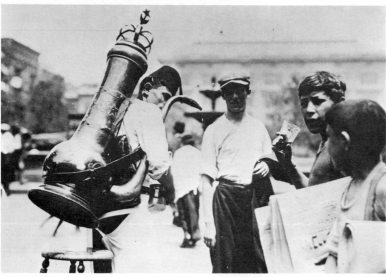

A Syrian selling cold drinks in New York, about 1910. (Photograph by Bain, Library of Congress)

A Syrian restaurant and lodging house on Washington Street, New York, 1894. (Drawing by W. Bengough, Nostalgia Press, Inc.)

St. Joseph's in Lee Street, the first French-Canadian Church in the Archdiocese of Boston, 1868.

6

From Across the Borders

Although Europe remained the chief source of immigration to the United States, additional currents from within the Western Hemisphere joined the flow after 1880. There were Canadians, Mexicans, and West Indians, who retained enough ties to their nearby birth places to affect significantly their adjustment to life in the United States.

There had always been a good deal of movement, in both directions, across the unguarded border between the United States and Canada. By 1870 about five hundred thousand natives of the Dominion had become residents of the Republic. The number increased steadily thereafter. In 1930 it was more than 1.25 million. Among these immigrants, those of British stock were scarcely visible. Some of them simply blended with the native American population; others developed associations with the English and Scottish immigrants close to them in culture and habits.

The French-speaking newcomers from Quebec, however, stood apart. The crowded little farms of that province had never afforded their occupants a rich livelihood; in the 1870s, the rewards of labor were hardly adequate to sustain the large families of these devout Catholics. Increasingly the young men looked to the south, and once a few of them had tried their fortune in Massachusetts and Rhode Island, word got about quickly: there was more work and better wages across the border. Soon a fever—*le mal des États-Unis*—spread throughout the townships, and thousands joined the migration.

Most of the newcomers settled in New England where they took jobs in the textile mills and other factories. They developed solid communities, within which a stubborn loyalty to the language and to the Catholic Church sustained an autonomous culture. The eleven journals they regularly published in New England in 1900 were a sign of the group's cohesion. There were clusters in such big cities as Boston, Fall River, and Manchester, and a few outposts in Kansas, Illinois, and Michigan.

Their proximity to home enabled these newcomers to preserve their group identity long after they settled down. Individuals traveled back and forth, and families maintained connections across the border. Organizations like l'Union Saint-Jean Baptiste and l'Association Canada-Américaine had branches on both sides of the frontier. The communities in the United States turned to Quebec, and also to France and Belgium, for priests to serve in their churches and teachers to conduct their parochial schools. Although the French-Canadians became an influential political force in some localities,

Cover of *Charette's March*, published in Lowell, Massachusetts, 1898, to honor a naval hero of the Spanish-American War and recipient of the Congressional Medal of Honor.

Lumbermen in northern New England, early twentieth century. (Harvard University Social Ethics Collection)

they were far from having merged with the rest of the population by 1930.

A somewhat similar movement operated from across the southern border. There had been a Spanish-speaking population in the Southwest ever since the acquisitions of the Mexican War. The position of these Hispanos changed little until the twentieth century when they were joined by Spanish-speaking people of quite another sort —poor Mexican immigrants.

Profound changes in their own society set the Mexicans moving. The Revolution of 1910 touched off two decades of political conflict and uncertainty. Moreover, in the same period, the modernization of agriculture weakened communal controls over the land and displaced many peasants. Some of them wandered to the cities; others made an even longer journey north to take jobs as agricultural laborers in the United States.

Conditions were ripe for their reception. Commercial farming was replacing the family homestead, particularly in the Southwest; and the growers of fruits and vegetables, of cotton and sugar beets, felt a seasonal need for hands at harvest time. Furthermore, Mexicans, like other residents of the Western Hemisphere, were exempt from restrictive quotas that excluded Europeans and Orientals after 1920. The resulting demand for labor lent an impetus to the northward movement.

A substantial visa fee imposed in 1925 limited the number who entered legally, but this simply forced others to cross the border surreptitiously. The number of wetbacks who filtered into the United States was never known precisely, but it was certainly large.

Ninety percent of the Mexican immigrants lived in Texas, California, Arizona, New Mexico, and Colorado, and there was also a colony in Chicago. Concentrated in their own districts "across the tracks," they remained largely apart from the dominant culture about them. Very few troubled to become American citizens or indeed were conscious of having changed countries by coming north. They preserved in the United States not only the language and culture of the land of their birth but also the habits of poverty.

Yet patterns of life that were tolerable in a village in Michoacán had disastrous consequences in the United States. The traditional Mexican family structure could not withstand the shock of migratory labor or industrial society. The birth rate remained high, but children dropped out of school early so that opportunities were closed to them. Frugality and the habits of saving were alien to these people, and this further hurt their chances. Without hope, there was little incentive to resist the temptations of gambling, drink, drugs, and petty thievery. Mexicans also suffered from a protein deficiency and from high rates of tuberculosis and infant mortality.

French-Canadian immigrants are the tenants of this grim wooden barracks in Lowell, Massachusetts, about 1900. (Harvard University Social Ethics Collection)

"Little Canada"—the French-Canadian district of a mill town, about 1900. (Harvard University Social Ethics Collection)

Snow covers the tenement's dirt, but adds to the hardships of the mill town poor. (Harvard University Social Ethics Collection)

Youngsters are much on their own in "Little Canada." (Harvard University Social Ethics Collection)

Clotheslines are ubiquitous where French-Canadian children play, about 1900. (Harvard University Social Ethics Collection)

Mexican-Americans in San Antonio, Texas, 1875. (New York Public Library)

Mexican and Chinese mingle in California. (*Harper's Monthly*, December, 1882, New York Public Library)

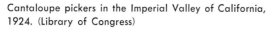

Cantaloupe pickers in the Imperial Valley of California, 1924. (Library of Congress)

A copper town in Clifton, Arizona, 1903. (Library of Congress)

Natives of Nevada, 1906. (Library of Congress)

Mexican cotton pickers on a Texas plantation, 1919. (United Press International)

Mexican immigrants packing broccoli. (United States Department of Agriculture)

Labor officials from the United States and Mexico discuss methods of preventing illegal immigration, 1925. (United Press International)

Cuban women workers in a cigar factory. (Photoworld)

These immigrants from Guadeloupe, French West Indies, arrived on the S.S. *Korona*, 1911. (National Park Service, Sherman Collection)

Mexican immigrants were unable to break out of their cycle of poverty because a large percentage of them depended on migratory labor, wintering in the city and then following the crops across the country. Only slowly did they begin to find more stable jobs, as track laborers, or in steel mills, packing plants, and tanneries. The inability to settle down and the closeness of Mexico delayed the adjustment to new conditions and inhibited the development of communal institutions. Occasional strikes, as by the Imperial Valley fruit pickers in 1928, brought some gains. But efforts to organize a federation of mutual-benefit societies or a labor union came to nothing. The promoters were too influenced by Mexican models and inadequately aware of the different situation in the United States.

World War I and exemption from the quota laws also stimulated a small movement out of the West Indies. Some Cuban cigar workers had come to Key West, Florida, earlier. But after 1914 the flow increased and included mostly colored people. These newcomers settled in port cities like Boston and New York, where they formed a group or, rather, groups—distinct not only from the dominant whites, but also from native American Negroes.

The Puerto Ricans were sometimes counted in this category although they were American citizens and, properly speaking, not immigrants. More distinctive were the natives of Haiti, Martinique, and Guadeloupe, many of them workers in the fur industry, who clung together out of the desire to preserve their French culture.

Most numerous were the arrivals from the British West Indies. The American Negroes generally considered these "monkey chasers" uppity and aggressive, resenting the success of the newcomers in business and their intrusion into the professions. Small local associations drew together the people from Nevis or Jamaica or Trinidad.

The best-known West Indian of the 1920s was Marcus Garvey, a printer who arrived from Jamaica in 1916, bringing with him the dream of returning to Africa, through which the colored men of the Western Hemisphere would achieve liberation. His Universal Negro Improvement Association at its peak enrolled several million members, supported a newspaper, and struggled to develop a black economy complete with its own shops, factories, and steamship line. Garvey, pending the blacks' return to their homeland, also proclaimed himself provisional president of Africa, and established a court and an army. All these dreams collapsed when the U.N.I.A. ran into financial difficulties and Garvey was imprisoned in 1925 for using the mails to defraud. The response to Garvey's scheme revealed the desperation of many American Negroes. But Garvey's ideas were the products of his Caribbean upbringing.

Paradoxically, as with the Mexicans and Canadians, the proximity of the West Indians to the countries they left affected their adjustment to the society they entered. These immigrants encountered problems analogous to those of other newcomers to the United States. But the shock of migration was not as decisive as for Europeans; the people who crossed the nearby borders were not immediately aware of the change in their situation.

Workers from the Bahamas sort and pack celery at a Belle Glade, Florida, plant, where they help meet a local labor shortage. (United States Department of Agriculture)

Jamaican bean pickers at a farm in Madison County, New York. (United States Department of Agriculture)

The S.S. *General Goethals*, purchased by Garvey and the Universal Negro Improvement Association to carry back Negroes to Liberia. Crowds paid 50 cents per person to go aboard and inspect the boat. (Photoworld)

Marcus Garvey and his staff in full regalia. (Brown Brothers)

Commodore Matthew C. Perry lands at Gore-
Hama, 1853, to open Japan to the West.
(United Press International)

7

The Japanese and Other Orientals

The Orientals who trickled into the United States between 1880 and 1930 shared many of the characteristics of the European immigrants. Most of the Far Easterners, like their European counterparts, were agriculturists who came temporarily to earn some money to take home. But they, too, in time settled down, sent for their wives, and built institutions to help them in their permanent transfer to the New World. Like many of the European immigrants in the half century after 1880, the Orientals suffered from the developing racism and xenophobia in American society, but to a greater degree because of the visibility of their physical characteristics.

Dislike of the Chinese led in 1882 to a federal law excluding them for a period of ten years; when the measure expired, Congress made the bar permanent. The coolies, it was charged, were able to subsist on such a low standard of living and were so unwilling to adopt the habits of the country in which they were sojourners, that it was best to prevent any more of them from entering the United States. Americans justified the exclusion of Chinese immigrants by what they considered their shortcomings, rather than because of an antipathy to all Orientals.

In fact, for a while, many Americans regarded the Japanese most favorably. Under Commodore Perry in 1854, the United States had opened the mikado's islands

to Western influence, and therefore stood in a special relationship to the people thus freed from centuries of isolation. American missionaries and technical-aid experts helped in the process of development with which they sympathized. The rapid modernization of the Nipponese seemed almost American in quality; yet there were also the romantic associations with the land of cherry blossoms, expressed in the writings of Lafcadio Hearn and in such short stories as John L. Long's "Madame Butterfly," which was the basis for Belasco's dramatization and for the libretto of Puccini's opera.

At the start of the twentieth century, these sympathies were still firm. Americans applauded the Japanese victories in the wars against China and Russia, evidence that a modern power, though small, could whip old despotisms, though great.

There had been little concern in the United States therefore at the arrival of a few hundred Japanese annually—from 1885 on, when the mikado's government relaxed its rules against emigration. Only about twelve thousand had come by the end of the century. The men arrived first as laborers, and when they were settled, the women followed. The number increased after 1900; about ninety thousand entered the country between 1901 and 1910.

The Japanese settled down to a stable family life, the

John L. Long. (New York Public Library)

A group of Japanese immigrants arriving at Vancouver, Canada, on the way to California. (Brown Brothers)

Japanese farm workers in California. (Brown Brothers)

great majority finding homes in California. They played a useful role in agriculture and opened thriving businesses. Prone to imitating the Americans, they were eager to educate their children in the ways of their adopted country.

The associations they formed aimed to ease their settlement. Prefectural clubs, labor unions, newspapers, farmers' cooperatives, and mutual-aid societies helped them deal with specific economic and social problems. Like other immigrants, they wished to preserve the language and religion of their old homeland; to do so they supported shrines and afternoon schools that taught Japanese. But even those were adapted to the American context rather than simply transferred from Japan.

The other Asian immigrants, the Hindus and the Filipinos, were even less numerous than the Japanese and at first no more troublesome. Perhaps six thousand Hindus appeared along the Pacific Coast in the first decade of the twentieth century. Mostly Sikhs from the Punjab, they were migrant laborers in the rice and cotton fields of the Sacramento and Imperial valleys of California. A few also found jobs in Oregon lumber mills. A handful of temples and the Khalsa Divan, a mutual-aid society, were their first steps toward communal organization.

As for the Filipinos, American expansion in the Pacific opened the way to the appearance of a few thou-

The ranch of a prosperous Japanese farmer in Florin, California. (Sidney L. Gulick, *The American Japanese Problem*, New York, 1914)

Japanese picking celery in California. (Photoworld)

Left, above and below: Japanese farm laborers in California picking strawberries and packing them for shipment. (Sidney L. Gulick, *The American Japanese Problem*, New York, 1914)

Japanese immigrants in Downey, California, 1913. (National Park Service, Oshiki Collection)

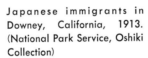

Hindu farm workers in California. (Brown Brothers)

The pupils of a Japanese school in California. The children studied in the public schools during the regular hours and went to the Japanese school in the late afternoon to learn the language of their parents. (Sidney L. Gulick, *The American Japanese Problem*, New York, 1914)

East Indian immigrants arriving in the United States. (Brown Brothers)

Arizona farmers hold a mass meeting to force out Japanese and Hindu farmers from the Salt River Valley, 1934. (United Press International)

Filipino leaders meet to resist the efforts to limit immigration from the Philippines, 1935. (United Press International)

Filipino lettuce cutters in the Imperial Valley of California, 1939. (Photograph by Dorothea Lange for the Farm Security Administration, Library of Congress)

A Filipino and a Mexican worker bunching carrots. (United States Department of Agriculture)

sand who found employment along the Pacific Coast. Some of these Spanish-speaking Catholics, Malay by origin, came by way of Hawaii. Others came directly, among them *pensionados*—students on government fellowships. Their numbers increased markedly after World War I. Many had enlisted in the United States Navy in Manila and, once exposed to the life of the mainland, wished to remain. Others were attracted by jobs in Idaho, California, Oregon, and Washington, where there were demands for hands to pick apples, beets, hops, and potatoes. Still others became porters and domestic servants. Yet the total never rose much above fifty thousand.

Filipino soldiers who fought for the United States receive American citizenship in a ceremony at Fort Dix, New Jersey, 1942. (United Press International)

President Harry S. Truman signs an amendment to the immigration law that extends the right of citizenship to Filipinos and East Indians already in the United States and assigns annual immigration quotas of 100 each to the Philippines and to India, 1946. (United Press International)

After 1900 the criticisms once leveled at the Chinese were increasingly directed against all Orientals. The mixture of stocks created no difficulty in Hawaii. But in California, the presence of the Asians became a political issue; prejudice against the Japanese mounted steadily and spread in time to make victims of all non-Europeans.

There had been some calls for the exclusion of the Nipponese in 1901. But the question became serious in 1905 when Mayor Eugene E. Schmitz and Abraham Ruef, the bosses of the dominant San Francisco political machine, ordered ninety-three Japanese children into segregated schools. They did so in order to divert attention from the findings of a grand jury then investigating the misdeeds of the municipal government. But the calls to prejudice found a responsive audience, and anti-Japanese sentiments spread like wildfire.

The commotion embarrassed the national administration, which had been working for a diplomatic understanding with Japan in the interest of collaboration in the Far East. President Theodore Roosevelt, eager to soothe ruffled feelings in Tokyo without antagonizing California voters, sponsored an informal "Gentlemen's Agreement" in 1907–1908, by which the Japanese government undertook to prevent laborers from leaving for the United States in return for assurance that American law would not stigmatize the mikado's subjects as inferiors. Such voluntary restraint did not, however, appease the prejudiced on the Pacific Coast. Local land and school statutes discriminated against the Japanese, and, periodically, fulminations in the press and from the podium warned that the "little yellow men" were bringing in picture brides with the intention of multiplying to take over the country.

The hatred spread to other Orientals as well. Between 1907 and 1910 there were sporadic riots against the "ragheads," as the Hindus were called, in Washington, California, and Oregon. Resentment against Filipinos, too, flared out in a variety of forms. California authorities, for instance, held that such people were Mongolians, and refused to license their marriage to whites. Labor pressed for their exclusion.

Since the Filipinos were nationals of the United States, they could not be barred until 1935 when the Philippines became a commonwealth. But there were no such inhibitions when it came to other Asians. Congress responded to this prejudice in 1917 when it created the "Asiatic barred zone," all natives of which were denied admission to the United States. The culminating measure was the abrogation of the Gentlemen's Agreement by the Immigration Act of 1924, which formally excluded Japanese immigrants. Since none were actually en route, congressional action simply expressed a desire to state openly that the United States regarded yellow men as inferior and did not want them.

These acts of prejudice blocked efforts to develop understanding between the United States and Japan. Moreover, they complicated the adjustment of the immigrants already here. Rejection by American society came as a profound shock to those who had been eager to conform to the ways of their adopted country. Hostility forced them to look inward, to withdraw to the closed circle of the group and the family, and, to some extent, even to turn their sights back to Tokyo in the quest for guidance. Significantly, the sense of having been rejected by the Americans increased the immigrants' dependence upon Japan. After 1908, for instance, the Japanese Association strengthened its ties with the mikado's government.

The mounting determination to halt the immigration of Asians was not simply an expression of color prejudice, significant though that was. The emotions that led some Americans to call for the exclusion of Japanese and to riot against Hindus were also feeding a demand for an end to all immigration. Unanticipated conditions of life on the prairies and in the slums lent some plausibility to the argument that the United States in the twentieth century had arrived at a point at which the policies of the eighteenth century were no longer viable.

Japanese students in a California public school. This photograph was used by both the opponents and supporters of Japanese immigration to the United States. The anti-Japanese argued that it shows the menace of the invasion. The defenders of the newcomers argued that it shows the extent of their Americanization. (Sidney L. Gulick, *The American Japanese Problem,* New York, 1914)

Japanese laborers arriving in Hawaii, 1900. This old photograph was long used by anti-Japanese propagandists as evidence that immigrants were still entering the country after 1908 despite the Gentlemen's Agreement. (Sidney L. Gulick, *The American Japanese Problem,* New York, 1914)

Hindu immigrants. (E. A. Ross, *The Old World in the New,* New York, 1914)

An anti-Japanese campaign seeks to prevent the immigrants from settling in Hollywood, California, 1923. (United Press International)

JAPS KEEP MOVING THIS IS A WHITE MAN'S NEIGHBORHOOD.

Peasants in the great plains of eastern Europe found similarities to their homeland in the American West. (E. A. Steiner, *On the Trail of the Immigrant*, New York, 1906)

An immigrant camp in the West. (*Harper's Monthly*, October, 1879, New York Public Library)

8

The Prairie and the Metropolis

The social experience of the immigrants of the late nineteenth century had many similarities to that of their predecessors. The newcomers of the 1880s, like those of the 1840s, had to earn a livelihood, learn to manage households under unfamiliar conditions, and restructure their communities in a strange environment. But, in addition, the later arrivals also had to deal with unique problems created by the novel settings in which many of them lived. Both the Great Plains and the growing metropolitan cities imposed harsh requirements on the farmers and the industrial laborers who made their homes there after 1880. The strain long affected the adjustment between the immigrants and their adopted country.

However different Illinois and Wisconsin had been from Germany or Scandinavia, those American territories had still borne enough similarities to the places the immigrants had left so that there was some continuity in their lives. The prairies of the Great Plains, now fully open to the newcomers, were totally different. Treeless and flat, they stretched monotonously into the distance, offering their human occupants no familiar features to ease the strain of strangeness. Completely apart from the economic difficulties of fluctuating prices and

drought and capricious transportation costs, the farmers suffered from the harsh personal effects of the prairie environment. The railroads accelerated the speed of settlement and scattered people across great distances. The resulting loneliness oppressed all the settlers in the region, but particularly those who came from the close-knit villages of the Old World.

The metropolis was also a novel setting for human experience. The millions of people heaped together in New York were as ill prepared for the city as it was for them. The unprecedented density of settlement in the slums disorganized the residents. The districts in which the immigrant laborers lived became the breeding ground of poverty and of the attendant forms of delinquency. And the disease and crime that flourished there threatened to spread and infect the whole society. Such difficulties were general and occurred in cities with relatively few, as well as in those with many, foreign-born. But the effects were more visible, if not more virulent, among the immigrants.

Many Americans—old stock and new—retained their faith in the promised land. Those who did not yield to xenophobia looked beyond the immediate tribulations

Breaking the prairie in Nebraska. (New York Public Library)

Covered wagons crossing the Arkansas River. (*Harper's Monthly,* September, 1862, New York Public Library)

A pioneer home in Aberdeen, South Dakota, 1882. (Library of Congress)

Homesteaders await the opening of the Cherokee Strip on September 16, 1893. Thousands of home seekers all over the United States came for the signal that would send them into the territory where free land was available for the most fortunate arrivals. (Chicago, Rock Island & Pacific Railroad)

A settler's home in North Dakota, 1908. (Library of Congress)

A hot night on the East Side, 1893. The painting by Anthony gives a forceful impression of the dense residential life of the city. (New-York Historical Society)

The street is the children's playground. (United Press International)

A New York slum about 1890. (Photo by Jacob A. Riis, Library of Congress)

Faith in the New World. The drawing shows immigrants of all nationalities welcomed by Uncle Sam to the United States ark of refuge where they exchanged oppression for freedom. (Colored lithograph by Joseph Keppler in *Puck*, April 28, 1880, New-York Historical Society)

Mullen's Alley near Cherry Street, about 1888. (Photo by Jacob A. Riis, Library of Congress)

Children of nineteen different nationalities line up in a display of patriotism at Public School No. 1, Henry and Oliver streets, New York, 1926. (United Press International)

of the times and perceived a new and better land taking form out of the sacrifices of the moment. Some of them grasped the figure of speech made popular by Israel Zangwill's play *The Melting Pot* and conceived of their country as a crucible, from which would emerge the real American, "the fusion of all races, the coming superman." Others, critics like Randolph Bourne and Horace Kallen, were even more optimistic; the various elements that flowed into the nation would not lose their identity or be reduced to a flat uniformity, but would add richness and variety to a pluralistic whole.

Such people took heart from neighborhoods like that of Harlem in 1920, where twenty-seven nationalities coexisted without open conflict. A venturesome walker through those streets could see signs of the presence of old-stock Americans as well as Germans and Irish of an earlier era. But he would also meet Negroes beginning to move into the area and pass the shops of Chinese laundrymen, Gypsy phrenologists, and Greek and Syrian grocers. He would traverse blocks occupied by Italians,

Jews, and Turks, and become aware of little clusters of Finns, Russians, Rumanians, Swedes, and Yugoslavs.

There were problems. But the optimistic Americans who witnessed or read about the deterioration of life in the prairies and the slums regarded the problems as a challenge and responded by enlisting in the armies of reform. They determined to redeem American society either through politics or through direct action. The populists and progressives who sought through education, cooperation, conservation, scientific methods, and regulatory laws to ease the common difficulties of life on the prairies did not have to distinguish between native and immigrant farmers.

But the life of the foreign-born in the cities presented reformers with a distinctive problem. Moved to action by books that revealed how the other half lived, devoted men and women came to the slums to Americanize and also assist the children of the newcomers. Toynbee Hall in London furnished a model, but the American settlement houses adapted themselves to local conditions.

273

Horace M. Kallen, right, presents a certificate of merit to Oscar R. Ewing, federal security administrator, for leadership in the fight for betterment of the lot of the common man. Michael A. Stavitsky, president of the American Association for Jewish Education, looks on, 1950. (United Press International)

The Upper East Side, East 112th Street, New York, 1922. (United Press International)

A scene in the shadow of the Sixth Avenue El. The pessimists were dismayed at "the mongrel mixture of humanity"; the optimists were pleased by the richness and variety of the pluralistic whole. (New York Public Library)

Harlem before the First World War—125th Street, New York City, 1911. (Brown Brothers)

Harlem, looking south on Lenox Avenue, 1927. (United Press International)

An evening school in New York—twenty-seven nationalities were represented in the class. (New York Public Library)

A one-room school for scholars of all ages, 1910. (Library of Congress)

An Americanization class for steelworkers. (Photoworld)

The entrance to Toynbee Hall, London. (Harvard University Social Ethics Collection)

Stanton Coit's Neighborhood Guild (1886) in New York, Jane Addams's Hull-House (1889) in Chicago, Robert A. Woods's South End House (1891) in Boston, and Lillian Wald's Henry Street Settlement (1893) in New York were the best known of these efforts.

The immigrants themselves, in time, came to seek their own means of resolving their problems. When a second generation appeared, familiar with the English language and with American institutions, it was possible to begin to think of using trade unions and political parties to improve the conditions of life in the city and on the farm.

Between 1900 and 1930 such influences began to transform the relations of people to their government. In the West, the progressive movement focused upon preservation of natural and human resources and upon the regulation of big business. In the eastern industrial states, the sons of Irish immigrants like David I. Walsh of Massachusetts and Alfred E. Smith of New York and of German newcomers like Robert Wagner of New York struggled for measures such as workmen's compensation and factory and tenement-house inspection. But by the time these reforms became effective, serious doubts were also being raised about the validity of the whole concept of immigration.

Jane Addams, 1914. (Library of Congress)

The beckoning lights of Hull House, fifty years after its founding, 1941. (United Preses International)

The library of Hull House, Chicago. (Harvard University Social Ethics Collection)

The textile room in Hull House, Chicago. (Harvard University Social Ethics Collection)

An English class in a Chicago settlement house. (Harvard University Social Ethics Collection)

Lillian Wald. (Library of Congress)

Play in the schoolyard. (Henry Street Settlement—Urban Life Center)

A street festival in New York. (Henry Street Settlement—Urban Life Center)

Senator David I. Walsh of Massachusetts. (Library of Congress)

Even the older people learn English. (Henry Street Settlement—Urban Life Center)

Learning and playing in the settlement house class. (Henry Street Settlement—Urban Life Center)

Alfred E. Smith. On his right is Lillian Wald, on his left, Mrs. James Delano Roosevelt, mother of the President, 1934. (United Press International)

Robert F. Wagner, 1916. (Library of Congress)

The effects of unrestricted immigration—the Yankee, a curiosity in his own country, surrounded by foreign types. *(Frank Leslie's Illustrated Newspaper, September 8, 1888, Library of Congress)*

9
Closing the Gates

Not all Americans were optimistic. At the end of the nineteenth century, apart from the Oriental question, some doubters began to challenge the premises of the traditional policy of open immigration. The founders of the Republic had possessed the resources of an empty continent, and therefore had welcomed all who wished to come. Furthermore, with the slave trade ended, the arrivals of the revolutionary era had for the most part originated in countries with cultures very much like that of the United States. It had therefore not been necessary during Jefferson's generation to test the belief that any man could become an American. Were the same assumptions valid a century later when the country seemed fully populated and when the people crowding through its gates seemed totally alien to its way of life?

Earlier expressions of hostility to the foreign-born had not questioned the merits of immigration. The Know-Nothings of the 1850s, for example, had sought to restrict the political power of the immigrants and of the Catholic Church but had not expected to choke off the flow of newcomers.

But by the end of the nineteenth century serious men entertained the suggestion that the policy of open gates had outlived its usefulness. It was tempting to locate the source of the nation's problems in the alien elements that had penetrated. The faults of the time, they argued, were not due to defects inherent in the nation. Low wages, slum housing, overcrowded cities, intemperance, disregard for the Sabbath, the pervasiveness of vice, and crime and corruption in politics were all linked with the foreigners, just as the inadequacy of the currency and speculation were linked to the international bankers. The conclusion seemed to follow that the cure to all these ills lay in putting an end to the endless flow of newcomers, or at least in being selective about those admitted.

A respectable scientific theory offered the justification for a change in policy. Mankind, some biologists argued, consisted not of the descendants of a single pair of ancestors, as the Bible had asserted. Rather, the evolutionary process had generated a variety of biologically distinct races, some superior to others. The United

279

A Question of Labor. The drawing by W. A. Rogers shows an Irishman imported duty free by the great trusts to compete with American labor, while the articles the workingman uses are heavily taxed for the benefit of the monopolists. *(Harper's Weekly,* September 29, 1888, Nostalgia Press, Inc.)

With Uncle Sam's Compliments. A hostile drawing by W. A. Rogers suggests the return of assisted immigrants to Great Britain. *(Harper's Weekly,* June 25, 1887, Nostalgia Press, Inc.)

An early anti-episcopal cartoon. The picture shows New Englanders repulsing an effort to land a bishop in the New World. Fear of any kind of bishops long kept anti-Catholic sentiment alive. *(Political Register, 1768, Library of Congress)*

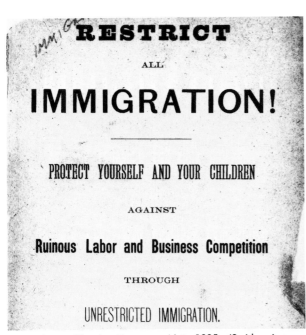

An anti-immigration pamphlet, 1885. (Smithsonian Collection of Business Americana)

The threat of immigration to American culture—at the left, the Catholic bishop threatens the public schools, at the right, American children worship at strange altars. *(Harper's Weekly,* August 30, 1873, Library of Congress)

States had been the handiwork of first-rate Anglo-Saxon or Teutonic peoples, and its institutions had been appropriate to their genius. The difficulties of the late nineteenth century were the results of the influx into the country of inferior breeds incapable of ever adjusting to American conditions.

A gigantic report by a government commission in 1911 seemed to supply the evidence for the biological argument. Few Americans read the forty-two-volume report with sufficient care to see through its prejudices. Most accepted the assurances of reporters that these tomes proved that the new immigrants—different from and inferior to the old—were responsible for the nation's ills. The remedy was clear: reduction in the total number of immigrants admitted and the exclusion of the races unfit for life in the Republic.

These ideas gained strength steadily. The Immigration Restriction League, founded in 1894, launched an educational campaign for the new policy. It evoked a favorable response in New England, a section which had already changed radically and which feared the effect of further migration. Southerners, their concern with race deepened by the problems of living with the freed Negroes, also tended to accept the restrictionist arguments. Conflicts between supporters of public and parochial schools, such as in Wisconsin and Illinois, revived anti-Catholic emotions and increased the membership of the American Protective Association (A.P.A.). In the 1890s, too, old stereotypes about the Jews began to acquire an anti-Semitic tone. An end to immigration would limit the number of Catholics and Jews. Finally, many skilled laborers and artisans were persuaded by the argument that restriction would end competition

with the foreign-born. Those favoring a change in policy may not have amounted to a majority of the population. But they carried increasing weight in Congress.

Immigration legislation in the nineteenth century had simply aimed to regulate the conditions of entry and to exclude obviously unfit applicants such as lunatics, polygamists, anarchists, the diseased, and persons likely to become a public charge. But the restrictionists sought a different kind of control and turned first to the device of a literacy test, which they assumed would be a reliable measure of the potentiality for citizenship. Congress three times yielded to such demands, in 1896, 1913, and 1915, only to see the bills vetoed by Presidents Cleveland, Taft, and Wilson, who objected to the radical departure from American policy.

When the literacy test was finally enacted in 1917 over President Wilson's veto, it proved a great disappointment to its sponsors. The Slavs and Italians, it turned out, could learn to read, and therefore could surmount the hurdle of the test. And after World War I ended, the flow of immigration resumed.

Nevertheless, the restrictionist forces gained strength after the war. The Bolshevik revolution abroad and the activities of anarchists at home touched off a great Red scare, which added emotional weight to the desire to exclude aliens. The turn toward isolationism after American disillusionment with the Treaty of Versailles led to a conviction that it was best to cut all ties with Europe and the outer world, including immigration. Xenophobia reached new heights as millions of frightened Americans, fearing the Catholics and Jews as well as the Negroes, enlisted in the Ku Klux Klan. That organization had reached the peak of its influence in 1924 and

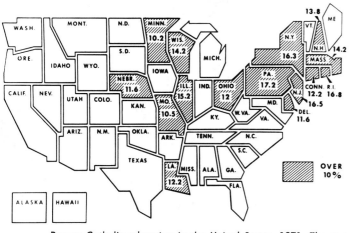

Roman Catholic education in the United States, 1971. The states shaded are those in which more than 10 percent of elementary and high-school students attend Catholic schools. (United Press International)

The Catholic Church sanctions the disorder launched by the labor movement. (Cartoon in *Puck*, Library of Congress)

Immigrants at Ellis Island take an intelligence test. (Brown Brothers)

The matron at Ellis Island administers the intelligence test to new arrivals. (Brown Brothers)

New arrivals await their turn on Ellis Island, 1920. At one point just after the war, congestion was so heavy that incoming immigrants could not be processed speedily enough to permit all of them to enter the building at the same time. (United Press International)

The Bolshevik threat, 1919. Béla Kun, leader of the Red rebellion in Hungary. (Photoworld)

Alien anarchists, socialists, and other radicals rounded up during the Red-scare raids in New York City arrive at Ellis Island for investigation and possible deportation, 1920. (United Press International)

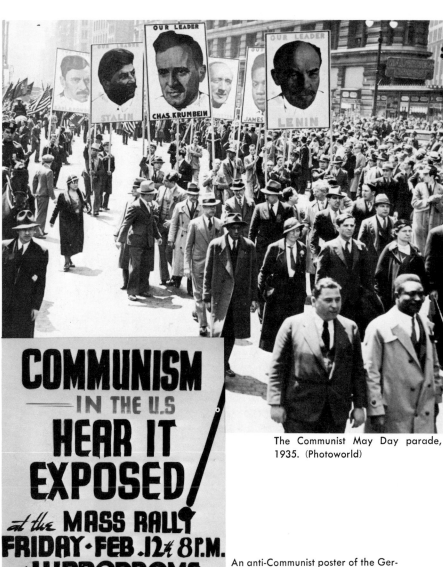

The Communist May Day parade, 1935. (Photoworld)

An anti-Communist poster of the German-American Bund. (Photoworld)

then declined. But by the time it did, animus against the foreigners had produced a total revision of the American immigration system.

Three laws passed in 1921, 1924, and 1929 established a new pattern. These measures set an absolute limit of 150,000 annually on all immigration other than that from the Western Hemisphere. The total was, moreover, divided into quotas assigned by a complicated formula to each nationality in accordance with its presumed contribution to the original American stock. Countries of the old immigration, like Britain, Germany, and Ireland, received high quotas; those of the new, like Italy, Poland, and Greece, received very low ones. As a result, the movement across the Atlantic was immediately reduced to a trickle.

In addition, conditions in postwar Europe had also changed. The population rise had begun to slacken, and restrictive regimes in Italy and Russia were forbidding their peoples to leave. The era of free immigration, which had contributed so notably to American development, had come to an end.

The effect of the quota law, 1923. Would-be immigrants who reached the United States too late for admission under the old system are sent back to their steamer from the dock at Ellis Island. (United Press International)

The effects of the early Ku Klux Klan. (Wood engraving by Thomas Nast, *Harper's Weekly*, October 24, 1874, Library of Congress)

Applicants for visas wait for their medical examination in the American Consulate General, Warsaw, 1932. Poland was one of the countries with a low quota so that visas after 1924 were difficult to secure. (The National Archives)

Despite the difficulties of getting away, Polish immigrants in 1927 still seek the right to depart. (United Press International)

IV
The Refugees
1930-Present

The European war dance, 1877. This lithograph illustrates the American view, still strong in 1917, of the propensity of Europeans to resort to war. The United States is neutral and trades peacefully amidst the hullabaloo. (Lithograph by Currier & Ives, Library of Congress)

1
War and Totalitarianism

The international order that made immigration possible came to an end after the First World War. But Americans and Europeans alike were slow to recognize the change. Few imagined that the idea of a single world with common interests that transcended national lines, one within which it made sense to move people and goods freely, would disappear soon after the restoration of peace. That idea had been so much a part of the assumptions of the century between 1815 and 1914 that its endurance seemed assured. The failure of the League of Nations, the spread of totalitarianism, and a second war even more destructive than the first characterized the new situation. Opportunities for migration disappeared, although the need remained; and American policy, for reasons of its own, conformed to the tendencies prevalent elsewhere.

After 1914 migration came to be considered an offense to nationalism. In the twentieth century, nationalism lost the liberal humanitarian connotation it had borne for the generation of Giuseppe Mazzini, the Italian patriot. Increasingly, society identified patriotism with a demand for total loyalty. Love of country was taken to mean complete obedience to the government, enduring attachment to the culture of the fatherland, and unquestioning respect for its language, customs, and beliefs. Indeed, by the 1920s some Europeans and Americans were asserting that true nationalism demanded also pure racial homogeneity among the people of a country.

From the point of view of the 100 percent patriot, emigration was an act of desertion and immigration was a means of introducing impurities into the society. A nation was a whole body that claimed its members by heredity, not an association to be joined or abandoned at will. Just as many Americans no longer found it tolerable to let anyone enter, so many Europeans were no longer ready to let anyone depart.

Furthermore, nationalism was sometimes associated with another current of thought that denied or limited the scope of personal rights. Increasingly critics in some countries attacked the concept that freedom of movement or indeed any other freedom was an inalienable right of man. Political theorists and propagandists of both the right and the left argued that claims to liberty were vestiges of a bourgeois interlude in world history, of no value in the twentieth century. Instead, these opponents of liberalism insisted upon the total subservience of the individual to the state. Obligations to society were more important than personal desires.

The rulers of the Soviet Union demanded unlimited state power after the Communist revolution. They were themselves not open nationalists, for their intellectual heritage had links to nineteenth-century humanitarian socialism. But as the Bolsheviks acquired control and faced the necessities of governing an immense country, their original ideals ceased to be the basis of an immediate program and receded into a remote utopian future. Someday when the revolution would be complete, the coercive instruments of government were to wither away. But meanwhile the need to win the civil war and to suppress class enemies required the methods of the police state. Under Lenin, and even more so under Stalin, the regime conscripted the citizen in peace as in war and therefore controlled the right of his departure.

The Fascist government of Italy under Benito Mussolini also rejected the idea that there were any boundaries to its power. There, too, the disregard for parliamentary procedures, the denial of human rights and individual freedom, and the brutal use of force produced a sharp curtailment of emigration.

The depression that settled on Europe and America after 1929 reinforced restrictive policies. The liberal attitudes of the past vanished in the crisis. Each country raised its tariff barriers and closed its borders to the movement of people and goods in the effort to save itself—regardless of what happened to others.

Large-scale international migration came to a halt. The totalitarian character of the Soviet and Fascist regimes deepened in the 1930s. In the same decade a still more virulent version of totalitarianism appeared in Germany when Adolf Hitler's National Socialist German Workers' party took power. The Nazis combined extreme nationalism with complete denial of human rights and utter ruthlessness, and established absolute control over the populace. They claimed the loyalty of the *Volksdeutsche,* or Germans, "by race," whether they lived in the Reich or not, including those in the United States. By 1933, branches of the party in several American cities engaged in vigorous propaganda on behalf of the Führer. In addition, a front organization, The Friends of New Germany, enlisted the support of sympathetic Americans. The older German-American associations in time mobilized to counteract the Nazi campaign for race-consciousness in the United States. But there was no comparable capacity for resistance to Hitler within Germany.

The climax came with the outbreak of World War II in September, 1939. Each state conscripted its citizens, either for the battlefield or for the production front, and the free movement of populations came to a complete halt. The belligerent governments nevertheless did not hesitate to shift about hundreds of thousands of people when military advantage or ideological objectives made it desirable to do so. The end of the fighting therefore left millions of displaced persons scattered across the continent of Europe.

Postwar changes in the character of many regimes created further problems. In much of Eastern Europe the old political and social systems disappeared with the collapse of the German empire and the advance of the Soviet Union and its satellites. Hordes of miserable people were homeless and placeless. Yet the restrictive barriers of the preceding decades prevented them from finding refuge.

The immigration laws enacted between 1921 and 1929 impeded the American response to these crises. These measures not only limited the total eligible to enter the United States (there were years thereafter when departures actually exceeded entries), but in practice were deliberately racist.

Despite its humane aspirations, the New Deal administration could not conceive that an alteration in the basic policy was possible. The depression seemed to foreclose any significant change. To open the gates to outsiders might only add to the millions already unemployed. Furthermore, there was reason for concern that any tampering with the status quo might ignite the explosive hatreds that already endangered American society. Incited by a host of demagogues like Huey P. Long, Theodore G. Bilbo, Gerald L. K. Smith, and Father Charles E. Coughlin, millions of confused and desperate men had enlisted in proto-Fascist organizations—the Silver Shirts, the White Shirts, the Christian Front, and others. Renewed immigration of Jews or Catholics might stir them into violence. In any case, isolationism remained strong throughout the 1930s, and its supporters blocked any effort at renewed political, economic, or social connections with Europe.

American entry into the war did not immediately

The immigration office in Wejherowo, Poland—still active despite the hostility of the Polish government, 1927. (United Press International)

Nationalistic Rumanians in New York, outside the Rumanian consulate where they seek passports that will enable them to go home. (Photoworld)

Lenin speaks to the soldiers in Moscow in the early days of the revolution. (Photoworld)

The Russian Red Guard at a mass meeting in defense of the revolution, 1918. (Photoworld)

A bread line during the Great Depression. (Photoworld)

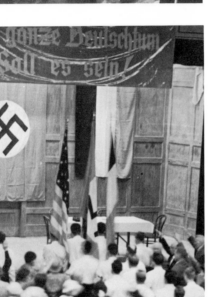

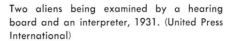

Lining up for a free meal during the depression. (Photoworld)

Two aliens being examined by a hearing board and an interpreter, 1931. (United Press International)

◄ Meeting of the Friends of New Germany at Los Angeles, 1934. (Photoworld)

German displaced persons camp in a courtyard in Vienna. There was no hope of securing American visas under the quota laws. (Photoworld)

Polish refugees driven by the war to distant Iran. (Photoworld)

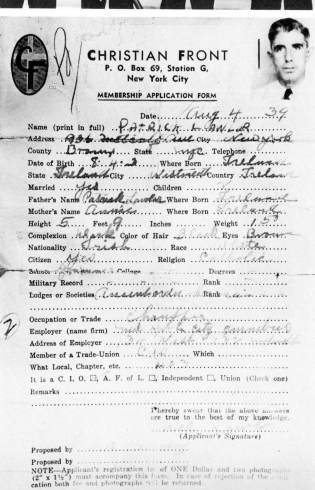

Theodore G. Bilbo stumps for re-election to the United States Senate from Mississippi on a native white supremacy platform, 1946. (United Press International)

Thousands of homeless and displaced persons on the roads of Germany in the aftermath of war, 1945. (Photoworld)

Members of the United Christian Front, 1940, ready for action. (United Press International)

An application form for membership in the Christian Front, 1939. (United Press International)

An anti-immigration cartoon implies that a liberal policy would make citizens of alien criminals, 1940. (United Press International)

Japanese-Americans relocated at the reception center, Salinas, California, 1942. (Photograph by Russell Lee for the Farm Security Administration, Library of Congress)

transform the situation. In time, the call to national unity and the revelation of Hitlerite atrocities would arouse the conscience of the country; but any potentially divisive step still seemed dangerous while the struggle for survival was in doubt. A tragic incident in January, 1942, revealed the depth of existing racial prejudice. The war emergency became the excuse for the mass evacuation of one hundred thousand Japanese-Americans, including those who were citizens, from the Pacific Coast. Confined to relocation camps, these victims were evidence of the persistent fear of foreigners.

Nor were the ethnic groups with ties to Europe in a position to press for policy changes. For instance, although the American Slav Congress, formed in 1942, drew together thirteen national elements, it suffered from internal conflicts and fell under the control of Communists, who were also influential in the International Workers Order. American Jews were able to cooperate in some relief measures, but Zionists and anti-Zionists sought divergent objectives.

The result was a pathetic lack of response to the needs of the refugees from totalitarianism. Even when quotas were available, as was the case for German citizens, the American consuls were slow to grant visas. The United States participated in an international conference at Évian, which, however, achieved nothing but the creation of an intergovernmental committee on refugees. A proposal to admit twenty thousand children in 1939 and 1940 could not secure a majority in Congress.

Indeed, isolationism as well as the depression of the 1930s led to a tightening rather than a loosening of existing law. In 1930, President Hoover had ordered administrators stringently to enforce the provision against admitting persons likely to become a public charge so that, in effect, only applicants with substantial financial resources could secure admission. In 1940, control of immigration was transferred from the Labor to the Justice Department in the expectation of more rigid enforcement of the law. Aliens were thereafter required to register annually.

During the war, the only consequential change in the immigration law was repeal of the Chinese Exclusion Act in 1943. The gesture, intended to placate an ally in the struggle against Japan, cost little. It simply made a hundred and five quota places available annually, and few Chinese were in a position to use the privilege thus extended to them. When one thousand European refugees were given emergency shelter in Oswego, New York—which was declared a "free port" for the purpose —they were subject to endless surveillance, and President Roosevelt was forced to announce that he had no intention of making the United States a haven for the homeless.

Japanese-Americans unloading at the Santa Anita reception center, 1942. (Photograph by Russell Lee for the Farm Security Administration, Library of Congress)

Japanese-Americans sort themselves out in a relocation camp. (Photoworld)

Aliens lining up to register in the New York City General Post Office, 1940. (United Press International)

Hungry children in Bratislava, Czechoslovakia, 1946. (Photoworld)

Refugees provisionally admitted to be held at Fort Ontario, Oswego, New York, 1944. (Photoworld)

Nor did the postwar era bring any immediate softening of the law. The Internal Security Act of 1950 barred anyone ever affiliated with a Communist or Fascist movement from entry into the United States and set up severe rules for deportation. The McCarran-Walter Act, passed in 1952 over President Harry S. Truman's veto, was the culmination of the restrictive policy established thirty-five years earlier. That law did eliminate the discriminatory provisions against all Asians and thus made each country in that continent eligible for 100 quota

places. But otherwise the Act hardened existing barriers to immigration, confirmed the quota system, and set up harsh administrative procedures to control aliens.

As a result, the United States was as ill prepared to deal with the postwar refugees as it had been to assist the fugitives from the prewar dictatorships. It no longer welcomed the tired huddled masses of the Old World. Indeed, it looked with suspicion even upon the people of ability and genius who were ready to contribute to its own welfare.

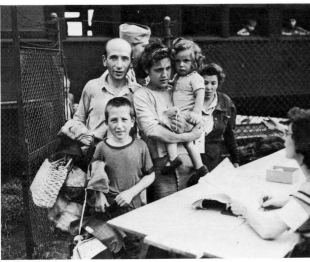

A refugee family reaches Oswego by way of Italy. (Photoworld)

Refugees housed at Oswego, New York, receive their first American meal. (Photoworld)

Aliens crowd the New York office of the Hebrew Immigrant Aid Society to register under the requirements of the McCarran immigration act, 1953. (Photoworld)

Immigrants suspected of Nazi or Fascist affiliation are held for screening at Ellis Island, 1950. (United Press International)

Immigrants debarking in New York.
(United Press International)

2

Fugitives from Dictatorship

The restrictive attitudes of the years between the two world wars set the limits of the welcome which the United States accorded the fugitives from the troubled societies of Europe. The number who secured admission in those twenty years was smaller than that of 1907 alone. The reduced scale of migration altered the situation the newcomers faced after 1918. Moreover, the arrivals of the 1920s and 1930s were no longer the peasants or laborers of an earlier era. The few who possessed the resources to surmount the hurdles of the quota system had more in common with the eighteenth-century liberals than with the nineteenth-century immigrants. That difference also influenced the character of resettlement in the interwar decades.

Each totalitarian regime forced some of its victims to move. But America was not always the favorite refuge of the fortunate minority that escaped. The free countries of Europe were more attractive than the United States to the intellectuals, professionals, and aristocrats who formed a large proportion of the émigrés. Residence in France or England caused less of a break in their social and cultural life than was involved in crossing the Atlantic. Furthermore, there was an advantage

to being closer to the homeland, as long as the exiles still hoped for a restoration of the old regimes or an ouster of the dictators. The first destinations of the fugitives therefore were Paris, London, Berlin, Prague, Riga, and, for some Russians, Shanghai. Relatively few recognized at the outset that greater safety and wider opportunities awaited them in the United States.

The Revolution was but the most spectacular of the disasters that befell Russia after 1917. Large areas suffered from the passage of German armies, first in victory, then in retreat. War with Poland followed and in 1921 a devastating famine struck the land. And then at last the white forces of resistance and counterrevolution collapsed in Siberia.

The peasants and the industrial laborers lacked the means to leave and, in the 1920s at least, continued to hope that the new Communist system would improve their lot. Most of the 1.5 million Russian refugees therefore were aristocrats, professionals, intellectuals, and middle-class people. In the first few years after the Revolution, the Reds were eager to get rid of such dissidents and put few obstacles in their way if they had the means to escape.

By the 1920s the immigrants who arrived at Ellis Island were no longer the depressed peasants of the past. (United Press International)

An immigrant being branded with indelible ink, 1921. This procedure was intended to prevent the misuse of passports and visas, feared by American officials when the laws became increasingly restrictive. (United Press International)

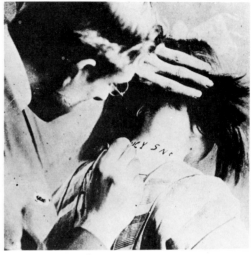

Refugees from the Soviet Union. This group of Russians reached Boston on the S.S. *Pittsburgh* en route to the Pennsylvania mining district, 1922. (United Press International)

Orphans arrive in New York from the Soviet Union in charge of an agent of the Hebrew Immigrant Aid Society. The children were left without parents by the revolutionary atrocities and were adopted by American families, about 1920. (Photoworld)

Polish refugees wait in Danzig for transportation to America, 1920. (United Press International)

Russian soldiers at Ellis Island. (National Park Service, Sherman Collection)

The first refugees to reach the United States from the Soviet Union. The Teperow family arrives in New York on the way to Boston. (Photoworld)

Igor Sikorsky. (Sikorsky Aircraft Corporation)

Alexander Kerensky, as Minister of Justice of the Russian provisional government. (Library of Congress)

Although most Russian refugees remained in Europe or the Far East, some came to the United States. Igor Sikorsky, for instance, arrived in 1919, abandoning in emigration a prestigious position as director of an aviation factory. Well educated—his father was a psychologist, his mother a physician—he had been interested in the problems of flight since youth. Landing in a foreign country at the age of thirty, he had to support himself by teaching mathematics to immigrants. After four years he accumulated the funds to open a factory in which he built all-metal planes and developed the clippers that in 1937 made possible transoceanic flights. Two years later, he succeeded in constructing a successful helicopter and laid the groundwork for that industry.

Sikorsky never lost his attachment to the culture of the country of his birth. He thus remained a devoted communicant of the Russian Orthodox Church and, in several books, probed the spiritual dilemma of modern man.

Many of his countrymen also retained an emotional connection with Russia, although political persecution drove them away. Alexander Kerensky, premier of the provisional government displaced by the Bolsheviks, and the historian Michael Karpovich were among those who found refuge in the United States, but who continued to have a great interest in their homeland.

In the 1930s, however, the attitude of the Soviet Union changed. It turned ever more frequently to terror to maintain control and therefore feared the effect on opinion abroad of the news that refugees might carry away with them. As his fears of the opposition grew, Stalin preferred to liquidate rather than to exile his opponents. Thereafter only the desperate and ingenious escaped.

About seventy thousand Italian refugees fled fascism. Many intellectuals, like other groups, at first regarded the Black Shirts as something of a joke and acquiesced in the new system because they did not take its rhetoric seriously. The full implications of Mussolini's rule unfolded slowly. Violence and the infringement of personal rights were characteristic from the start, but there were some grounds for hope of improvement until 1938 when the government launched an anti-Semitic campaign. Many exiles therefore at first chose to remain nearby in France or Switzerland.

Others were uncertain and moved back and forth across the Atlantic for years. Arturo Toscanini, for instance, resigned in 1929 as director of La Scala, in Milan, because he refused to play the Fascist hymn. A proud man, he valued integrity in life as in music, and he defied Il Duce's thugs. Since he had earlier made frequent visits to the United States, Toscanini had no difficulty in securing an engagement as conductor of the New York Philharmonic. Still, he loved his native country and went back several times before he realized the hopelessness of living freely under totalitarianism. So too, the physicist Enrico Fermi, whose wife was Jewish, reluctantly accepted the life of exile in 1939.

Enrico Fermi, Nobel Prize winner. (United Press International)

A group of German refugees arrives in Boston just after the outbreak of war in Europe, 1939. (United Press International)

Arturo Toscanini, still vigorous at the age of 83 when this photograph was taken. (Photoworld)

Anti-Semitic banner in Greifenberg, in Pomerania, Germany, 1935. The slogan reads, "The Jews are our misfortune." The slogan coined by the Nazi Julius Streicher was the regular headline of his newspaper, *Der Stürmer*. (Photoworld)

On the other hand, Gaetano Salvemini knew at once that the Fascists were the enemies of men of liberal sentiments. That distinguished historian had early known the meaning of tragedy when the great earthquake in Messina in 1908 destroyed his whole family. Yet he remained a humane and sensitive scholar, dedicated to learning and conscious of his obligations to society. Having once been arrested and released, he surreptitiously left his beloved Florence and, after a stay in London, came to teach at Harvard, where he wielded a vigorous pen in defense of liberty.

The largest group of refugees were the fugitives set in motion by Adolf Hitler. At his assumption of power in 1933, he purged the civil service and the universities of Jews and "leftists." The more perceptive opponents of nazism then understood that life in Germany was hopeless for them and fled. The number who sought escape increased year by year as the regime grew more repressive. In 1938 the seizure of Austria added to the ranks of the fugitives. By the time full-scale war broke out in September, 1939, more than a million men and women had fled the territory of the Third Reich. Of these, some two hundred thousand had come to the United States, about half of them Jewish.

Among the exiles were men with international reputations who brought with them immensely valuable talents. Thomas Mann, for instance, was the best-known German novelist. Once a conventional nationalist, he now perceived the destructive implications of nazism and left voluntarily. His later writings groped for an understanding of the universal values of man's existence.

Such speculations had much earlier engaged Albert Einstein. That gentle mathematician whose formulas had revealed to the twentieth century a totally new vision of the universe had always rejected nationalism; and he abhorred violence. When Central Europe became intolerable, he found refuge in the Institute for Advanced Studies at Princeton. Ironically, he later became the intermediary who put before President Roosevelt the project to build the atom bomb and thus unleashed power theretofore unimaginable.

Thomas Mann, 1948. At his right is
Harold Ickes, former Secretary of the
Interior; at his left, Justice Felix
Frankfurter of the United States Su-
preme Court. (Photoworld)

Albert Einstein in a public broadcast asks for
world disarmament. (Photoworld)

Dr. Eugene Paul Wigner receiving the medal
for merit from Secretary of War Robert P.
Patterson, 1946. (Library of Congress)

Dr. John von Neumann (right)
and Robert Oppenheimer, 1954.
(United Press International)

Dr. Franz Alexander of Berlin
(right) chats with another prominent psychoanalyst, Oskar Pfister,
1930. (United Press International)

As the shadow of Hitlerism darkened the face of Europe, the scientists of other countries also fled to America. Eugene Wigner, a theoretical physicist who later
won the Nobel Prize, John von Neumann, a profound
mathematician, and Franz Alexander, a famous psychoanalyst, were all Hungarians. When that unhappy
land fell under the control first of Béla Kun, the Communist, and then of Admiral Nicholas Horthy, the Fascist, they left for Berlin. When the Nazis made that
sanctuary unsafe, the United States was the last hope of
these scientists.

The migration from Germany also included prominent figures from the world of art. The architects Mies
van der Rohe and Walter Gropius, the composers Arnold Schoenberg and Kurt Weill, the conductors Bruno
Walter and Otto Klemperer, and the writers Franz Werfel and Lion Feuchtwanger were among those who
sought a haven in the United States.

Such men, whose reputations preceded them, were
the most fortunate immigrants. There was no doubt that
they were bona fide artists or teachers of higher education, and they therefore qualified for exemption from
the quota provisions of the law. Furthermore, they could
legally secure positions in advance so that no immigration official would venture to challenge them on the
ground they were likely to become a public charge.

But hundreds of talented people less well known
faced endless tribulations in migration. Those who managed to secure admission arrived in a country deep in
depression. The universities, short of funds, were desperately cutting their staffs; hundreds of native Ph.D.'s
were unemployed. All the professions seemed overcrowded, not because there were too many practitioners

Walter Gropius, 1954.
(United Press International)

Kurt Weill. (Columbia Records Photo)

Franz Werfel, just after arriving in the United States. (United Press International)

A violinist from Budapest who fled the reign of terror after Nazi troops moved across the Hungarian border plays for a fellow passenger on a ship that brings them to the United States. (Photoworld)

German refugees wait at the purser's desk of their liner for the valuables they were allowed to take with them from Germany, 1938. (United Press International)

An exiled Greek physician, a specialist in tropical diseases, works as a laborer in a Cleveland greenhouse, 1950. (United Press International)

Vladimir Nabokov. (United Press International)

A qualified Polish doctor in the United States as a displaced person, working as a menial servant in Reading, Massachusetts, 1949. (United Press International)

to fill the nation's needs but because there was no money for fees.

The harried refugees, struggling to reconstruct their lives, found some help from voluntary committees hastily set up to assist. But the exiles also encountered widespread apathy and even hostility. Professors who had once lectured in distinguished European universities eagerly grasped at any teaching post or, if necessary, accepted menial jobs in libraries and laboratories. Experienced physicians were grateful for the chance to take qualifying examinations, which opportunity some—but not all—states offered. Lawyers rarely were able to exercise their calling, for they were unfamiliar with American codes and practice, and only citizens were admitted to the bar.

For businessmen, managers, and engineers, it was an uphill struggle, given the hard times of the depression decade. Often they had to leave their wealth behind, and whatever they saved from confiscation was difficult to invest. Skills learned in other contexts were rarely applicable to the New World. Few refugees therefore felt secure about the future when war in 1939 swept away the last vestiges of their past. Although they had begun to form communal associations of their own and although they enjoyed some professional and academic contacts with American colleagues, they could not escape the consciousness that they were regarded as objects of benevolence rather than as assets to the national culture.

In the two years between the outbreak of war in Europe and Pearl Harbor, the ranks of the refugees swelled. The novelists Vladimir Nabokov and Sigrid Undset, the dramatist Maurice Maeterlinck, the painter Marc Chagall, and the composers Igor Stravinsky and Darius Milhaud were among those who then escaped to the United States, either from their original homes or from previous places of refuge. But the numbers were pathetically small measured against the masses whom dictatorship and war made victims in Europe.

Maurice Maeterlinck, 1899. (New York Public Library)

Marc Chagall, returned to Paris, watching the installation of his stained-glass windows representing the twelve tribes of Israel, 1961. (Photoworld)

Sigrid Undset (left) with Pearl Buck, both Nobel Prize winners, 1942. (United Press International)

Igor Stravinsky conducting in Rome in 1951. (United Press International)

The westward movement, modern style. A group of Italian-Americans leave Springfield, Massachusetts, to resettle in Fresno, California, 1947. (United Press International)

3

Postwar Migration

The outbreak of war in Europe reduced the already meager flow of transatlantic immigrants, and restrictive laws kept the volume low thereafter. Yet in the United States the war also created a serious manpower shortage, which persisted into the 1950s. Despite automation, booming industry and mechanized agriculture still required an abundant supply of labor. The demand was met by movements of people through alternative channels already opened in the 1920s.

The largest shift of population was internal, from rural to urban areas, from the South to the North and from the East to the Pacific Coast. The Negroes and whites transplanted in the course of that movement now encountered the problems of settlement and adjustment that had earlier tried the European immigrants. A similar displacement brought to New York and other mainland cities thousands of American citizens from Puerto Rico. In the 1940s and 1950s, cheap air transportation enabled more than five hundred thousand islanders to take up the tasks for which the foreign-born were no longer available.

The largest international movement of labor came from across the Mexican border. Economic development in Mexico had not relieved the pressure of poverty and of a rising population. The government was therefore willing to organize the recruitment of *braceros* for seasonal labor in agriculture and industry. In the five years after 1942, some 220,000 entered on these terms. In addition, countless individuals came on their own, either legally or as wetbacks across the border. By 1945,

there were some 2.5 million Mexican-born persons in the United States.

Their life fell mostly within the patterns their predecessors had already established; the majority lived in the Southwest and made the big swing through the vegetable and cotton fields or wielded the pick and shovel in construction gangs. Los Angeles, El Paso, and San Antonio were the centers of urban residence. But in time there were also substantial numbers concentrated in permanent settlements in such northern cities as Detroit and Chicago, where they gained more stable employment in industry. Relations with other Americans were uneasy. The zoot-suit riots of 1943 in Los Angeles showed the underlying resentment of the Anglos against the aliens and their children who seemed to escape the burdens of the war. In the 1950s, however, the Mexican communities began to gain stability as the number of new arrivals declined, while the second generation became increasingly important and learned to make its way in an environment not as strange to them as it had been to their parents. In a few places, members of the group reached for political power in order to protect the interests of *la raza,* the race.

Overseas immigration after 1939 remained small in total volume. As long as the law was unchanged, there was no possibility of reviving the old forms of free movement. Yet isolation proved impractical—in population as well as in diplomacy.

Minor exceptions, once made for special purposes,

Migratory potato pickers board a truck that takes them to work in New Jersey, 1940. (United Press International)

Migrant farmers waiting to hitch a ride north either by freight train or auto, 1940. (United Press International)

A Puerto Rican family in New York, about 1950. (Photoworld)

Customs official inspecting the luggage of Puerto Ricans arriving in New York by boat, about 1948. (Photoworld)

Mexican braceros at work in Salinas, California, 1963. (United Press International)

Home of a migratory Mexican fieldworker in the Imperial Valley, California, 1937. (Photograph by Dorothea Lange for Farm Security Administration, Library of Congress)

Mexican laborers topping sugar beets near Stockton, California, 1943. (Library of Congress)

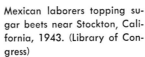

An illegal Mexican immigrant caught trying to cross the border under the hood of an automobile, 1954. (United Press International)

Campsite for Mexican potato pickers in Siskiyou County, California, 1939. (Photograph by Dorothea Lange for Farm Security Administration, Library of Congress)

Wives of Mexican laborers do the family wash in the communal laundry of a modern camp, about 1948. (United States Department of Agriculture)

Only a handful of visitors use the Ellis Island ferry about 1949. (Photoworld)

A Negro soldier with his Japanese wife and son register in the American Consulate General in Tokyo, about 1949. (Photoworld)

provided the entering wedge for a gradual reconsideration of attitudes. In time, the accumulation of experience showed the need for a thorough review of basic policy.

The war provided the first occasion for reassessment. Young men and women, stationed overseas to fight or for occupation duty, early took to fraternizing with the local population. Romance sprouted in Italy, France, Germany, Japan, and, later, Korea. Soon there were marriages and offspring, of which the United States had to take cognizance. The war brides, with their husbands and children, returned to the United States, their way eased by special regulations. In the seven years after the end of the war, about 125,000 such persons were admitted, and they adjusted to life in their new homes with remarkable ease.

A greater involvement resulted from the American stake in the peace of the world after 1945. There was no escape to isolationism as there had been twenty-five years earlier. Troops remained abroad to guard the unsettled borders; the United Nations grappled with recurrent problems; and Americans realized that they could not wash their hands of the world's troubles with any simple treaty of peace. Military aid and economic assistance were essential to the reconstruction of Europe if the sacrifices of the war were not to be in vain. The Truman Doctrine, the Marshall Plan, and the action in Korea were evidence that no detachment was possible in a nuclear age.

Given these commitments, the displaced population of Europe was a standing challenge to the United States. When the fighting stopped, some 40 million people were homeless. They had been moved about at the whim of their rulers, and now many of them had not only no dwellings but also no countries to return to. Shifts of boundaries made them foreigners in the places of their birth, and changes in regime left them enemies in their homelands. Until they settled down, there could be no stability in the continent.

Repatriation was no solution for millions of them. Frenchmen, Netherlanders, and Italians could go home. But few Jews were willing to return to Central or Eastern Europe. The survivors could not forget that 6 million of their coreligionists had perished in the concentration camps and that their erstwhile neighbors had often joined in anti-Semitic orgies encouraged by the Nazis. Many citizens of the Baltic states had fought against the invading Russians and were unwilling to trust themselves to Stalin's tender mercies now that he was in undisputed control. That was also the case in the other Red satellites—Poland, Hungary, and Rumania in particular. Millions of Germans streamed westward out of the provinces handed over by the Soviet Union to its Polish puppet; and the flow in the same direction continued as the Communists strengthened their grip on East Germany.

Furthermore, other crises displaced new groups as the old ones came to rest. Italy and Greece suffered from an excess of population that impeded economic progress for more than a decade. Floods in the Netherlands in 1953 and earthquakes in Greece in 1955 led to serious setbacks and emphasized the urgency of finding places for surplus people.

The United States had invested so many lives and so much effort in the well-being of Europe that it was foolish to block off the needed relief immigration would extend. Yet the restrictive laws of the 1920s seemed so permanent that help appeared within reach only through the expediency of creating temporary loopholes to let limited and strictly controlled numbers in.

As a result of pressure from interested religious and philanthropic organizations, Congress in 1948 finally passed the Displaced Persons Act, which authorized the entry, outside of the normal quotas, of four hundred thousand persons in the next four years. Compared with the greater efforts and the smaller resources of other countries, this was a miserly record. Yet even that help was precious and cost the United States nothing. When the law expired, it was replaced by the Refugee Relief Act of 1953, under the terms of which some 210,000 immigrants entered the country outside the quota system.

Despite criticism from Presidents Truman and Eisenhower, however, the permanent American immigration system remained inflexible and Congress obdurately refused to consider any modification. The Russian suppression of a flicker of independence in Hungary in 1956 therefore inevitably created a new crisis. Two hundred thousand anguished Freedom Fighters fled westward into Austria, and many of them dreamed wistfully of a refuge in the United States, but there were only quotas for a handful. President Eisenhower nevertheless managed to contrive a device that admitted some of them on parole. In the end, about thirty-five thousand Hungarian refugees entered the United States. Private philanthropy somewhat offset public rigidity; some hundred colleges, for instance, made scholarships available to the children of the exiles.

Cuba, which was even closer to home, passed through a disquieting revolution two years later. It was not surprising that the supporters of Batista should flee when the dictator fell; but many liberals, democrats, and radicals who had at first supported the revolution soon joined in the flight. Castro refused to hold the elections he had promised, and instead, after liquidating the opposition, drifted into the Communist fold. Rash economic experiments depressed the standard of living and compounded the hardships of many Cubans. The number of fugitives mounted and, in the decade after 1958, reached a total of about one-half million. A sizable colony grew up in Miami, Florida, which was their first stopping place.

The need for a refuge persisted in the 1960s. Emergencies continued to challenge Americans. Some provision had to be made for the Chinese fugitives, who in 1963 fled from famine and political persecution to Hong Kong, and for the Czechs who found the Russian invasion of 1968 intolerable.

Other connections with the outer world applied unexpected, though smaller, pressures to the immigration system. By the Fulbright Act of 1948, the United States had launched a novel program of international educational exchanges. Thereafter thousands of scholars and students from every part of the world spent one or several years in American hospitals, universities, laboratories, and libraries. Some of them decided to stay, either because they had established marital or academic connections while in the United States, or because they discovered that the conditions of life or work were superior to those in their own countries. Although the numbers were difficult to fix with precision, the brain drain became a subject of substantial controversy. The situation in medicine was particularly dramatic. About three hundred doctors arrived annually from Latin America alone in the 1960s; and in 1966 about 25 percent of the fourteen thousand foreign students doing graduate medical work in the United States planned to stay on.

One way or another, at least one hundred thousand nonquota immigrants were finding their way into the United States each year. That is, usually more newcomers entered outside the system than through it. The Italian quota, for instance, was 5,666; the average number admitted was 15,000. The discrepancy was an indication that a reconsideration of the basic law was long overdue.

Revision finally came in 1965 with the support of President Lyndon B. Johnson. The new law rested on the principle of equal access, with admission primarily on a first-come, first-served basis. All racial and ethnic preferences disappeared. On the one hand, the law abolished the national origins quota system; on the other, it imposed for the first time a numerical limit on immigrants from the Western Hemisphere. The new statute established annual overall ceilings of 120,000 for the Americas, and 170,000 for the rest of the world, within which no single country could claim more than 20,000 places in a year. Three categories of applicants received favored treatment—certain members of the families of United States citizens or resident aliens, people with skills needed to fill manpower shortages, and refugees. These exceptions rested on the needs of Americans, not upon prejudice.

A Negro sailor and his Japanese bride take the marriage oath at the American consulate in Tokyo, 1952. (Photoworld)

The adopted Vietnamese daughter of an American soldier and his Japanese-born wife takes the citizenship oath in Cincinnati, 1970. (United Press International)

German refugees arrive in the United States. (Photoworld)

A Czech refugee and his wife arrive at La Guardia by air on their way to Ohio, where they will live on their son's farm. (Photoworld)

The first contingent of displaced persons from the Butzbach camp leave by train for Bremen where they will embark for the United States, 1948. (United Press International)

President Truman signs a bill bringing the United States into the International Refugee Organization. The law authorized a contribution of $73,-500,000 toward the care of displaced persons, 1947. (United Press International)

Refugees arriving in New York, 1947. Among the 576 passengers of the S.S. *Marine Flasher* were 400 orphans. (Photoworld)

A group of Estonians and Latvians reach Florida on a 54-foot schooner after a 5,000-mile trip from Sweden, 1947. (United Press International)

Sixty-seven orphans from Latvia, Estonia, and Lithuania arrive by air at Idlewild Airport from Hamburg, Germany, about 1950. (Photoworld)

Young refugees from Communist-controlled Latvia, Lithuania, and Poland arrive in Boston on the S.S. *Masen*, 1950. (United Press International)

A train bearing a group of displaced persons bears a sign welcoming them to the United States. (Photoworld)

President Dwight D. Eisenhower signs the Refugee Relief Act opening the doors of the United States to more than 200,000 fugitives from behind the Iron Curtain, 1953. (United Press International)

Polish Jews who had fled to Siberia when the Nazis invaded their country come west to join their son in Brooklyn, about 1948. (Photoworld)

Eighty-four Italian refugees arrive in the United States and are welcomed by Judge Juvenal Marchisio, 1951. (United Press International)

Displaced persons, on the deck of the United States Army transport *General Black*, enter New York Harbor. (Photoworld)

Refugees crowd the deck as their ship passes into the harbor of New York, 1953. (Photoworld)

Hungarian refugees arrive at the Brooklyn Army terminal, 1957. (United Press International)

President Eisenhower's personal aircraft *The Columbine* brings a group of twenty-one Hungarian refugees to America, 1956. (United Press International)

Cuban refugees arrive in Mobile, Alabama, 1964. Determined to escape from the Castro terror, they took to sea in a fishing boat which sank in the Gulf of Mexico, but were rescued and brought to the United States. (United Press International)

The first Chinese refugee family enters the United States via Hong Kong under amendment to the Refugee Relief Act, 1962. (United Press International)

Two members being sworn into the Board of Foreign Scholarship, which administers the International Exchange Program, under the Fulbright Act, 1953. From left to right they are Samuel Brownell and Philip Willkie. With them are Senator J. W. Fulbright and Raymond D. Muir. (United Press International)

German-born scientists employed at the Redstone Arsenal, Huntsville, Alabama, take the oath of allegiance as citizens of the United States, 1954. (United Press International)

President Lyndon B. Johnson signs into law the new immigration bill, 1965. The ceremony took place on Liberty Island in New York harbor. At the left is Vice-President Hubert H. Humphrey; at the right, Senators Edward and Robert Kennedy who were active in support of the new law. (United Press International)

A group of Russian "old believers" arrive in New York, 1963, from Turkey, seeking the space to lead the distinctive life the faith of their sect requires. (United Press International)

The enactment of the new law was evidence that the issues created by nineteenth-century immigration had vanished. The old free movement of people had practically ended in the 1920s; and the suspicion and fear immigration had aroused had left a legacy, in the national origins quota system that inhibited American responses to the problems of the 1940s and 1950s. The statute of 1965 accommodated the policy of the United States to the realities of the world situation. Unlimited immigration was impractical. But a moderate movement of under four hundred thousand a year could help the country and be useful to worthy people in other parts of the world.

In practice the course of immigration during the 1960s conformed to the pattern the law described formally. The total number of entries fluctuated between three and four hundred thousand a year, with about half coming from the Western Hemisphere. The balance consisted of arrivals from Europe and Asia, with the percentage of the former steadily falling and that of the latter steadily rising.

Since the newcomers became citizens at about the same rate as fresh immigrants appeared, the number of resident aliens in the United States remained constant —about 3.5 to 4 million at any given time. In 1970, the largest portion of these, about a million, were natives of Mexico and Canada. Some five hundred thousand were born in the countries of the old immigration, Britain and Germany. Italy was the birthplace of 241,000, Cuba of

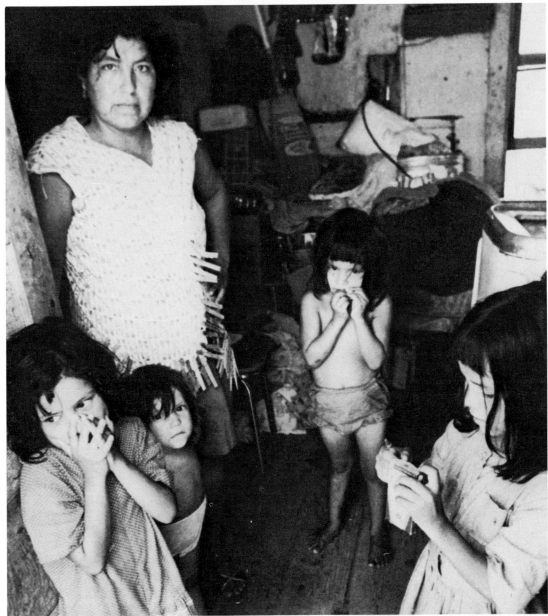

The family of a Mexican migratory worker in Mathis, Texas, 1970.
(United Press International)

Citizenship by way of marriage, 1970. A Yugoslav immigrant whose visa was about to expire advertised for a wife who would gain him an extension of residence in the United States. He was able to select from among 171 applicants. (United Press International)

395,000, and Poland of 118,000. The other aliens represented lands in every corner of the earth.

Immigration in the 1960s thus became a normal feature of American life. For centuries the movement of peoples into the Western Hemisphere had been the means of settling an empty continent. That process was over. Now immigration served another purpose. The United States had now become a great power, and it made room within its boundaries for the individuals and groups drawn to it by its connections and responsibilities in every part of the world.

A swearing-in ceremony of new citizens at the Washington Monument. (United Press International)

President Richard M. Nixon addresses a reception of newly naturalized citizens in Chicago, 1970. (United Press International)

Aliens registered under the Alien Address Program, 1970. (United States Department of Justice, Immigration and Naturalization Service)

State of residence	Grand Total	Total permanent residents	Mexico	Canada	United Kingdom	Cuba	Italy	Germany	Poland	Philippines	China 1/	Portugal	Greece	Dominican Republic	Japan	Colombia	Jamaica	Ireland	All other permanent residents	Oth tha perma resid
Total	4,247,377	3,719,750	714,509	398,310	298,881	288,118	235,842	216,593	120,074	94,325	85,979	77,796	66,503	65,647	58,843	52,903	51,496	50,646	843,285	527,
Alabama	6,179	5,061	77	541	904	222	82	1,281	28	49	109	15	105	7	139	67	29	70	1,336	1
Alaska	3,626	3,201	104	949	340	10	12	420	19	222	57	2	25	–	190	24	15	40	772	
Arizona	49,303	46,171	34,075	3,741	1,609	88	200	1,173	100	371	569	16	103	9	272	64	28	94	3,659	3
Arkansas	2,568	2,213	110	254	357	55	51	494	40	45	88	3	16	4	104	11	3	13	565	
California	981,842	916,365	379,951	86,191	61,685	21,187	13,772	33,806	2,887	38,207	38,255	17,513	4,307	490	24,065	7,885	1,300	5,166	179,698	65
Colorado	22,936	20,584	3,234	2,559	2,250	448	597	3,033	395	203	360	17	317	16	584	168	39	129	6,235	2
Connecticut	109,349	101,479	248	19,575	12,650	2,195	15,192	4,638	11,689	370	407	5,862	2,433	198	239	1,253	2,512	1,747	20,271	7
Delaware	5,910	5,184	25	566	1,009	308	402	517	296	139	167	16	114	3	81	55	57	118	1,311	
D.C.	18,394	12,577	228	435	1,395	437	365	546	55	343	733	91	508	202	100	249	940	127	5,823	5
Florida .:....	290,237	207,194	2,114	21,398	12,400	130,011	1,460	5,456	711	617	542	223	725	821	672	4,925	2,228	297	22,594	83
Georgia	17,234	13,541	200	1,471	2,7:3	1,420	138	2,893	46	194	300	37	188	18	327	200	55	104	3,237	3
Hawaii	53,003	48,164	118	1,391	1,233	40	45	657	10	25,122	1,966	129	15	4	13,531	16	22	36	3,829	4
Idaho	4,942	4,398	1,100	945	388	6	46	318	12	60	88	1	41	–	149	10	2	25	1,207	
Illinois	263,935	232,754	47,738	13,862	12,606	7,971	16,175	21,263	25,744	5,563	2,778	86	8,651	464	2,462	2,521	1,405	4,788	58,677	31
Indiana	30,262	25,232	4,552	2,797	3,103	583	442	2,991	1,028	455	428	17	1,054	41	319	118	89	201	7,014	5
Iowa	11,012	7,787	711	1,280	922	175	194	1,295	95	240	63	1	194	3	94	33	4	19	2,464	3
Kansas	11,860	8,950	2,450	890	960	357	105	1,420	68	135	180	5	55	15	230	100	15	50	1,915	2
Kentucky	7,472	5,704	88	773	818	181	125	1,582	38	192	82	5	49	9	122	89	29	–	1,522	1
Louisiana	23,207	17,774	745	1,013	1,606	2,579	730	1,320	59	197	258	17	125	34	180	443	41	112	8,315	
Maine	20,414	18,096	38	14,503	920	30	162	494	147	71	61	33	110	5	77	17	11	123	1,294	2
Maryland	48,023	39,908	412	2,807	5,125	1,686	2,668	4,388	1,116	1,063	1,189	190	1,755	160	563	656	663	692	14,775	8
Massachusetts ..	168,516	152,550	334	14,155	14,154	2,608	16,024	4,704	7,379	535	3,286	29,905	6,379	480	530	1,045	1,335	5,350	24,347	15
Michigan	145,740	133,263	5,590	44,528	14,076	1,164	7,678	10,355	11,830	727	1,071	29	2,462	85	660	364	381	1,059	31,204	2
Minnesota	22,291	17,722	517	4,306	2,387	231	166	2,001	377	279	371	2	149	1	157	65	32	151	6,080	5
Mississippi	3,620	2,826	86	241	527	50	78	515	20	66	301	16	39	4	84	43	7	70	679	
Missouri	23,828	18,631	1,460	1,910	2,306	502	1,552	2,896	542	409	378	16	492	32	435	179	51	296	5,175	5
Montana	3,858	3,353	217	1,301	369	13	57	337	65	53	16	1	47	–	63	5	2	33	774	
Nebraska	6,451	5,267	411	617	667	158	158	907	114	109	86	16	91	–	125	35	10	46	1,717	1
Nevada	9,171	8,509	1,634	1,483	942	768	177	677	35	188	256	34	84	1	194	60	7	76	1,893	
New Hampshire ..	13,087	12,190	33	7,780	1,020	49	110	464	421	47	70	77	520	16	61	36	24	104	1,358	
New Jersey	232,967	197,097	617	9,616	16,488	33,946	28,932	15,398	13,618	1,314	2,055	6,327	4,371	2,313	887	4,584	2,163	3,548	50,920	35
New Mexico	14,989	13,642	10,171	601	669	143	88	566	15	105	94	9	51	3	125	23	10	33	936	1
New York	820,578	717,222	3,152	46,634	59,048	47,482	94,962	35,221	25,520	3,476	19,499	4,238	19,779	49,489	2,871	23,221	35,509	20,842	226,279	103
North Carolina .	13,678	10,828	147	1,361	1,879	472	142	2,044	55	150	242	17	669	23	496	86	24	58	2,963	2
North Dakota ...	2,404	1,967	27	710	231	4	14	233	21	70	20	1	12	–	37	6	–	17	564	
Ohio	97,929	86,194	1,675	8,642	8,936	1,094	7,371	9,966	4,405	1,355	1,165	85	3,229	82	731	313	568	734	35,843	11
Oklahoma	9,964	7,600	1,042	984	1,093	172	76	1,527	56	82	185	7	61	4	230	77	15	83	1,906	2
Oregon	24,237	20,730	1,433	6,320	2,199	340	255	1,588	176	312	966	39	217	8	680	26	19	185	5,967	3
Pennsylvania ..	109,970	95,724	598	6,134	11,746	1,973	17,261	9,551	6,573	1,066	1,669	1,019	3,573	104	686	750	1,170	2,036	29,815	14
Rhode Island ...	26,314	24,710	22	2,957	1,750	188	2,865	561	837	118	225	11,421	355	108	117	245	50	374	2,517	1
South Carolina .	7,941	5,715	63	738	1,250	267	81	1,054	28	156	93	12	232	9	207	62	14	63	1,386	2
South Dakota ..	1,464	1,173	23	247	157	22	10	151	12	36	27	2	13	–	38	4	–	8	423	
Tennessee	8,524	6,365	108	945	1,103	241	125	1,133	58	149	260	8	106	10	207	81	22	39	1,770	2
Texas	257,876	242,288	200,004	5,170	6,596	3,141	703	6,827	294	873	1,508	65	508	71	988	821	142	434	14,143	15
Utah	12,788	10,509	823	1,723	1,505	16	168	1,561	15	12	334	–	306	3	361	15	1	41	3,625	2
Vermont	8,160	6,990	26	4,793	619	20	128	281	104	17	54	1	27	8	32	3	2	41	834	1
Virginia	30,805	25,269	295	2,517	4,783	1,659	529	3,608	162	805	582	59	582	48	567	455	130	298	8,190	5
Washington	63,248	56,861	2,710	20,237	7,276	229	857	4,866	353	2,716	1,753	47	433	6	2,245	75	56	441	12,561	6
West Virginia ..	5,615	4,567	60	326	500	85	643	456	301	180	96	9	181	7	57	30	7	39	1,590	1
Wisconsin	34,868	29,599	2,139	2,698	2,574	425	1,499	6,527	2,065	399	475	26	591	10	300	197	130	163	9,381	5
Wyoming	2,097	1,639	372	275	188	2	32	162	12	11	61	5	37	1	46	1	–	14	420	
U.S. terr. & poss.:																				
Guam	12,042	6,428	15	44	87	–	7	52	1	4,609	49	–	7	–	98	1	–	4	1,454	
Puerto Rico ..	51,548	40,857	379	264	366	20,584	121	311	27	26	47	21	7	10,030	25	1,074	25	13	7,537	10
Virgin Islands .	19,101	9,578	8	112	6,397	81	10	108	–	17	5	3	3	188	3	17	103	2	2,521	9

1/ Includes Taiwan.

United States Department of Jus
Immigration and Naturalization Se

310

V Immigrant Contributions

Fiorello H. La Guardia. (Photoworld)

Joel Chandler Harris (right) with James
W. Riley. (New York Public Library)

To assess the contributions of immigrants to the civilization of the United States is difficult because, in the largest sense, the history of immigration is the history of America. Every inhabitant of the country is either himself a newcomer or the descendant of an ancestor who arrived from elsewhere. Generation after generation of wanderers shaped the national experience.

In a narrower sense, the immigrant contributions may be measured through the lives of the first two generations, that is, of those who themselves made the crossing and their children. True, the effects of transition and of connections with the land of origin were often perceptible also in the third generation and beyond. But the immediacy of the contact with parents who had themselves come from one world and entered another put the second generation in a special, marginal position. The results were evident in the political careers of such men as Louis D. Brandeis, Fiorello H. La Guardia, Robert F. Wagner, and Alfred E. Smith, and were expressed in literature by Joel Chandler Harris, Eugene O'Neill, Theodore Dreiser, and Carl Sandburg.

But to treat all these types in their full variety and complexity would require far too large a canvas. The full story, even of the second generation, would encompass much of the history of the nation. Here it will be enough to focus upon the contributions of the immigrants in the most restricted meaning of the term, those who themselves were foreign-born and themselves

crossed over to a new life in the United States. In number they amounted to about forty million. They helped settle the continent; they developed the industry of the country; they confirmed the pluralism and freedom of American society; and they made substantial contributions to the transfer of culture from the Old to the New World.

Always, the great majority of immigrants were plain people, driven by circumstances over which they exercised little control, searching in the New World for the means of reweaving the torn fabric of an old life. The contribution of any one of them was petty. But the sum formed a mighty force that gave a distinctive shape to the American economy and to American society.

For a long time the immigrants imparted an expansive quality to agriculture. In the eighteenth century, the Scotch-Irish and, to a lesser extent, the Germans pushed outward to the edge of settlement, planting themselves in New Hampshire, New York, Pennsylvania, Virginia, and Carolina on the rim of the populated districts. Some of their nineteenth-century successors, like the Scandinavians in Minnesota or the Dakotas, also ventured into the emptiness and brought the virgin land under cultivation.

But more usually, in the period of high immigration, the foreign-born farmers played another role. The Europeans left the initial penetration of the unfamiliar fron-

312

Theodore Dreiser. (Photoworld)

Carl Sandburg, 1941. (Library of Congress)

Connecticut settlers entering Ohio. (Drawing by Howard Pyle, New York Public Library)

Massachusetts emigrants on the way to Connecticut—a romantic picture by S. E. Brown, about 1878. (New York Public Library)

The emigrants—a symbolic drawing. (New York Public Library)

Western progress—the farm, the steamboat, the railroad and the oil well. (Tinted lithograph in *Beaver Country Pennsylvania Atlas*, 1876, Library of Congress)

A New England autumn—cider making. (Lithograph by Currier & Ives, 1866, from a painting by G. B. Durrie, Library of Congress)

Italian vine grower in Tennessee. (E. Lord, J. J. D. Trenor, and S. J. Barrows, *The Italian in America*, New York, 1905)

Apple pickers, 1910. (Library of Congress)

tier to the native Americans, but contributed capital and labor to the conversion of the first rude clearings into permanent settlements. Often the Kentuckian or Yankee who moved into Ohio and Indiana was impatient and speculative, reluctant to make do with what he had and quite willing to sell out to a German or Englishman. The proceeds enabled the American to push on to Iowa or Missouri, so that the contributions of the immigrants helped speed the westward advance of settlement.

Occasionally also immigrant farmers brought with them specialized skills. Swiss from Ticino introduced grapes for wine to the Napa Valley in California in 1860. Cultivation of the sugar beet owed much to Joseph Seemans and of "everlasting clover" to Wendelin Grimm. So, too, new strains of sturdy wheat found their way to Kansas in the baggage of German Mennonites.

To industry, the mass of newcomers contributed only

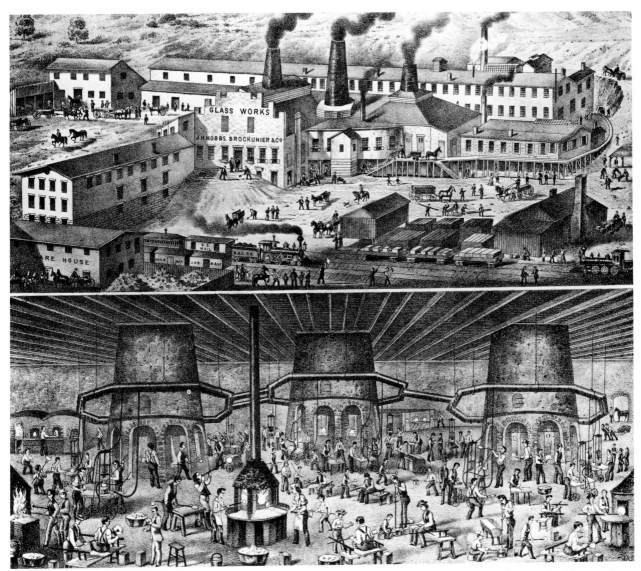

Glassworks in Wheeling, West Virginia. (*Illustrated Atlas of the Upper Ohio River Valley,* 1877, lithograph, Library of Congress)

their labor. But that was invaluable. The United States, in the nineteenth century, was an underdeveloped country dependent upon Europe for manufactures and hampered by a new country's shortage of workers. The immigrants who flocked into American cities created a pool of eager employees, willing to accept wages and conditions so advantageous to the entrepreneur that their presence alone was a temptation to expand. Furthermore, industrialization did not pauperize the native population, as it did in some other countries. The men, women, and children who toiled for a pittance in the factories and the mines were the recent arrivals. Those already here, and established, tended to rise in status and gained as the flood of goods from the new mills lowered prices and raised the level of real incomes.

Immigration also stimulated social mobility more generally, and therefore had a loosening effect upon the whole society. The flood of newcomers, entering at the bottom of every community, tended to lift up those already there. The mass of alien laborers and farmers created opportunities for teachers, merchants, lawyers, and doctors whose services they needed. With time, the foreign-born and their children too could profit from the arrival of more recent immigrants. Rarely indeed did anyone move in a single leap from rags to riches. But it was often possible through diligence, saving, and luck to make moderate advances—into the retail trades, or into the ranks of managers and foremen, or into skilled handicrafts. And those immigrants who did not themselves succeed could at least clutch the realistic hope that their offspring would move a rung or two up the ladder of success.

Immigration thus emphasized the fluidity of American society. Wilderness conditions were always uncon-

Philadelphia factory workers, proud of their seniority, 1920. (United Press International)

Logging near Tacoma, Washington. (Library of Congress)

Immigrant workers in a shoe factory. (Brown Brothers)

Coming up from the shaft of a copper mine in Calumet, Michigan. (Library of Congress, Detroit Collection)

would-be aristocrats. The steady flow of newcomers into the country stimulated movement and thus inhibited tendencies toward rigidity of place or position.

In a society so much in motion, institutions took root easily, but rarely were able to preempt the soil. Anyone could gather a church on the frontier, but no church after the seventeenth century dominated its community or commanded the adherence of worshipers, except of their own will. Scores of faiths existed side by side by the time of the Revolution, and each group of immigrants thereafter added to the number and variety. No single system of education or philanthropy served all Americans; nor did the ways in which they expressed themselves and communicated with one another fall within a single pattern. Pluralism early became characteristic of American life, and immigration confirmed and strengthened it.

As a result, a multitude of ethnic groups retained their identity for many decades. A traveler in Burke County, North Carolina, in 1920, who observed pictures of Garibaldi and Mazzini alongside those of Jefferson and Washington, would learn that he had hit upon a set-

genial to fixed lines of rank or status. In the frontier settlements, family connections, titles of nobility, and even wealth were less important than what a man could himself achieve. For a long time, the speed with which people moved about, from place to place and up and down the social hierarchy, continued to discount the value of inherited qualities and to deflate the pretensions of

The labor force of the Remington Typewriter factory—most foreign-born. (Brown Brothers)

Church and State—No Union Upon Any Terms. Thomas Nast's cartoon shows the multiplicity of sects in the United States. The German Reform, the Chinese, the Quaker, the Roman Catholic, the Mormon, and the Jew can worship after their own fashion, as long as none of them requires a special privilege in relationship to the state. (*Harper's Weekly,* February 25, 1871, Library of Congress)

A Shaker encampment in England. (*Illustrated London News,* August 31, 1878, New York Public Library)

Religious dance at a Shaker meeting. (*The Graphic,* May 14, 1870, New York Public Library)

tlement of Waldensians—French-speaking Presbyterians who had come from Italy by way of Uruguay. Hundreds of such picturesque clusters dotted the country; every great city had its own colorful patchwork of neighborhoods. That diversity was not only a reminder of the historic origins of the American population; it was also a restraint upon the tendencies toward conformity that developed as the nation modernized. Remote as they were from the standards of the majority, groups like the Shakers deserved toleration. Americans had to accept differences and also often had to use voluntary cooperative associations for common purposes instead of depending wholly upon government.

A few foreign-born individuals played a prominent role in American politics. The Englishman Thomas Paine and the Scot James Wilson, the Swiss Albert Gal-

A singing meeting of the Shakers. (*Frank Leslie's Illustrated Newspaper*, December, 1885, New York Public Library)

James Wilson. (New York Public Library)

Albert Gallatin. (New York Public Library)

Franklin K. Lane, Secretary of the Interior. (Library of Congress)

John P. Altgeld, governor of Illinois, 1892–1896. (Library of Congress)

latin, the Germans J. P. Altgeld and Carl Schurz, the Canadian Franklin K. Lane and the Austrian Felix Frankfurter were among those who held high office or influenced critical decisions. But the larger impact of the immigrants was through their participation as voters in the political process.

The great mass of newcomers came from societies that had offered them no experience in democracy. Yet within five years of arrival they qualified for citizenship and had the same right to the ballot as natives. Doubts about their ability to exercise properly the franchise again and again worried Americans who feared the appearance of demagogues or the spread of corruption. The concern proved vain. Pluralism permitted the immigrants, ill prepared as they were, to develop their own associations and, ultimately, to use the instruments of American democracy for their own interests. The ma-

The Fourth of July at Tammany Hall, New York. (*Harper's Weekly*, July 11, 1868, Library of Congress)

Chicago women of foreign birth, voting for the first time in 1919. (Brown Brothers)

Felix Frankfurter, Justice of the United States Supreme Court. (Library of Congress)

chines and the bosses who ruled the cities in the nineteenth century were certainly guilty of abuses from time to time. But they also understood the needs of the people they served and gradually they learned how to use the machinery of government for the welfare of their constituents. In the twentieth century, pressure from the immigrants upon the progressive movement and the New Deal helped to shape a new conception of what the state owed its members.

Pluralism also enriched American culture. The habits people from the Old World carried with them were centuries old, and they had no desire to discard them. Often the peasant from Norway or Greece cherished a costume from home, although he might actually wear it only on the festivals observed according to the homeland calendar. Tastes in food and drink also persisted after the crossing, as did the rhythms of the traditional song and dance.

The result was not a homogeneous blending in which differences disappeared but rather an accommodation in which one group borrowed from another so that the whole of American life gained in richness and color. The awareness that Santa Claus was Dutch in origin or the Christmas tree German did not prevent families of other antecedents from adopting them; just as Italian, Mexican, Chinese, and East European dishes became familiar components of the American cuisine.

The general effect of drawing together many different strands in a common culture was to soften the characteristics of a society long influenced by Puritanism and the wilderness. The Sabbath lost its harsh features, the rigid control of personal behavior yielded to a more permissive attitude, and the emphasis upon utility gave way to recognition that there was a place in life for sensuality, leisure, and fun.

Hence, immigrants readily found a place in the world of entertainment that encompassed the stage, the music hall, the movies, and the athletic field. The Shubert and the Warner brothers, William Fox, Dion Boucicault, John Drew, Barney Williams, and Charlie Chaplin were but a few of the numerous newcomers who helped shape American theatre, vaudeville, and the movies. And John

An evening reading class for immigrants in a New York City public school, 1920. (Brown Brothers)

Immigrants from Israel, Poland, the Dominican Republic, Russia, Austria, and Greece meet as students in an adult education citizenship program in New York, 1952. (United Press International)

Immigrants at Ellis Island wearing old country costumes as they buy their railroad tickets. (Brown Brothers)

Girls of Dutch descent polish the streets of Holland, Michigan, in preparation for the annual tulip festival, 1949. (United Press International)

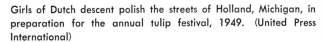

A Norwegian dancing club in Chicago in a parade, 1949. (United Press International)

Magyar peasant immigrant. The embroidery on her apron reads: "If I am pure and good, I expect to be honored." (E. A. Ross, *The Old World in the New,* New York, 1914)

Jacob J. (left) and Lee (right) Shubert, who dominated the theatrical life of New York for many years, 1960. (United Press International)

Greek-Americans march in their folk costumes despite the rain of New York, 1970. (United Press International)

The Warner brothers, Jack, Harry, and Albert, in 1956, having agreed to sell their film holdings for almost $70 million. They began their careers in 1903 when they opened their first theatre in a vacant store in New Castle, Pennsylvania. (United Press International)

John Drew as "The Irish Emigrant," a role he made famous. (New York Public Library)

John Morrissey. (New York Public Library)

Charles S. Chaplin. (Photoworld)

Morrissey, who arrived from Tipperary in 1853 to make a fortune in boxing, was the first of the strong men who earned fame—at least—by the display of physical prowess.

Culture had a double connotation in the nineteenth century. It referred to the broad patterns of thought and the habitual practices of the whole society. But it also referred to the learning, art, and manners particularly associated with the educated and gentle classes in society. In that narrower sense, the mass of immigrants were people of no culture.

However, a small but significant number of uncommon immigrants served as bearers of such culture. Their role was important because the United States stood in a dependent relationship to Europe after the Revolution as before it. In science and the fine arts, the country had been backward and provincial, however much Americans boasted that theirs would be the culture of the future. National pride and lack of technical skill kept them from catching up at a leap. A few exceptional immigrants helped bridge the gap.

Native American scientists of the eighteenth and nineteenth centuries were generally self-educated amateurs who worked alone and who were often cut off from the advanced knowledge and techniques of Europe. Migration, therefore, created a refreshing channel of contacts with the outer world. Joseph Priestley, for instance, had already established a reputation as a chemist when he arrived from England in 1794. That was also true of the mathematician Richard Price, and of Louis Agassiz, the Swiss zoologist. Other notable contributors to American science were the geographer A. H. Guyot, the ornithologist J. J. Audubon, and, in medicine, Simon Baruch, Jacques Loeb, Joseph Goldberger, and Alexis Carrel.

Americans did have a bent for tinkering, and there was no lack of native inventors and engineers. Yet a number of immigrants made significant contributions in these areas, too. John Roebling, John Ericsson, and Gustav Lindenthal were among the best-known engineers. The Scotsman Alexander Graham Bell took time from teaching the deaf in Boston to invent the telephone. The Belgian Leo H. Baekeland, having first discovered how to make a photographic paper, Velox, then went on to lay the foundation of the plastics industry with Bakelite. The Irishman Humphrey O'Sullivan invented the rubber heel. The work of the Serb Michael

Dr. Richard Price, 1723–1791. (*London Magazine,* June 1, 1776, New York Public Library)

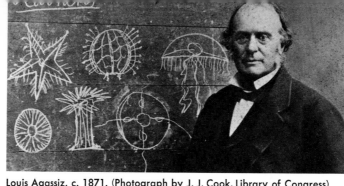

Louis Agassiz, c. 1871. (Photograph by J. J. Cook, Library of Congress)

Arnold Henry Guyot, 1884. (New York Public Library)

Dr. Alexis Carrel, 1913. (Library of Congress)

John J. Audubon. (Engraving after the painting by Chappel, Library of Congress)

Dr. Simon Baruch, father of Bernard Baruch. (United Press International)

John A. Roebling. (*National Cyclopedia of American Biography,* 1899)

Alexander Graham Bell. (Photograph taken in 1904, Library of Congress)

Leo H. Baekeland. (Photograph by Bain, Library of Congress)

Charles P. Steinmetz, 1912. (New York Public Library)

Ole Rölvaag. (Brown Brothers)

Jacob A. Riis, 1904. (Photograph by Pach Brothers, Library of Congress)

E. L. Godkin. (Brown Brothers)

Joseph Pulitzer. (New York Public Library)

Edward Bok, 1909. (Photograph by Pirie MacDonald, Library of Congress)

John Ericsson, standing to the right of pole, among his American scientist colleagues. (Painting by Christian Schussele, The National Gallery of Art, Washington, D.C.)

An array of the great American newspapers and their editors. Pulitzer is in the center column, third down. (Library of Congress)

Pupin, and of the German Charles P. Steinmetz, advanced the understanding of electricity.

The creative figures in the arts made their marks in fields in which Americans tended to be weak. The foreign-born were less prominent in literature than in music. But, there were some novelists of importance; Ole Rölvaag's *Giants in the Earth* and Abraham Cahan's *The Rise of David Levinsky* illuminated the experience of the Great Plains and of the city slums. The Dane Jacob A. Riis and the Englishmen E. L. Godkin and James E. Scripps, the Hollander Edward Bok, and the Hungarian Joseph Pulitzer were among the immigrants important in American newspaper and magazine life. But the main lines of American literature were firmly rooted in native and English traditions to which foreign-born writers did not easily conform.

By contrast, the American tradition was weak in both religious and secular music, and there were few opportunities for performers or composers to perfect their techniques. The United States long lacked the organized operatic and concert life and the aristocratic patronage that in Europe encouraged young people of talent to perfect their techniques. As a result, the field was open to musicians who had acquired their training abroad.

Often the careers of such people were international. They were not, properly speaking, immigrants, but art-

ists who simply arranged American stops on tours that took them to every part of the world. The acclaim that greeted the appearance of Jenny Lind, the Swedish nightingale, in 1842 led numerous virtuosos and companies to follow in her footsteps.

More important were the artists who struck roots in the United States and whose efforts resulted in the beginnings of an indigenous music life here. Theodore Thomas, Serge Koussevitzky, Arturo Toscanini, Walter Damrosch, and Bruno Walter were among the conductors who perfected orchestras in American cities. And Jascha Heifetz, Jean de Reszke, and Mischa Elman were among the performers who enriched the country's musical life.

The other arts in the United States were neither as dependent on foreign talent as was music nor as independent as was literature. The immigrants Karl Bitter and Augustus Saint-Gaudens were notable sculptors; and Emanuel Leutze and G. T. Berthon were well-known painters. But they were not as important in the American art world as the musicians nor as isolated as the novelists.

The career of one aspiring musician showed the interplay between the talent of the immigrant and the opportunity of the New World. Victor Herbert had been born in 1859 in Dublin, a city that offered no scope to a

324

A Ukrainian concert at Ellis Island, June 4, 1916. (National Park Service, Sherman Collection)

The scene at Castle Garden, New York, at Jenny Lind's first concert, 1850. (*Ladies' Home Journal,* November, 1890, New York Public Library)

Theodore Thomas. (Library of Congress)

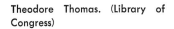

Bruno Walter. (Columbia Records Photo)

Walter Damrosch. (Library of Congress)

Jean de Reszke. (New York Public Library)

Mischa Elman. (Drawing by Spurr, 1916, Library of Congress)

Karl Bitter. (National Cyclopedia of American Biography, 1899)

Panel from the Carl Schurz Monument, New York City, Karl Bitter, sculptor, 1914. (American Architecture, 1914, New York Public Library)

The famous Washington Crossing the Delaware by Leutze has a firm place in American art. (Courtesy of the Metropolitan Museum of Art, Gift of John S. Kennedy, 1897)

serious cellist. Herbert left home, studied in Germany, and by the time he was twenty-three, was playing with Johann Strauss in Vienna. That modest success did not satisfy him. In 1886 he moved to New York, where he found a place in the Philharmonic Symphony Orchestra.

He had left Europe because his true ambition was to become a composer; and competition against the well-established Germans and Austrians seemed hopeless. In New York, the field was open. Yet the concerts, operas, and symphonies on which Herbert lavished his efforts were failures. This was not his style.

In 1893 he was thirty-four and still far from the renown of which he dreamed. In that year he compromised; he accepted the post of bandmaster of the Twenty-second Regiment of the New York National Guard. Turning his back upon the classics, he now took up the military march and the popular song and dance.

From these chores he derived a sense of what the American audience wanted; his Viennese experience had shown him how to supply it. Light opera proved his medium and earned him fame. *The Wizard of the Nile, The Fortune Teller, Mlle. Modiste, The Red Mill,* and *Naughty Marietta* won the affections of a generation of Americans. He put together these gay little plays out of casual borrowings from the masters of European comic opera and out of traditional themes. But he tied them together with wit, urbanity, and skill. For more than thirty years, the nation whistled and hummed his songs, which provided a bridge between the innocent minstrelsy of the nineteenth century and the elaborate musical comedy of the twentieth.

Herbert was representative of the men who brought to the United States a skill and found an opportunity. Like the other uncommon men who made the crossing, he established a link between the culture of his new home and that of the Old World.

But he was also representaive of the much more numerous body of immigrants who were common men and who lacked skill. They, too, by their willingness to risk migration and their capacity to work and endure, helped to bring the promised but undeveloped land in which they arrived into a place of prominence in the world. In good measure, its economy and its society were a product of their efforts.

Augustus Saint-Gaudens. (Library of Congress)

Victor Herbert. (Brown Brothers)

A scene from one of Herbert's popular shows, *Mlle Modiste.* (New York Public Library)

Three immigrants on Ellis Island, about 1910, looking across the Bay at the Statue of Liberty. (Brown Brothers)

Bibliography

General

Davie, Maurice R. *World Immigration, with Special Reference to the United States.* New York, 1936.

Handlin, Oscar. *Race and Nationality in American Life.* Boston, 1957.

———. *The Uprooted.* Boston, 1951.

Hansen, Marcus L. *The Immigrant in American History.* Cambridge, 1940.

Jones, Maldwyn Allen. *American Immigration.* Chicago, 1960.

Stephenson, George M. *A History of American Immigration, 1820–1924.* Boston, 1926.

Taft, Donald R. *Human Migration.* New York, 1936.

Wittke, Carl. *We Who Built America: The Saga of the Immigrant.* New York, 1939.

Documentary Collections

Abbott, Edith. *Historical Aspects of the Immigration Problem.* Chicago, 1926.

———. Immigration: *Select Documents and Case Records.* Chicago, 1924.

Handlin, Oscar, ed. *Immigration as a Factor in American History.* Englewood Cliffs, New Jersey, 1959.

From the Beginnings (1607–1820): The American Indians

American Heritage Book of Indians. New York, 1961.

Debo, Angie. *A History of the Indians of the United States.* Norman, Oklahoma, 1970.

Driver, Harold E. *Indians of North America.* Chicago, 1961.

Hagan, William T. *American Indians.* Chicago, 1961.

La Farge, Oliver. *A Pictorial History of the American Indian.* New York, 1956.

Mc Nickle, D'Arcy. *They Came Here First: The Epic of the American Indian.* Philadelphia, 1949.

Prucha, Francis P., ed. *The Indian in American History.* New York, 1971.

European Migration and Its Background

Baird, Charles W. *History of the Huguenot Emigration.* 2 vols. New York, 1885, 1966.

Browning, Charles H. *Welsh Settlement of Pennsylvania.* Philadelphia, 1912.

Dunaway, Wayland L. *The Scotch-Irish of Colonial Pennsylvania.* Chapel Hill, North Carolina, 1944.

Graham, Ian C. C. *Colonists from Scotland: Emigration to North America, 1707–1783.* Ithaca, New York, 1956.

Hansen, Marcus Lee. *The Atlantic Migration, 1607–1860.* Cambridge, Massachusetts, 1940.

Hirsch, Arthur H. *The Huguenots of Colonial South Carolina.* Durham, North Carolina, 1928.

Johnson, Amandus. *The Swedish Settlements on the Delaware . . . 1638–1664.* Philadelphia, 1911.

Leyburn, James G. *The Scotch-Irish.* Chapel Hill, North Carolina, 1962.

Marcus, Jacob R. *Early American Jewry.* 2 vols. Philadelphia, 1951–1952.

Myers, A. C. *Immigration of the Irish Quakers into Pennsylvania, 1682–1750.* Swarthmore, Pennsylvania, 1902.

Smith, Abbot E. *Colonists in Bondage: White Servitude and Convict Labor in America, 1607–1776.* Chapel Hill, North Carolina, 1947.

Africans

Blake, W. O. *History of Slavery.* Columbus, Ohio, 1857–1860.

Drake, Richard. *Revelations of a Slave Smuggler.* New York, [1860].

DuBois, W. E. B. *Black Folk, Then and Now: An Essay in the History and Sociology of the Negro Race.* New York, 1939.

———. *Suppression of the African Slave Trade to the United States, 1638–1870.* Cambridge, Massachusetts, 1896.

Franklin, John Hope. *From Slavery to Freedom.* New York, 1967. First eds., 1947, 1956.

Mannix, Daniel P. *Black Cargoes: A History of the Atlantic Slave Trade, 1518–1865.* New York, 1962.

Phillips, U. B. *American Negro Slavery.* New York, 1918.

Redding, J. Saunders. *They Came in Chains.* Philadelphia, 1950.

Woodson, Carter. *The Negro in Our History.* Washington, D.C., 1962. (This is 10th ed. prepared by Charles H. Wesley)

The Revolution and American Nationality

Arieli, Yehoshua. *Individualism and Nationalism in American Ideology.* Cambridge, 1964.

Boorstin, Daniel J. *The Americans: The National Experience.* New York, 1965.

Crèvecoeur, Michel G. J. de. *Letters from an American Farmer.* London, 1782.

Echeverria, Durand. *Image in the West.* Princeton, 1957.

Jones, Howard Mumford. *America and French Culture, 1750–1848.* Chapel Hill, North Carolina, 1927.

Peasants in a New World (1820–1880): Refugees

Childs, Frances S. *French Refugee Life in the United States, 1790–1800.* Baltimore, 1940.

Lerski, Jerzy J. *A Polish Chapter in Jacksonian America: The United States and the Polish Exiles of 1831.* Madison, Wisconsin, 1958.

Lonn, Ella. *Foreigners in the Confederacy.* Chapel Hill, 1940.

———. *Foreigners in the Union Army and Navy.* New York, 1951.

Wittke, Carl. *Refugees of Revolution: The German Forty-Eighters in America.* Philadelphia, 1952.

Zucker, A. E., ed. *The Forty-Eighters.* New York, 1950.

Irish and Britons

Adams, William F. *Ireland and Irish Emigration to the New World from 1815 to the Famine.* New Haven, 1932.

Berthoff, Rowland T. *British Immigrants in Industrial America, 1789–1950.* Cambridge, Massachusetts, 1953.

Brown, Thomas N. *Irish-American Nationalism.* New York, 1966.

Conway, Alan, ed. *The Welsh in America: Letters from the Immigrants.* Minneapolis, 1961.

Ernst, Robert. *Immigrant Life in New York City, 1825–1863.* New York, 1949.

Ford, Henry J. *The Scotch-Irish in America.* Princeton, 1915.

Gibson, Florence E. *The Attitudes of the New York Irish Toward State and National Affairs, 1848–1892.* New York, 1951.

Handlin, Oscar. *Boston's Immigrants: A Study in Acculturation.* Cambridge, Massachusetts, 1941; rev. ed., 1959.

Hartmann, Edward G. *Americans from Wales.* Boston, 1967.

Rowse, A. L. *The Cornish in America.* New York, 1969.

Shannon, William V. *The American Irish.* New York, 1963.

Todd, Arthur C. *The Cornish Miner in America.* Truro, England, 1967.

Wittke, Carl. *The Irish in America.* Baton Rouge, 1956.

Germans

Cunz, Dieter. *The Maryland Germans.* Princeton, 1948.

Faust, Albert B. *The German Element in the United States.* 2 vols. New York, 1927.

Hawgood, John A. *The Tragedy of German-America.* New York, 1940.

Von Grueningen, John P., ed. *The Swiss in the United States.* Madison, Wisconsin, 1940.

Walker, Mack. *Germany and the Emigration 1816–1885.* Cambridge, 1964.

Wittke, Carl. *The German-Language Press in America.* Lexington, Kentucky, 1957.

Scandinavians and Hollanders

Andersen, Arlow W. *The Immigrant Takes His Stand: The Norwegian-American Press and Public Affairs, 1847–1872.* Northfield, Minnesota, 1953.

Blegen, Theodore C., ed. *Land of Their Choice: The Immigrants Write Home.* Minneapolis, 1955.

———. *Norwegian Migration to America, 1825–1860.* Northfield, Minnesota, 1931.

———. *Norwegian Migration to America: The American Tradition.* Northfield, Minnesota, 1940.

Hoglund, A. William. *Finnish Immigrants in America 1880–1920.* Madison, Wisconsin, 1960.

Jalkanen, Ralph J., ed. *The Finns in North America: A Social Symposium.* Hancock, Michigan, 1969.

Janson, Florence E. *The Background of Swedish Immigration, 1840–1930.* Philadelphia, 1931.

Lucas, Henry S., ed. *Dutch Immigrant Memoirs and Related Writings.* 2 vols. Assen, Netherlands, 1955.

———. *Netherlanders in America: Dutch Immigration to the United States and Canada, 1789–1950.* Ann Arbor, Michigan, 1955.

Mulder, Arnold. *Americans from Holland.* New York, 1947.

Mulder, William. *Homeward to Zion: The Mormon Migration from Scandinavia.* Minneapolis, 1957.

Qualey, Carlton C. *Norwegian Settlement in the United States.* Northfield, Minnesota, 1938.

Riis, Jacob A. *The Making of an American.* Ed. Roy Lubove, New York, 1966.

Sabbe Philemon D., and Buyse, Leon. *Belgians in America.* Lannoo, Tielt, Belgium, 1960.

Stephenson, George M. *Religious Aspects of Swedish Immigration.* Minneapolis, 1932.

The Great Migration (1880–1930)

Erickson, Charlotte. *American Industry and the European Immigrant, 1860–1885.* Cambridge, Massachusetts, 1957.

Evans-Gordon, W. *The Alien Immigrant.* New York, 1903.

Henry, John R. *Some Immigrant Neighbors.* New York, 1912.

Hourwich, Isaac A. *Immigration and Labor.* New York, 1912.

Roberts, Peter. *The New Immigration.* New York, 1912.

Ross, E. A. *The Old World in the New.* New York, 1914.

Shriver, William P. *Immigrant Forces.* New York, 1913.

Steiner, E. A. *The Broken Wall.* New York, 1911.

———. *From Alien to Citizen.* New York, 1914.

———. *The Immigrant Tide.* New York, 1909.

———. *On the Trail of the Immigrant.* New York, 1906.

Warne, Frank J. *The Tide of Immigration.* New York, 1916.

Woods, Robert A. *Americans in Process.* Boston, 1902.

———. *The City Wilderness.* Boston, 1899.

Jews

Antin, Mary. *The Promised Land.* Boston, 1969.

Brandes, Joseph. *Immigrants to Freedom: Jewish Communities in Rural New Jersey.* Philadelphia, 1971.

Glanz, Rudolph. *Jews in Relation to the Cultural Milieu of the Germans in America up to the Eighteen Eighties.* New York, 1947.

Handlin, Oscar. *Adventure in Freedom.* New York, 1954.

Hapgood, Hutchins. *The Spirit of the Ghetto.* Ed. Moses Rischin, Cambridge, Massachusetts, 1967.

Hirshler, Eric F., ed. *Jews from Germany in the United States.* New York, 1955.

Joseph, Samuel. *Jewish Immigration to the United States from 1881 to 1910.* New York, 1914.

Rischin, Moses. *The Promised City: New York's Jews 1870–1914.* Cambridge, Massachusetts, 1962.

From Southern Europe

Foerster, Robert F. *The Italian Emigration of Our Times.* Cambridge, Massachusetts, 1919.

Lord, Eliot, Trenor, J. J. D., and Barrows, S. J. *The Italian in America.* New York, 1905.

Musmanno, Michael A. *The Story of the Italians in America.* Garden City, New York, 1965.

Nelli, Humbert S. *The Italians in Chicago 1880–1930.* New York, 1970.

Rose, Philip M. *The Italians in America.* New York, 1922.

Taft, Donald R. *Two Portuguese Communities in New England.* New York, 1923.

Vaz, August M. *The Portuguese in California.* San Francisco, 1965.

Watts, George B. *The Waldenses in the New World.* Durham, North Carolina, 1941.

Williams, Phyllis H. *South Italian Folkways in Europe and America.* New Haven, 1938.

Eastern Europe and Asia Minor

Balch, Emily G. *Our Slavic Fellow Citizen.* New York, 1910.

Burgess, Thomas. *Greeks in America.* Boston, 1913.

Čapek, Thomas. *The Cechs (Bohemians) in America.* Boston, 1920.

Davis, Jerome. *The Russian Immigrant.* New York, 1922.

———. *The Russians and Ruthenians in America.* New York, 1922.

Elkholy, Abdo A. *The Arab Moslems in the United States: Religion and Assimilation.* New Haven, 1966.

Fairchild, Henry P. *Greek Immigration to the United States.* New Haven, 1911.

Fox, Paul. *The Poles in America*. New York, 1922.

Govorchin, Gerald G. *Americans from Yugoslavia*. Gainesville, Florida, 1961.

Greene, Victor R. *The Slavic Community on Strike: Immigrant Labor in Pennsylvania Anthracite*. Notre Dame, Indiana, 1968.

Haiman, Miecislaus. *Polish Past in America, 1608–1865*. Chicago, 1939.

Halich, Wasyl. *Ukrainians in the United States*. Chicago, 1937.

Hitti, Philip K. *The Syrians in America*. New York, 1924.

Konnyu, Leslie. *Hungarians in the United States: An Immigration Study*. St. Louis, 1967.

Kutak, Robert I. *Story of a Bohemian-American Village*. Louisville, Kentucky, 1933.

Malcom, M. Vartan. *The Armenians in America*. Boston, 1919.

Miller, Kenneth D. *The Czecho-Slovaks in America*. New York, 1922.

Prpic, George J. *The Croatian Immigrants in America*. New York, 1971.

Saloutos, Theodore. *The Greeks in the United States*. Cambridge, Massachusetts, 1964.

Thomas, William I., and Znaniecki, Florian. *The Polish Peasant in Europe and America*. 2 vols. Chicago, 1918–1920, reprinted New York, 1958.

Warne, Frank J. *The Slav Invasion and the Mine Workers*. Philadelphia, 1904.

Wood, Arthur E. *Hamtramck, Then and Now*. New York, 1955.

Wytrwal, Joseph A. *Poles in American History and Tradition*. Detroit, 1969.

Xenides, J. P. *The Greeks in America*. New York, 1922.

From the Americas

Ducharme, Jacques. *The Shadows of the Trees: The Story of French-Canadians in New England*. New York, 1943.

Gamio, Manuel. *Mexican Immigration to the United States*. Chicago, 1930.

Handlin, Oscar. *The Newcomers*. Cambridge, Massachusetts, 1969.

Kibbe, Pauline S. *Latin Americans in Texas*. Albuquerque, 1946.

Mc Williams, Carey. *North from Mexico*. New York, 1961.

Mills, C. Wright, et al. *The Puerto Rican Journey*. New York, 1950.

Padilla, Elena. *Up From Puerto Rico*. New York, 1958.

Rand, Christopher. *The Puerto Ricans*. New York, 1958.

Reid, Ira de A. *The Negro Immigrant, His Background, Characteristics and Social Adjustment, 1899–1937*. New York, 1939.

Senior, Clarence. *Our Citizens from the Caribbean*. St. Louis, 1965.

Taylor, Paul S. *Mexican Labor in the United States*. 3 vols. Berkeley, 1928–1934.

Wessel, Bessie B. *An Ethnic Survey of Woonsocket, Rhode Island*. Chicago, 1931.

Oriental Immigration

Barth, Gunther P. *Bitter Strength*. Cambridge, Massachusetts, 1964.

Coolidge, Mary R. *Chinese Immigration*. New York, 1909.

Grodzins, Morton. *Americans Betrayed: Politics and the Japanese Evacuation*. Chicago, 1949.

Gulick, Sidney L. *The American Japanese Problem*. New York, 1914.

Ichihashi, Yamato. *Japanese in the United States*. Stanford, California, 1932.

Kung, S. W. *Chinese in American Life*. Seattle, 1962.

Lasker, Bruno. *Filipino Immigration to Continental United States and to Hawaii*. Chicago, 1931.

Miller, Stuart C. *The Unwelcome Immigrant: The American Image of the Chinese, 1785–1882*. Berkeley, 1969.

Sandmeyer, Elmer C. *The Anti-Chinese Movement in California*. Urbana, Illinois, 1939.

Ten Broek, Jacobus, Barnhart, Edward N., and Matson, Floyd W. *Prejudice, War, and the Constitution*. Berkeley, 1958.

Thomas, Dorothy S. *Japanese American Evacuation and Resettlement*. 3 vols. Berkeley, 1946–1958.

Tupper, Eleanor, and Mc Reynolds, G. E. *Japan in American Public Opinion*. New York, 1937.

Immigration Restriction

Bernard, William S., ed. *American Immigration Policy*. New York, 1950.

Billington, Ray Allen. *The Protestant Crusade, 1800–1860: A Study of the Origins of American Nativism*. New York, 1952.

Desmond, Humphrey J. *The A.P.A. Movement*. Washington, D.C., 1912.

Divine, Robert A. *American Immigration Policy, 1924–1952*. New Haven, 1957.

Garis, Roy L. *Immigration Restriction: A Study of the Opposition to and Regulation of Immigration to the United States*. New York, 1927.

Hartmann, Edward G. *The Movement to Americanize the Immigrant*. New York, 1948.

Higham, John. *Strangers in the Land: Patterns of American Nativism, 1860–1925*. New Brunswick, New Jersey, 1955.

Solomon, Barbara M. *Ancestors and Immigrants: A Changing New England Tradition*. Cambridge, Massachusetts, 1956.

Modern Times

Davie, Maurice R., et al. *Refugees in America*. New York, 1947.

Fermi, Laura. *Illustrious Immigrants: The Intellectual Migration from Europe, 1930–41*. Chicago, 1968.

Fleming, Donald, and Bailyn, Bernard, eds. *The Intellectual Migration: Europe and America, 1930–1960*. Cambridge, Massachusetts, 1969.

Heberle, Rudolf. *Displaced Persons in Louisiana and Mississippi*. Baton Rouge, 1950.

Kent, Donald P. *The Refugee Intellectual: The Americanization of the Immigrant of 1933–41*. New York, 1953.

Vernant, Jacques. *The Refugee in the Post-War World*. New Haven, 1953.

Immigrant Contributions

Adamic, Louis. *A Nation of Nations*. New York, 1945.

Bowers, David F., ed. *Foreign Influences in American Life*. Princeton, 1944.

Brown, Lawrence G. *Immigration: Cultural Conflicts and Social Adjustments*. New York, 1969.

Eaton, Allen H. *Immigrant Gifts to American Life*. New York, 1970.

Glazer, Nathan, and Moynihan, Daniel P. *Beyond the Melting Pot*. Cambridge, Massachusetts, 1963.

Handlin, Oscar, ed. *Children of the Uprooted*. New York, 1966.

————. *The Positive Contribution of Immigrants*. Paris, 1955.

Park, Robert E. *The Immigrant Press and Its Control*. New York, 1922.

————, and Miller, Herbert A. *Old World Traits Transplanted*. New York, 1921.

Wheeler, Thomas C., ed. *The Immigrant Experience: The Anguish of Becoming American*. New York, 1971.

Index

Italic page numbers indicate illustrations.